MW00638193

Advance Praise for
Cornfields to Gold Medals

"Don Showalter is a tremendous coach, teacher, ambassador, and mentor to countless basketball players and coaches who've benefited immensely from his guidance and principles that are shared in this book. *Cornfields to Gold Medals* takes readers on an improbable journey filled with an elite level of winning, continuity of leadership, and, most important, incredible purpose."—*Mike Krzyzewski, former Duke University and USA Senior National Team head men's basketball coach*

"From developing USA Basketball grassroots initiatives to achieving coaching excellence with the USA Men's Junior National Team program, Don's handprints have been all over our organization. His positive impacts as a teacher and coach are far-reaching. As it shares his journey, this book captures Don's passion and enthusiasm for the game at all levels."—*Jim Tooley, chief executive officer, USA Basketball*

"Don Showalter epitomizes all of the values of a great coach and teacher. From Iowa high school players in the heartland to future NBA stars, all have been influenced by his approach to teamwork, competition, and hard work. He teaches winning, on and off the court."—*Fran Fraschilla, ESPN*

"I'm so glad this book about Don Showalter has been written. There are more famous coaches, but there isn't a better one than Don. He is a selfless servant of the game, and I've never been around a better teacher, coach, and person. This book details exactly why Don Showalter is the model of what every coach should aspire to be."—*Jay Bilas, ESPN*

"As one of our game's most respected teachers, Coach Showalter reflects the best of our profession. He is a gifted tactician and a valued mentor to me in my quest to be a better leader. This book offers the reader some of the great lessons he has absorbed in a career devoted to teaching young men not just our game but proven methods to positively impact those around them."—*Jay Wright, former Villanova head men's basketball coach, assistant coach of the USA Basketball Olympic team, and Naismith Hall of Fame member*

"Don Showalter is, without question, one of the best coaches and, more important, one of the best individuals I've met in my 40 years in college basketball. His leadership running USA Basketball has been outstanding, and there is no one better to lead our sport and our nation on the global stage. I am proud to know him and call him my friend."—*Fran McCaffery, University of Iowa head men's basketball coach*

"I would not be where I am today without the teachings, guidance, and leadership Don Showalter has provided me since the summer of 1974, when he introduced me to the game of basketball. Coach Showalter possesses the rare quality of being able to lead people of all ages. Players and coaches gravitate to him due to his willingness to give back to the game that he loves and has dedicated his life to."—*Steve Forbes, head men's basketball coach, Wake Forest University*

"The USA Basketball Junior National Team would not be what it is today without Don Showalter. He started the program with structure and attention to detail, and he provided disciplined coaching to a generation of elite players. Don has given so much to the game of basketball and has never asked for anything in return—a true basketball lifer!"—*Sean Ford, USA Basketball Men's National Team director*

"I have been around the game of basketball my entire life, it seems, and I know of no better teacher than Don Showalter. His ability to connect, correct, and lead is unmatched. To lead a group that has all of the pressure *not* to lose and to teach every young man how to win with class is truly a remarkable task, and one Show made look easy; he is called Mr. Perfect for a reason. And he has always been that way. From Iowa to Colorado Springs to the world, Coach Show is someone who every player, coach, and fan can look at as the example of how to be a true winner!"—*Mike Jones, associate head coach, Virginia Tech men's basketball*

"A remarkable true story of a person's passion for basketball. A must-read for any coach and those in evolving leadership roles. Readers will enjoy this story of compassion, leadership, and success."—*Don Logan, executive director, Iowa Basketball Coaches Association*

"This is a man who fell madly in love with basketball. He has tirelessly promoted the game, coaches, players, and fans. He is a true evangelist and extraordinary coach. This is the story of a most unique human being."—*George Raveling, member, Naismith Memorial Basketball Hall of Fame*

CORNFIELDS
to
GOLD MEDALS

COACHING CHAMPIONSHIP BASKETBALL, LESSONS IN LEADERSHIP, AND A RISE FROM HUMBLE BEGINNINGS

Don Showalter
and Pete Van Mullem

TRIUMPH
BOOKS

Library of Congress Cataloging-in-Publication Data

Names: Showalter, Don, author. | Van Mullem, Pete, author.
Title: Cornfields to gold medals: coaching championship basketball, lessons in leadership, and a rise from humble beginnings / Don Showalter and Pete Van Mullem.
Identifiers: LCCN 2023000138 | ISBN 9781637272046 (Cloth)
Subjects: LCSH: Showalter, Don. | Basketball coaches—United States—Biography. | Coaches (Athletics)—United States—Biography. | Basketball—Coaching. | Basketball for children—Coaching. | BISAC: SPORTS & RECREATION / Coaching / Basketball | EDUCATION / Leadership
Classification: LCC GV884.S456 A3 2023 | DDC 796.323092 [B—dc23/eng/20230202
LC record available at https://lccn.loc.gov/2023000138

This book is available in quantity at special discounts for your group or organization. For further information, contact:
Triumph Books LLC
814 North Franklin Street
Chicago, Illinois 60610
(312) 337-0747
www.triumphbooks.com

Printed in U.S.A.
ISBN: 978-1-63727-204-6
Design by Patricia Frey

All photos courtesy of the author

To my lovely wife and best friend, Vicky, for sharing every game. To my assistant coaches, both in high school and with USA Basketball. To all the players who I had the privilege to coach. And to my family, especially Melissa and Brent, for all their support along my coaching journey.

—Don Showalter

To the coaches I played and worked for, you are cherished mentors for life. To the players I coached, thank you for letting me share my passion for basketball with you. To my parents, who supported me in finding my own path.

—Pete Van Mullem

Contents

Introduction

The dominance of Team USA in international basketball competition often made us the favored team. The 2018 gold medal game against France was no different. Yet France presented a formidable opponent. In their previous six games leading up to the 2018 FIBA Under-17 Basketball World Cup final in Argentina, France bested opponents by double-digit scoring margins, with only their semifinal matchup against Puerto Rico a single-digit win: 78–73. Led by future pros Malcolm Cazalon, Killian Hayes, and Théo Maledon, France had their best chance to pull off an upset.

This would be my 10ᵗʰ and last gold medal game leading the Junior National Team. I struggled to grasp the finality of the moment because I was still living it, coaching the game I loved.

The 2018 USA Basketball Junior National Team featured the best young talent in the United States, future stars in the game like Jalen Green, who earned NBA All-Rookie first-team honors as a freshman in 2022 for the Houston Rockets; Jalen Suggs, who led the Gonzaga University Bulldogs to the 2021 NCAA national title game; Scottie Barnes, the 2022 NBA Rookie of the Year for the Toronto Raptors; and Vernon Carey Jr., who earned second-team All-America honors as a freshman for Duke University in 2020.

Both teams started slow, but we took an early lead, 8–5, on a De'Vion Harmon layup, his third bucket. The game remained tight as Cazalon banged home a three off an assist from Maledon to cut our lead to three with 1:24 left in the first quarter. Then Jalen Green followed with a three of his own, and we finished the quarter on a 7–1 run, capped by a thunderous dunk from Carey with four seconds left on the clock to end the period up 23–14. We struggled to score in the second quarter. With seven minutes to go, Cazalon scored a layup and France cut our lead back to five, 23–18. We needed a timeout.

We increased our defensive intensity coming out of the timeout, outscoring France 20–5 to take a 45–25 lead into the halftime break. Even with the breakthrough at the end of the second quarter, I was not satisfied. At halftime, we made adjustments and I reminded our players who they were representing as members of Team USA. Coaching the Junior National Team went beyond winning gold medals; it served as a training program for the Senior National Team, where winning Olympic gold took on a higher level of importance.

We opened the third period with three different players scoring buckets to expand our lead to 51–27. When Green caught a shovel pass from Suggs with 3:05 left in the third quarter and dunked over a defender, we almost doubled France's scoring output to lead 69–35.

I began to realize the finality of it all. I never crafted a plan as a young coach to be on the podium accepting a gold medal, nor did I think about what coaching moves I needed to make along my journey to get there. I grew up on a small family farm in southeastern Iowa and had a passion for basketball. When my playing career ended, I transferred my enthusiasm for playing the game to coaching it. Coaching basketball allowed me to continue being a part of the game I loved and provided me an opportunity to share my passion for the game with others. Early in my coaching career, my passion drove my interest in pursuing opportunities. As my knowledge of the game and my skills as a teacher of the game began to align with my enthusiasm, more opportunities came my way.

The buzzer sounded. USA 95, France 52.

"The Star-Spangled Banner" played, and I glanced toward the young men next to me. I had been here before; for each of them, it was a new experience. I reveled in their moment, just watching them. The emotion and pride of representing the US as the head coach of the Junior National Team—a tenure that finished with a 62–0 record and 10 gold medals—overcame me. I could feel my eyes starting to well up. I blinked a few times to keep my emotions from spilling out, but one drop of moisture escaped. I held back the urge to wipe the tear away as I glanced toward a smattering of spectators and caught the eye of my high school sweetheart, my partner at every step of my journey, Vicky. We exchanged a smile; we both knew this would be the last time. A career that began among the cornfields of rural Iowa would end with another gold medal.

How did I go from being the son of a farmer and a night-shift hospital worker, growing up on a single-family farm among the cornfields of Iowa, to standing on the gold medal stand, coaching the best young basketball talent in the world? How did I cultivate my passion for basketball and my desire to share that passion with others to become an international ambassador for the sport? How did I keep family, faith, and basketball in perspective along my journey? I hope by sharing my story and the lessons I learned along the way, it will help you along your own personal and professional path.

—Don Showalter

CHAPTER 1

Donnie

Donnie steadied himself on a chair. His long arms stretched above his head as he placed strands of masking tape in a circle on a large metal beam. The beam rose between the kitchen and the sitting room, a structural support for the Showalters' farmhouse. After securing the tape, Donnie bounded off the chair and rejoined his brother Doug, who had just finished wrapping tape around a rolled-up sock. With the circle as a hoop and the rolled-up sock as the ball, a game of one-on-one basketball ensued.

Makeshift hoops were scattered about the Showalter farm: on the backs of doors, the light pole in the driveway, on the side of the barn, and inside the hay barn and corncrib. Rarely did Donnie miss a day shooting baskets. Often his brother Doug and good friend Fred Mishler joined him. Fred's family managed a farm a mile from the Showalters' place, and he and Donnie grew up together.

"Hey, Fred, let's head up to the hay barn," shouted Donnie as Fred jogged toward him with a basketball cradled in one arm. The hay barn, rented by the Mishler family, laid claim to a nonregulation full court. Fred's older brothers had nailed down wooden boards and Doug, Fred, and Donnie pushed the hay bales off to the side to play. Fred tossed the ball to Donnie, now only a few feet away and said, "Naw, let's go to the corn crib instead. There is quite a bit of hay in the barn right now. We'd spend more time pushing bales than playing."

1

An enclosed structure, the corn crib attached to the side of the Showalters' barn. Half of the barn housed hogs and the other half with ears of corn except for a 15 foot cement slab, an open space to allow for a truck or tractor to pull in and load corn. It was the perfect place for a basketball hoop, except that above the slab protruded a large funnel to assist with the loading of corn. Because the funnel hung out over the slab, its presence played with the amount of arc one could place on his shot.

"Sure," said Donnie, with a slight grin. "I have too much arc on my shot right now, it would be good to flatten it out a bit." He and Fred laughed and took off a on run, across the snow, toward the corn crib.

DONALD "DONNIE" MONROE SHOWALTER was born to Donald and Iva Showalter in 1952 in Wellman, Iowa. The first of five sons, Donnie felt drawn to the competitive, social, and physical qualities offered by sports, especially basketball. A happy, easygoing disposition made Donnie approachable and likable—a charisma built on action more than words. He made others comfortable being themselves when in his presence. Donnie never seemed to be short of friends, one of whom was Dan Bontrager. They shared a love for sports and competition. "Donnie was easy to be friends with, because he was fun to be around," recalled Dan.

Donnie bounded down the stairs from his second-story bedroom. He did not want to be late. He had lost track of time, preoccupied by the printed images of Ted Williams, Yogi Berra, Willie Mays, and two from his favorite team, Roger Maris and Mickey Mantle, otherwise known as the New York Yankees' M&M boys. He had been captivated by the hundreds of other baseball cards sorted, stacked, or strewn about his bedroom floor and mesmerized by the baritone voice coming through his transistor radio of the legendary Minnesota Twins radio play-by-play announcer Herb

Carneal, describing the action of his favorite player, Tony Oliva, right fielder for the Twins. Skipping the final three steps, Donnie hit the hardwood floor in stride and raced toward the front door. He flung open the door, leaving it to dangle wide-open, exposing the Showalter farmhouse to the hot summer afternoon breeze. The urgency of his pace quickened outside as he skirted around his mom's garden, which took up most of the front yard, and headed in the direction of the turkey barn, where his father was working. His destination was in sight; he was going to make it. On his last stride, he slowed and leaped for the low step on the tractor. Then in one motion, like a seasoned farmhand, he pulled his body up by the steering wheel and twisted his torso into the metal tractor seat. He started the tractor and at only nine years of age headed out to the fields to assist with the hay, bean, and cornfields.

He had been introduced to farm chores at an early age. He cleaned the turkey barn, minded the yard and garden around the farmhouse, worked with the pigs and cattle, and tended to the 4-H calves. For both his parents, farming is what they knew and also how they met. Donald was the oldest of four siblings, which included a younger sister, Dorothy, and two younger twin brothers, Darrel and Dale. They all grew up farming. Iva was the second of five siblings, with an older sister, Rose, two younger twin brothers, Kenneth and Keith, and a brother nine years younger, Rowen.

Iva's father, Monroe Hochstedler, started as a schoolteacher, then purchased a farm in 1940 to raise turkeys and dairy cows. When Iva was 13, her parents purchased a second farm with 120 acres and a two-story house. Monroe employed farmhands to take care of the turkeys on the range. One summer he hired 17-year-old Donald Showalter. Iva was smitten by the new hire. "He spoke well and I knew he was smart," said Iva. "Plus, it was the way he looked at me with those honest blue eyes." Their young love simmered for the next two years, before Donald and Iva began a courtship.

Donald's work ethic made an impression on Monroe, and when Iva and Donald announced their engagement, he gifted them the second farm. They wed in 1951 and moved into the farm's two-story house. It had running water and a shower in the basement but no indoor toilet. Hot-water bottles placed at the foot of their bed warded off the chill of the winter wind as it seeped into the upstairs bedrooms.

For the next 40 years, Donald and Iva made the farmhouse their home. They added an indoor bathroom and shutters for the windows; remodeled the kitchen/dining area; paneled walls; screened in a porch; constructed a garage; painted; and landscaped with trees, bushes, and flowers. After Donnie's birth in 1952, the family grew again in 1954 with the arrival Doug. Then three more times with three more sons: David in 1959, Dean in 1966, and Dennis in 1968. Iva and Donald were a team when it came to raising their family. They supported their children, both in education and the activities they were involved in and they always made sure that family came first; together they modeled an approach to living one's life that later influenced how Donnie lived his.

DONNIE'S LEGS BOUNCED UP and down. The view from the dugout bothered the 12-year-old. With each passing minute, he became more agitated by his coach's decision to have him sit on the bench. Donnie followed the action on the field, clapping and cheering with his teammates in the dugout, his true emotions masked. He often pitched, and when someone else pitched, Donnie played shortstop. But on this day, he played neither. After the game, in the presence of his parents, Donnie uttered his frustration.

"Why didn't the coach put me in?" Donnie pouted. "I always get to play."

"I don't want to hear any more about it," scolded his father. "I am sure he had a good reason for not playing you today."

Donald Showalter presented a calm, easygoing manner in the presence of others. He listened first, then spoke in turn. He was a man of action who served as an elder in the East Mennonite Church, where he taught Sunday school and led church activities; later he served on the Mid-Prairie School Board. He exhibited an intense work ethic and liked order, and he set high standards for his five sons, expecting them to give their best effort until a task was complete.

As a father, Donald was distant at times. He did not regularly play ball with his kids and shied away from displays of fatherly affection, such as hugs and kisses. Yet he displayed unwavering support of their educational interests and passion for sports. An avid softball player himself, Donald understood the allure of competition and always made time to attend each of his son's athletic contests.

Iva took great pride in caring for her children, serving in the traditional role of homemaker. She combined a determined, sincere devotion to doing what was right for her family with a strong curiosity about the world. She did not want the limitations of rural farm life in Iowa to squelch her sons' opportunities to learn; she made sure there were books in the house and there was time to read. A young bride, Iva never finished formal high school. In time, she earned a GED and trained for a career in nursing at Kirkwood Community College in Cedar Rapids. Using her degree, she spent 25 years working the graveyard shift at the University of Iowa Hospital, a 16-mile commute from the family farmhouse.

Whereas Donald held a quiet presence over the house, Iva was more direct, serving as both the disciplinarian and the first source of emotional support. To be present for her children was important to her, which is why she worked the graveyard shift: to be around her children before and after school each day. Both Donnie's parents left an imprint on his future and allowed him to discover who he would become.

ONCE DONNIE HAD HIS heart set on a brand-new 1961 Schwinn Speedster. But he felt apprehensive about asking his father for the bike because he knew it was expensive. One day he finally mustered the courage. His father considered the request and replied, "I'm sure I can find you a good used bike from one of the neighbors."

Donnie paused, not willing to give up on the idea of a new bike, and said, "Dad, I really want a new Schwinn Speedster—a black one."

His father glanced in his direction, paused, and answered, "We'll see."

A few weeks later, Donnie noticed his father and sometimes his mother away from the farm in the early morning hours, not something either one of them normally did. This happened for about a week, then both resumed their morning routines about the farm. A short time later, his parents surprised him with a brand-new black Schwinn Speedster. Donnie later learned that his parents had cleaned up the school grounds around the one-room country schoolhouse he attended to pay for the bike.

Both Donald and Iva reinforced the importance of hard work and taught all five of their sons how to be independent. After school, homework came first, then chores. Donald pushed all his sons on the farm, but he understood when they needed a break just to be kids and he would give them an afternoon off to go fishing or play with their friends.

For Donnie and his friends, sports became a place to discover who they were and who they could become, a place to develop a sense of identity. In Donnie's case, his passion for basketball became quite apparent to his family and friends—a part of how they knew him and interacted with him, a part of who he was.

Dan Bontrager remembered thinking Donnie had it pretty good in that regard. "My dad made me help on the farm quite a bit. It seems to me that Donnie got to go play basketball a lot in the summertime," said Dan jokingly. "I always envied that a bit."

Much of Donnie's extended family was nearby, including Donald's younger brother Darrel and his wife, Janet. With Donnie being the oldest, and with no children of their own at that time, Darrel and Janet became especially close with Donnie, attending Donnie's games as a player and later coach when their son Craig played for him.

For 43 years, Darrel worked at the University of Iowa Hospital as a supply manager, which earned him two discounted staff tickets to all University of Iowa athletic events. One Saturday in the early 1960s, the couple was taking Donnie and his younger brother Doug to a Hawkeyes football game. Darrel fiddled with the radio dial until he landed on the voice of Jim Zabel. Zabel, known as "Z," did play-by-play of both Hawkeye football and basketball games for close to 50 years on WHO 1040-AM. Donnie glanced toward the bag resting below his Aunt Dorothy's feet, as she always brought snacks for the game. She often accompanied Darrel and Janet to football games and also had access to discounted ticket working as a staffing clerk at the University of Iowa. His eyes caught a glimpse of aluminum foil inside, and he sat back, satisfied. They were there: hot dogs, neatly wrapped in foil—his favorite. Donnie's focus shifted to football as Iowa Stadium came into view.

They easily found a seat at the 50-yard line, as Iowa football had fallen on hard times. The team had won only 14 games over six seasons from 1962 to 1967. Darrel pulled out his transistor radio and tuned to the game. Rarely did Darrel leave home without the radio when he attended Iowa games, a practice he would continue at Donnie's high school basketball games. For the next three hours, the action on the field, the food in Aunt Dorothy's basket, and family time together created fond memories for all.

IN IOWA, BELIEF SYSTEMS dot the landscape like coffee shops occupy urban street corners. For the Showalter family, the Mennonite faith guided their spiritual life. Like the Amish, the Mennonite way of life is rooted in strong conservative values that focus on humility, hard work, cooperation, and building a sense of community among their own—a self-sufficient approach to protect their community from the sins and perceived corruption of the outside world. In contrast, the Mennonites are considered more liberal and progressive than the Amish, more willing to adapt to the ever-changing world in the 20th century.

One area of particular concern for the Mennonites was the education of their young people. There was a growing sentiment in the 1930s among the Mennonite community that the public schools were an immoral environment that challenged Mennonite teachings by exposing their youth to adolescent sins, such as tobacco and alcohol. Furthermore, the public schools encouraged participation in extracurricular activities, which took time away from farm work. These concerns drove the Mennonites of southeastern Iowa to construct their own school, and in 1945 the Iowa Mennonite School, which became known as IMS, opened its doors to Mennonite youth.

Under the guidance of the Mennonite faith, both Donald and Iva instilled and modeled the value of education with all their sons. Donnie knew they expected him to attend college, as had their siblings. Iva's younger twin brothers, Kenneth and Keith, both attended a community college in Kansas, for instance, but it was Iva's youngest brother, Rowen, who acted on his own curiosity when it came to higher education, in a manner that captured Donnie's interest the most.

Rowen was only nine years older than Donnie, and from a young age he was intent on carving out a different future for himself, one removed from the daily grind of farm life. He desired to experience a bigger world and break free of the strict doctrine established by the Mennonite faith. "Growing up, your options were to be a farmer, teacher, minister, or a doctor," said Rowen. "Because becoming a doctor was a wide-open field and my mother had lots of faith in my local doctor, I mapped out a plan that I would attend a Mennonite college and go premed and then to medical school."

Rowen roomed with the son of a Harvard divinity professor his first years at Goshen College, a private Mennonite college in Indiana. With the urging of his roommate, Rowen applied to Harvard, an act that challenged traditional Mennonite beliefs. He told no one in his family. About midsummer between his freshman and sophomore year at Goshen, Rowen received an acceptance letter from Harvard. At this point he knew he needed to tell his parents. Although his father cautioned him on making the move, they let him go.

Rowen graduated from Harvard premed and attended New York University to become a psychiatrist. He practiced psychiatry for more than 50 years. He set an example that showed Donnie that he too could carve out his own future.

DONNIE RUSHED UP THE stairs, a couple steps ahead of his father. Donald paced himself on the climb up the staircase hidden beneath the arena seats, a stairwell that connected the lower concourse level with the upper deck. Donnie looked toward the court gleefully in anticipation of the game. Completed in 1927, with a seating capacity of close to 14,000, the Iowa Field House was a venue Donnie loved. The talents and abilities of the Hawkeyes players on display nurtured his passion for the game. Often he attended with his father or his uncle Darrel, and later his high school friends. But tonight, the 1966 NCAA Men's Basketball Mideast Regional Tournament was in town, featuring the Dayton Flyers, Kentucky Wildcats, Michigan Wolverines, and Western Kentucky Hilltoppers. The rosters were dotted with future household names: Pat Riley. Louis Dampier. Cazzie Russell. Clem Haskins. Henry Finkel.

With his eyes fixed on the court below, Donnie asked his father for the game program he had purchased as they entered the arena, and then perused the teams' rosters. With his transistor radio in hand, Donald listened and watched with his son as Dayton battled Kentucky in the first game. Coach Adolph Rupp strolled the sideline for Kentucky, in his 35th season. A living legend, Rupp already had four national championships. He became the first collegiate basketball coach to win more than 800 games, ending his career with 876. The Wildcats went on a run in the last 10 minutes, winning 86–79.

The second game was a tight, thrilling contest between Michigan and Western Kentucky. In the final seconds of the game, the Wolverines took an 80–79 victory on a couple made free throws.

After the game, as Donald steered the family Volkswagen Bug along Highway 6, Donnie's mind raced with thoughts of the play on the court. He noticed how well the teams played together. He observed the presence the coaches had in leading their teams and the respect the players had for them. Just an eighth grader, Donnie wondered what it might be like to play for a coach like that and what it might be like to *be* a coach.

DONNIE'S RIGHT INDEX FINGER slid along the page of the Iowa City telephone book, scrolling for the last name Miller. There was more than one, but his finger rested on the listing MILLER, RALPH AND JEAN. He reached for the phone with his left hand, then pulled it back and glanced over his class assignment one more time before dialing.

"Hello," said the person on the line.

"Is this Coach Miller?" asked Donnie.

"Yes. Who's calling?" replied Coach Miller, gruffly.

"My name is Donnie Showalter, and I'm calling to see if you would answer a few questions for a class assignment about being a coach."

"Are you a reporter?" piped Coach Miller as if he did not hear him the first time.

"No, I'm a student at Iowa Mennonite School completing an assignment where we have to interview someone in a career we are interested in."

"Oh, okay," said Coach Miller. "Go ahead."

Unbeknownst to Donnie or anyone else at that time, he had just interviewed a coach who would become a key figure in college basketball history. A future Hall of Famer, Coach Miller connected the basketball past to the present: he was first at the University of Kansas, where he learned from the game's inventor, Dr. James Naismith, a guest lecturer in one of his college courses; then he played at Kansas for Forrest "Phog" Allen, widely referred to as the Father of Basketball Coaching; and later he influenced future basketball coaches with his full-court-pressing style of defense and fast-break passing style of offense. Donnie's interaction with Coach Miller on that phone call gave him much more than a passing grade on a class assignment; it would fuel his confidence to approach an iconic college basketball coach just a few years later.

DONNIE NEVER CONSIDERED WHERE he might go to high school. Only two miles from his house, the Iowa Mennonite School (IMS) was the easy choice. All three uncles on his mother's side, plus his mother, had attended IMS. On his father's side, his two twin uncles, Darrel and Dale, and his Aunt Dorothy, had gone there. Interestingly his father had not, instead graduating from nearby Parnell High School. Also, a majority of the children in his youth group at the East Mennonite Church would enroll at IMS. Going to IMS just seemed like the next step.

The Mennonites took great pride in their school and maintained tight control of the environment, which included a strict dress code, daily chapel service, and high standards for student behavior. For IMS students, there was also no interscholastic competition. No rivals, no pep bands, no cheerleaders, no raucous crowds, no bus trips, no pursuit of a state championship, and no consistent coaching presence. IMS only offered intramural sports. This was to protect the traditional Mennonite faith and ensure youth wouldn't be tempted by the outside influences found in public schools—values that did not align with, or might distract youth from, responsibility to education, faith, and family.

Although IMS never competed against local public high schools, there were occasional opportunities to compete against other Mennonite schools. As a sophomore, Donnie traveled with a team from IMS to Ohio for a tournament with three other Mennonite high schools, one each from Ohio, Pennsylvania, and Virginia. The four-day trip culminated in a first-place trophy for IMS, a proud moment for the school and the athletes.

The experience in Ohio whet Donnie's appetite for more competition, and he found it in a local church league. The five local Mennonite churches—Lower Deer Creek, West Union, East Union, Kalona Mennonite, and Wellman—plus a team from Iowa City, came together to form a competitive league, with each church represented by its congregation: a mix of young adults, middle-aged men, and high school kids. As a sophomore, Donnie competed for the East Union Mennonite Church. The increase in physical play, coupled with the savvy of older players, challenged him to develop his game while providing a place to showcase his skills to members of the Mennonite community. The word got around that Donnie had a knack for the game, and his family took notice of his athletic prowess. So much so that a consensus was growing that IMS limited Donnie's basketball opportunities and maybe he should consider transferring to the public Mid-Prairie High School just a few miles down the road.

The basketball coach there was Cal Hickman, and he fit the image of a young coach with something to prove; he exuded confidence that bordered on cockiness. He was only 5'7", but it did not take long for Hickman to stand tall in the eyes of the youth he led. Hickman's ability to teach the game and get them to work together as a team gave him credibility, garnering him a high level of respect in the community among athletes and parents.

Raised on a farm in Humansville, Missouri, Hickman found his career path early as a teacher and coach. In 1963 he signed a contract to serve as a physical education teacher, head boys' basketball coach, and assistant football coach at the new consolidated Mid-Prairie School District in southeastern Iowa.

In the spring of 1968, the Mid-Prairie Golden Hawks completed their best season under Coach Hickman, winning 17 games, capped with a conference and district championship. "Donnie's father would go over to IMS to watch the Friday games and realized that IMS did not really focus on athletics," recalled Iva. "He recognized that Donnie was not really being coached."

It is unknown whether it was Cal Hickman or Donald Showalter who initiated the conversation about Donnie transferring to Mid-Prairie, but on a summer evening in 1968, Donald invited Hickman to dinner at the Showalter farm, and Cal, Donald, and Iva shared a conversation about how a transfer would work.

Donnie had never thought of transferring to Mid-Prairie. His friends went to IMS; that is just what you did. However, when discussion started among his family about leaving IMS and the opportunities it could provide him on the basketball court, Donnie felt comfortable with the thought of attending another school. It was settled: Donnie had become a Golden Hawk.

CHAPTER 2

Vicky

Donnie pushed the pedal to the floor; dirt sprayed from the rear wheels and dust billowed around the Dodge Coronet Super Bee. He sped up, only easing off the gas when the tires began to skip off the tips of the washboard ripples, bouncing the car side to side, or when he skidded sideways on a patch of loose gravel. *How fast will this go?*, he wondered. He loved the power and the speed of the muscle car, but like with most teenagers, the car represented a sense of freedom.

Donnie used money he earned from 4-H projects, church activities, and odd jobs, along with some assistance from his parents, to purchase it. Donnie and his Super Bee were inseparable; they'd become synonymous with one another. The flashy car surely garnered him attention among his peers, especially the girls. But by the middle of Donnie's junior year, only one girl had his full attention—a pretty brunette in his class, Vicky Joan Bauer. The Bauer family had been a part of the West Chester community since 1857, growing corn and beans, and raising hogs.

Vicky was born in 1952 to Joe and Janet Bauer, and she experienced an idyllic upbringing, nurtured in the delicate balance between the potential prosperity and poverty associated with supporting a family through farming. Her parents sheltered her; her older brother, Robert; and her two younger twin sisters, Jane and Judy, from this expected rise and fall by keeping the kids occupied in activities that centered around education, church, and family. Vicky participated in youth church group activities, piano lessons, and dance lessons. Her mother served as a leader in 4-H, and Vicky participated there in sewing, home furnishings, and food and nutrition.

The Bauers were a close family, and they spent quite a bit of time together, which included trips to the nearby town of Washington to visit the public library, eat dinner, or get ice cream. One summer, in 1962, the family drove from Iowa to Seattle to attend the World's Fair. "Vicky was a supportive, compassionate, and reliable big sister, but she could also be opinionated and a bit bossy," said Judy, chuckling.

Vicky embraced the structure of school, where she could assert herself and take on leadership roles. She first gravitated to music and chorus, then cheerleading in junior high and high school. In high school she was also involved with Future Teachers of America, the National Honor Society, yearbook staff, band, and choir. School became an important part of Vicky's identity during adolescence, and she easily found a supportive peer group—a core group of friends that became almost inseparable in social settings away from school. Donnie connected with Vicky's group of friends early on in his junior year at Mid-Prairie. "Donnie just fit right in with our group. It did not seem like he was a new kid coming to our school," recalled Vicky. "When basketball started, we were together more in the same group of friends, because I was a cheerleader and he was a basketball player."

In February 1969 Vicky and Donnie had their first date: a trip to Iowa City for dinner at Pagliai's Pizza, followed by a movie. A trip to Iowa City became a popular date night, but the couple spent much of their time together at the Bauer farm, and rarely alone. Jane and Judy both were dating older boys at that time, and after ballgames, friends from school frequently congregated at the Bauers' place in West Chester. "Our house was the fun place to be growing up," said Judy. "We often played cards with our boyfriends. My mom had snacks and plenty of food for everyone to eat."

WITH ONLY SECONDS ON the clock, the Keota Eagles led the 1969 sectional championship game by one point. As the Mid-Prairie Golden Hawks returned to the floor, center Dan Dickel positioned himself on the end line 84 feet from the Mid-Prairie basket to inbound the ball. Donnie was nearest Dickel, a couple feet behind the free-throw line. The Eagles matched up man-to-man, placing a defender on Dickel and leaving Donnie one-on-one with an Eagles defender. All attention in the gymnasium centered on what would transpire in the next few moments, as the winner would advance to the district tournament in Ottumwa.

The official blew his whistle and handed the ball to Dickel. Instantaneously, Donnie broke toward Dickel diagonally across the backcourt. Dickel delivered a bounce pass to his right, which Donnie caught in stride. With enough space to maneuver along the sideline, Donnie dribbled up past the half-court line. Without changing his stride, he plucked the ball off the dribble, planted his left foot, and leapt in the air, his right arm extended, releasing the ball toward the basket. Time paused. All eyes in the gymnasium traced the arc of the ball as it drifted toward the basket. The buzzer blared as the ball fell through the net.

The victory placed Mid-Prairie in the district tournament against Ottumwa Walsh, a private Catholic high school. Their Fighting Gaels prevailed 73–60, ending Mid-Prairie's season, despite Donnie's 28 points. Donnie only played half a season his junior year due to Iowa High School Athletic Association (IHSAA) transfer rules, which required a student-athlete to wait 90 days before competing in interscholastic competition. But Donnie's play in the postseason hinted at exciting things to come in his senior year—a season that would capture the interest of the community in a manner nobody had experienced before, with Donnie leading the way.

CHAPTER 3

Hickman

A neat, trimmed crew cut exposed Cal Hickman's boyish face and made him, at least in appearance, approachable to the youth he coached and taught. For many of the locals, Hickman felt like a familiar face; he looked like he grew up on a farm just a country mile down the road. But really he grew up 300 country miles to the south in Missouri, on a family farm near the Ozarks. There he developed a strong work ethic and learned traits such as cooperation and self-discipline, which he later instilled in the boys he coached. With his unpretentious upbringing, occasional down-home chuckle, and struggle with a slight speech impediment, the outsider seemed to fit right in, and the locals accepted him as one of their own.

During competition, Hickman's temper could ignite. He would jerk out of his seat and jump up and down, stomping his feet. At times his face darkened another shade of red as he continued stomping, almost rhythmically, creating what his athletes later described as a clapping sound. Hickman provided direct feedback to his team and rarely spared his words to make a point; sometimes he could get right in your face.

Influenced by Ralph Miller's up-tempo style of play with the Iowa Hawkeyes in the late 1960s, Hickman employed his squad to push the ball and pressure the other team. Thus, the Golden Hawks utilized a full-court zone press to generate turnovers and easy fast-break buckets. The energy and excitement of the new style of play earned the team the nickname the Hustlin' Hawks. On offense Hickman spread the court to best utilize the skills of his players—a pass-and-cut style that employed motion offensive concepts. His style of play made him fun to play for, and because he taught his players how to play, their confidence in themselves, and him as their coach, grew as they got better. Hickman expanded the game of basketball for youth, running some of the first summer basketball camps in southeastern Iowa. For Donnie, his teammates, and the community, Coach Hickman had changed the attitude about what it meant to play basketball at Mid-Prairie High School. During the 1969–70 season, the Golden Hawks reached new heights, generating a level of excitement for basketball in the local community for future generations.

The Golden Hawks' roster for the 1969–70 season featured both size and experience. The 6'3" Dan Dickel, described as "rugged" by sports reporters at the time, often finished the game as the leading rebounder and occasionally the top scorer. Jerry Kron joined him in the front court. Mainly a role player, the lanky, 6'3" Kron took advantage of opportunities to score high-percentage shots around the basket. Dick Ehrenfelt, a 6'4" sophomore, provided a presence in the post to complement Dickel.

Donnie occupied a wing, opposite junior Steve Mast, a transfer from Indiana. Mast, the most naturally skilled player on the squad, had a knack for scoring and a nose for the ball. Dan Jirsa shared the point guard duties with senior Byron Miller. Jirsa, the 5'10" quarterback and seasoned leader of the football team, brought an element of toughness and competitive fire. Senior, Dave Spreacker figured to be in the mix by the end of the season, but the 5'10" guard was still recovering from a knee injury he'd sustained late in the football season.

After a 2–2 start, that experience kicked in and Mid-Prairie walloped University High of Iowa City 74–47. Both 6'3" Dan

Dickel and Donnie chipped in 22 points, with Dickel adding 19 rebounds. Over the next three games, the Hustlin' Hawks averaged 86 points per game to up their record to 6–2.

Donnie's good attitude and even-keeled manner made him a quiet star, sometimes hiding his lethal ability to put the ball in the basket. He finished his senior year with 411 points for a team high of 18.1 points per game. His talents on offense overshadowed his lack of talent on defense. "Donnie could really shoot it, but he did not play defense worth a shit," laughed teammate Dan Jirsa at the memory. "I always had to guard the other team's best guard."

Mid-Prairie won their next six games, which included a school-record 117 points in a 66-point victory over West Branch, improving their record to 12–2. In the final week of the regular season, the Golden Hawks beat Solon High 98–74 in their second matchup to clinch the Eastern Iowa Hawkeye Conference (EIHC) title. They headed into the regular-season finale against Mt. Vernon with a record of 14–2.

DONNIE TURNED UP THE driveway to the Bauer farm, the hum of his Dodge Super Bee loud enough for Vicky to hear its approach. Donnie waved as he watched her bounce across the front yard toward him. He was beyond hooked at this point. She had a way about her that captured his affection—more than a crush or young love.

They were headed to the University of Iowa to watch Donnie's beloved Hawkeyes compete against the Purdue Boilermakers. The Boilermakers starred one of the nation's leading scorers in All-American Rick Mount, who averaged more than 30 points a game. Purdue entered the contest at 7–2, just one year removed from a runner-up finish to UCLA and Lew Alcindor in the 1969 National Championship Game. Coach Ralph Miller, in his sixth season with the Hawkeyes, had brought the exciting style of play with him from Wichita University (later Wichita State University), where he led the

Shockers to 220 wins in 13 seasons. The 1969-70 Hawkeyes, dubbed the "Miller six pack" due to the coach's tendency to only play his top six players, utilized a full-court pressure defense to energize their fast break. On January 3, 1970, they entered their contest against the Boilermakers with a 3–4 record. The game was the first conference game of the season for both teams.

Donnie parked in the parking lot, and he and Vicky strolled toward the entrance to meet their friends Dan Dickel and his girlfriend, Denise. Like Donnie, Dickel had fallen for someone who would later become his better half. Denise, also a cheerleader, and Vicky were grade school friends. Soon, all four of them became quite close. Donnie and Vicky waved when they noticed Dan and Denise approaching across the parking lot.

As the two couples approached the entrance, Dickel realized he had left his and Denise's tickets back at his house. They decided to go back and get them, and Vicky and Donnie headed into the Field House to find their seats.

The Hawkeyes' 1969–70 squad had the potential to be one of Iowa's best ever. And with the Field House packed beyond capacity, Donnie and Vicky witnessed the scoring prowess of Purdue's Rick Mount as he tossed in a career-best 53 points, an Iowa Field House record. Even with Mount's performance, though, Miller's Six-Pack prevailed 94–88. Donnie and Vicky never reconnected with Dan and Denise that evening. "Denise and I went to a movie instead," recalled Dickel, chuckling at the memory. "Which we ended up walking out of. I really blew that one."

That victory sent the Hawkeyes on a winning streak, finishing 14–0 in Big Ten Conference play, which included another victory over the Boilermakers in late February—in which Mount scored a Big Ten single-game record of 61 points—to take the outright Big Ten title. The Hawkeyes averaged 98.6 points a game, scoring more than 100 points 14 times that season.

Donnie thought how fun it would be to play for Coach Miller. He loved the fast-paced offense, with its many chances to shoot and score points, and the pressure defense. He knew Coach Hickman studied Coach Miller's system and style of play and used them with the team. Donnie was curious about the fast-paced, pressing defense style of play, and it became planted in the back of his mind, ready to use when he became a coach.

THE GOLDEN HAWKS CARRIED the swagger of a team confident in themselves heading into their final regular-season game of the year, having clinched the EIHC title one week prior and riding a 12-game winning streak. In the final scheduled game of the regular season, a matchup against the Mount Vernon Mustangs, the Golden Hawks controlled the game and led by two points with three minutes to go. With their 13th straight victory just minutes away, the Golden Hawks went cold and the Mustangs outscored them 20–8 in the fourth period to win 62–58. Mid-Prairie finished 14–3 overall and 12–2 in the conference.

The loss to the Mustangs provided a wake-up call heading into the sectional tournament. In 1970 Iowa established 64 sectional tournament sites, with the winner at each site advancing to the district tournament. Fortunately for Hickman's Hustlin' Hawks, Mid-Prairie hosted their sectional tournament. The Hawks wasted no time in their first-round game against Pekin-Packwood, winning by 60 points. In the second contest, Dickel went off for a season high 27 points against Sigourney and the Hawks won 79–51. In the final, five players scored in double figures and Hickman's team took the sectional championship against Keota 73–51.

At districts, against the Wilton Junction Beavers, Jerry Kron scored a career high 26 points, mainly on fast-break layups, and Donnie matched him with 26 of his own in a 96–78 victory. Then the following night, with a deft display of team shooting and behind a career high of 35 points from Donnie, they routed Aquin of Cascade, Iowa, 99–67 for the district title.

It would be difficult for Cal Hickman to find much fault in the Golden Hawks' play leading into the state qualifying game in Anamosa, Iowa. For Hickman, this certainly was his best team; only the undefeated 22–0 Bennett Bombers stood in the Golden Hawks' way of a state tournament berth. A few days before the game, Donnie discovered an infected wisdom tooth. He would play, but his time and effectiveness might be limited. Fortunately for Hickman, football star Dave Spreacker, recently returned to the lineup, had a key block late in the game against Bennett to send the game into overtime.

In overtime, Dickel scored a reverse layup to give Mid-Prairie a 61–60 lead with 28 seconds left. When the Bombers' last attempt bounced off the rim, the Mid-Prairie fans rushed the court. The win gave the Golden Hawks their first state tournament appearance in the school's 10-year history and the first appearance for a community team since West Chester High went to state in 1947.

The six straight victories in tournament play captured the community; momentum from each win fueled an interest in the play of the team. The players and coaches noticed the increased attention, and all anyone could talk about was the Hustlin' Hawks. The school district canceled classes on Thursday and Friday to allow students to attend the state tournament, and local businesses shut down. A caravan of fans followed the bus to Veterans Memorial Auditorium in Des Moines.

Vicky found herself caught up in the excitement of the moment. Her role as cheerleader and her relationship with Donnie drew her closer to the team and kept her emotionally involved. And what could have been a distraction for Donnie never became one; the passion of their high school relationship likely tempered by the deeper connection they already felt for each other. As the Golden Hawks arrived at the Fort Des Moines Hotel, Donnie had a Western

Union telegram waiting for him at the front desk, it read: *Don – Good Luck at State. Thinking of you and miss you. Lots of love always - Vicky.*

Mid-Prairie's first opponent in the state tournament was the 22–1 Manson Eagles. The Golden Hawks struggled early in the contest. Fortunately, Donnie kept them in it, shooting 5-for-6 from the field in the first quarter. He finished with 24 points and Mid-Prairie won by 14, 71–57.

The next morning, *Iowa City Press Citizen* sports editor Al Grady compared the Hustlin' Hawks to Miller's Hawkeyes, a team he covered extensively. "[Mid-Prairie] plays a pressing defense like Iowa, runs with the ball like Iowa, and passes the ball to the open man like Iowa." Grady continued with high praise for Donnie, "He has the quick release on a jump shot like Rick Mount.... Like Mount he seems to shoot best in heavy traffic."

In the Friday night semifinal, Mid-Prairie faced La Porte City. Utilizing an uncustomary half-court zone defense, the Golden Hawks jumped to an early 9–1 lead and never looked back, winning 91–73 for a berth in the State A Championship game. No one expected the Paullina High Panthers to be challenged in the State A Championship game. In their semifinal contest, the two-time defending state champion had cruised to their 75th straight win, getting 34 points from two-time all-state player Neil Fegebank. Still, the Hawks were playing their best basketball at a time when they needed it most.

Paullina went on a run and secured a 38–30 lead at the halftime break. Late in the fourth period, Paullina held a five-point lead, 71–66. On the next two Golden Hawks possessions, Donnie nailed back-to-back baskets to cut the score to 71–70 with a little less than three minutes to play. After a Donnie bucket, Steve Mast stole the ball from a Panthers guard and was fouled. If Mast made them both, all the pressure would be on Paullina.

Mast, a clutch performer and a junior on a team laden with senior talent, stepped to the line for his first free throw; he would have to hit the first one to get the second shot. Paullina fans roared; Mid-Prairie supporters kept quiet, fixated on Mast at the foul line.

Mast missed the free shot. Paullina rebounded the ball and finished the game with seven straight points for a 78–70 victory and their third straight state championship, extending their winning streak to 76.

Stunned, proud, and emotionally drained, both the Mid-Prairie team and the community turned disappointment into a celebration. As the team returned home, a welcome party greeted them. One might have assumed the Golden Hawks brought home the gold trophy. More than 1,000 people packed into the Mid-Prairie gym. Both Hickman and assistant coach Tim Grady spoke, and then Hickman introduced each member of the team, one by one, inviting them to the microphone to share a few words. When Donnie took the microphone, he stated, "Silver is just as good as gold any day." That statement reflected an appreciation of the moment and a recognition of their shared experience, while revealing his sense of humility.

Donnie shared co-captain first-team all-tournament honors with Fegebank and was a first-team all-EIHC selection. The Iowa Press Association named him third-team all-state. For Donnie the thrill of the state tournament lingered through the last few months of his senior year. The excitement of the senior prom and final moments with high school friends, experiences that create lifelong memories, could not quite surpass what he had shared with his Golden Hawks teammates and coaches at the state tournament in Des Moines.

FOR EVERY HIGH SCHOOL senior, graduation is one of life's key milestones, a transition point from adolescence to young adulthood. For teenagers already in constant pursuit of independence, what happens after graduation is a giant step toward their future. For those under the spell of teenage love, this step can present more challenges: commit to each other, break up, or manage a long-distance relationship. A tough decision to face for a high school couple like Donnie and Vicky as they neared graduation.

The future weighed heavily on Donnie's mind. They both graduated in a couple months. He would attend Wartburg College in Waverly, Iowa, where he had signed to play for Coach Buzz Levick. Vicky had been accepted at Iowa State University, with recognition for her hard-won scholastic achievements. She would be in Ames, not too far away—only a two-hour drive—but they would be apart, nonetheless. Vicky had her sights set on becoming an elementary school teacher, and Iowa State had a good education program. The opportunity at Wartburg gripped Donnie. Buzz Levick, in his fifth season, had the Wartburg Knights on the rise. In the 1969–70 season the Knights won 26 games and claimed their third straight conference championship. (Levick went on to a Hall of Fame career, leading the Knights for 28 seasons, winning 510 games, and capturing 14 conference championships.)

Donnie knew he wanted to be with Vicky, but in the moment he had more questions than answers about how a long-distance relationship might work. *With basketball it seemed simple*, he thought. *Why did life seem so messy?*

ON MAY 24, 1970, Mid-Prairie High School honored its 10th graduating class. Donnie, Vicky, and all their friends and family shared in the celebration. Shortly after the graduation ceremony, Donnie scrawled the following on the back page of his senior year scrapbook, reflecting on the experience:

These are my high school days filled with happiness of a basketball game and the sorrow of graduation. Vicky went through all of this with me.... We shared many things together in high school and I hope we will continue to do so during the coming four years.... College will be a test of both of us and I really hope that neither one of us will find the test too big to handle. There will be times when we may question each other and wonder if there isn't someone else better, but in the end I'm sure there won't be.... My past was great, but my future will be even greater, with some help.

DONNIE STARED STRAIGHT AHEAD, focused on Cal Hickman as he delivered a message to the young basketball players seated on the court before him at one of his summer basketball camps. Hickman always had a lesson to teach, and Donnie always listened. Still fresh off their memorable season together, he and Coach Hickman already had a special bond, but as Donnie's interest in coaching became more serious, Hickman became an important mentor.

After the 1969–70 season, Cal coached four more seasons at Mid-Prairie. Although none of his teams replicated the magic of the 1970 state tournament run, the Golden Hawks won three more conference titles and the 1971–72 team returned to Des Moines and finished fourth. After the 1974 season, Hickman left for a job in Blue Springs, Missouri. And after five seasons at Blue Springs High School, he returned to the family farm in the Ozarks. Coaching never left his blood, though, and he continued to coach at smaller-classification schools near the farm, eventually garnering more than 600 career wins.

AFTER SOME DISCUSSION, VICKY put forward the idea that she and Donnie would stay together but would give themselves permission to date other people at college. She told Donnie, "If we are meant to be—and I believe we are—then our relationship will thrive and survive during our time apart." They were both very optimistic about their odds.

Sometime the next week, Donnie presented Vicky with a small box. Inside was a small diamond ring—a promise ring to symbolize their commitment to each other. What the future held was unknown, but Vicky and Donnie knew they wanted to be together. Thus, they made a promise to each other and agreed to try the open relationship; they granted each other permission to participate in college life.

CHAPTER 4

Coach Showalter

With the Vietnam War still raging, the U.S. government instituted the first draft lottery since World War II on December 1, 1969; men ages 18 to 26 could be randomly selected to serve in the military based on their birth date. A provision in the draft lottery stated that undergraduate and graduate students, if drafted, could file for deferment as long as they were making progress toward a degree and still enrolled in college. Donnie enrolled at Wartburg College in the fall of 1970 to pursue his goal to teach and coach and continue his basketball career. He avoided the draft, but like his college classmates, the war in Vietnam occupied his thoughts between studies and social activities; he hoped the situation would be resolved before he graduated.

Away from home and his girlfriend, Donnie made quick friends with his dormmates, other freshmen also in search of new connections, even forming a band called the Sho-No-No's, a lip-sync group silently mouthing the songs of the Four Seasons and the Temptations. In the classroom he double-majored in biology and physical education. If his coaching career did not pan out, the biology major would allow him to go into physical therapy. On the court, Donnie found his niche on the freshman team under the guidance of John Kurtt, Buzz Levick's lead assistant coach.

A multisport athlete at Wartburg in the early 1950s, Kurtt's 6'2" athletic build sharpened his good looks. He understood the athletes' perspective, a desire to learn on the court and play through mistakes. Thus, his players enjoyed playing for him. He was well-liked on campus and fun to be around. Yet Kurtt led with a firm hand, demonstrating a deep pride for the orange and black of his alma mater, an expectation he also had of his athletes.

Kurtt's strengths as an assistant complemented the intensity of Coach Levick. A skilled teacher, motivator, and tactician, Levick's style kept him distant from his players at times. For Donnie, Cal Hickman had been the perfect high school coach—a coach who matched Donnie's enthusiasm for basketball, approached his role as a teacher of the game, and challenged his athletes to strive for maximum effort. At the same time, Hickman wanted to enjoy the moment with his athletes, a soft spot in his competitive nature that allowed him to connect with them. A trained educator, Buzz Levick also had a passion for basketball and loved to teach the game. Yet Levick's commitment to basketball seemed to take on a different meaning than Hickman's; Levick coached college ball. He had to build a winning program, and therefore most of his attention was on doing just that. He coached with vigor, a fire that established him as the man in charge; it was a disciplined approach, a style that earned him respect and results on the court but made him more difficult to connect with.

Coach Kurtt filled the void of Coach Hickman for Donnie, helping him transition from stardom at Mid-Prairie to one of many stars at Wartburg, where each player had been a top performer on his high school team. Furthermore, Kurtt nurtured Donnie's interest in becoming a coach.

DONNIE WAS BACK HOME working with Coach Hickman at the Southeastern Iowa Hawkeye Basketball Camp, and it felt good; it was his second summer working with Hickman. He had spent the previous week coaching at Buzz Levick's camp. There he worked with the junior and senior players, as well as local high school coaches. The experience opened his eyes to coaching—how much he did not know and how much he wanted to learn. Where Levick's camp challenged him and offered him a glimpse of his future as a coach, back home Donnie held celebrity status, especially to the young, aspiring basketball players; they remembered the euphoria around the 1970 team's postseason run, and they wanted to shoot and score like Donnie Showalter.

Steve Bontrager is arguably one of the greatest basketball players to come out of southeastern Iowa. He idolized Donnie. "I just loved him at these camps and just absolutely adored him," remembered Bontrager. "Donnie was a role model to me, and he was not even trying to be. He just instilled the love of basketball for me like nobody else could." The younger brother of Donnie's good friend Dan Bontrager, Steve recalled his first memory of Donnie: "I was in kindergarten when Dan and Donnie were in the sixth grade, and I would watch Donnie shoot baskets with Dan in the barn, and I thought, *Oh my God, if I could just be as good as Donnie.*"

Steve attended IMS in high school. Like Donnie, Steve's parents met with Cal Hickman about a potential transfer to Mid-Prairie, but they ultimately nixed the idea. Yet Steve's days at IMS ended. He did not want to play there anymore. He desired a greater challenge. "One day, I came out of my driveway and instead of turning right to go to IMS, I turned left and went to West High," laughed Bontrager. West High School in Iowa City won the State 3A Championship in 1973 with Bontrager able to showcase his knack for shooting to collegiate recruiters. He became a junior college All-American at Muscatine Community College and earned a scholarship to Oral Roberts University, where he led the Golden Eagles in scoring. After Oral Roberts, he embarked on a 14-year professional playing and coaching career. He later returned to Tulsa and became a highly sought-after shooting instructor. Bontrager never forgot about

Donnie Showalter from his childhood, and their paths in basketball would cross again.

THE ADJUSTMENTS TO COLLEGE life kept Vicky and Donnie busy, making the time apart more manageable. "I spent that year studying hard, going to classes, and being homesick and emotional about that and missing Don," recalled Vicky. "We saw each other on weekends when we could, we talked on the phone occasionally, but that was expensive, and so we wrote letters to each other—lots and lots of letters. It was a good year in our relationship, even though it was a tough year for me."

They knew a long-distance relationship would test their commitment to one another. While both engaged in college life, neither dated anyone else, even though they had given each other freedom to do so. As it became apparent that they truly wanted to be together, the next step in their relationship became quite clear.

A marriage proposal is like the state basketball tournament after a season of courtship: win or go home. During the season Donnie made the all-romance team. "In high school I had a charm bracelet that Donnie started, and so he would pick up appropriate charms from time to time," recalled Vicky. "He was very romantic insofar as he would show up for a date with a little gift for me." Yet his proposal performance earned him no postseason accolades. "We went ring shopping, and when the ring was ready, we went back and picked it up together," remembered Vicky. "Then he just gave it to me." Fortunately for Donnie, he and Vicky were already a couple that had matured through high school love and a year apart; they were both committed to each other and ready to work together to meet life decisions for years to come.

IN THE SPRING OF 1972, Donnie was finishing up his sophomore year at Wartburg and Vicky was at the University of Northern Iowa

(UNI) in Cedar Falls, where she had transferred after her freshman year to be closer to Donnie. Back home, Cal Hickman's Hustlin' Hawks made the state tournament behind the play of Donnie's brother, senior forward Doug Showalter. Described as a rugged player, Doug added a competitive spirit to the squad. "Doug was our muscle," recalled Bud Bender, who teamed with Doug and later worked for Donnie. "When he was determined to get a rebound, he got the rebound."

Whereas Donnie excelled with his instinctive understanding of the game and talent for shooting accuracy, Doug played to his athletic strengths: at 6'3" and a chiseled 180 pounds, he outhustled opponents for second-chance points, using his size, strength, and speed to gain position. Doug found success on the basketball court, but his talents seemed best suited for the football field. He attended Coe College in Cedar Rapids, pursued a degree in business, and played football for the Kohawks. Off the court, Doug and Donnie shared similar passions for muscle cars and girls. Doug had a green Plymouth Road Runner, which he used to pick up Judy Bauer, Vicky's younger sister, for a date night in Iowa City. In 1976 they married and began a life together in southeastern Iowa.

Just two years after the magical run in 1970, the Golden Hawks were back at state. They rolled to a 69–58 first-round win over Manson, then lost to Treynor 53–49 in the semifinals to set up a consolation final against the high-scoring Warriors from Central Elkader. The Warriors bested the Golden Hawks 108–95. The 203 combined total points set an Iowa state high school record for total offense in one game. In three seasons, Hickman's Hustlin' Hawks had been to two state tournaments, both led by the play of a Showalter. (It would take 24 years before Mid-Prairie experienced the thrill of a trip to Des Moines again, and once again a Showalter would be leading the way.)

ON AUGUST 26, 1972, Donnie and Vicky wed at the West Chester United Methodist Church. Following a quick honeymoon trip to the Colorado mountains, they began their junior year in college as a married couple. They lived in Waverly and Vicky made the short commute to Cedar Falls to continue her pursuit of a degree in elementary education and to earn her teaching certificate. Donnie prepared for his junior season playing for the Knights while continuing his pursuit of a double major in education and biology.

Donnie entered his junior season ready to compete for varsity minutes. After a sophomore season on the junior varsity marred by a nagging ankle injury, he had honed his game all off-season. The Knights roster, loaded with talent, would challenge for an Iowa conference title in the 1972–73 season, and Donnie wanted to contribute.

As a player, Donnie knew where to be on the court and when to be there, and he had an understanding of the proper space between other players, the correct angle to get open, and how to time a pass to a teammate in scoring position. His basketball instincts, coupled with an uncanny ability to shoot the ball, would likely earn him some varsity minutes. However, early-season injuries continued to limit his development. As his opportunity to contribute to the varsity team began to fade, Donnie got an unexpected start on his coaching career.

Coach Bud Bergman led the Waverly–Shell Rock High School Go-Hawks. A young coach at the time, Bergman coached the Go-Hawks for 26 seasons, winning more than 500 games. Although the 1972–73 basketball season had already begun, Bergman needed to replace an assistant coach in mid-December to help with both the varsity and the freshman team. Bergman knew of Donnie's interest in coaching through the Wartburg summer camp and asked him if he would like to join the coaching staff.

For Donnie the opportunity with the Go-Hawks seemed too good to pass up, but it left him wondering if he should leave the game he loved as a player to pursue his next step as a coach. Donnie consulted with Vicky, his parents, Coach Hickman, Coach Kurtt, and Coach Levick. They all encouraged him to pursue the opportunity, and Levick leveled with Donnie about his chances of seeing much court time with the Knights that season. Then, in a surprising move, Levick said he would honor Donnie's scholarship if he would help him with the Knights basketball program from time to time. Thus, Donnie's playing career ended and his coaching career began, oddly, in the middle of a season.

A year later, his senior year in college, Donnie immersed himself in his role as a coach, and Bergman treated him like a coach, welcoming him into the coaching fraternity unproven. Away from the court, Donnie delivered lumber part-time for the Spahn and Rose Lumber Co. in Waverly. Vicky worked part-time shifts at Fareway grocery store. They lived paycheck to paycheck, with the assistance of food stamps and cash back from coupons. (Fareway reimbursed patrons for the amount on their coupons.) Donnie and Vicky saved up coupons throughout the week, and occasionally Donnie's Aunt Janet sent some in the mail. The redeemed coupons could amount to $15 to $20 dollars a week. "I remember we were so poor," recalled Vicky. "Walking across the street for Dairy Queen ice cream was a big deal." The couple never thought much about what they did not have; they worked hard and enjoyed time with friends, both driven by the future they were building together.

On Saturday, March 23, 1974, Donnie gathered with a few friends at he and Vicky's Waverly apartment to watch the NCAA national semifinal game between the North Carolina State Wolfpack and the UCLA Bruins. The Wolfpack entered the game 28–1, ranked No. 1 in the Associated Press (AP) poll. The Bruins held a No. 2 ranking in the same poll at 25–3. UCLA had won the last seven national championships, dating back to the 1966–67 season, and had won nine titles in the previous 10 seasons. The Bruins featured two of college basketball's best players in Bill Walton and Jamaal Wilkes, both first-team All-Americans in 1974, with Walton earning recognition as the Naismith Player of the Year for the third straight season. NC State countered with David Thompson. During the 1973–74 season, Thompson averaged 26 points a game and was named the 1974 NCAA Tournament Most Outstanding Player.

After watching Marquette beat Kansas 64–51 in the first national semifinal game, anticipation among the young men had escalated for the second matchup. NBC play-by-play man Curt Gowdy and color analyst Tom Hawkins previewed the matchup, highlighting UCLA's quest for eight in a row and UCLA's dominance under head coach John Wooden. UCLA's run of 9 championships in 10 seasons from 1964 to 1973, including an 88-game winning streak (1972–74), placed Coach Wooden on the pedestal of college basketball coaches at a time when there appeared to be a transition from the past to the future taking place.

Adolph Rupp had retired after the 1971–72 season after winning 876 games at Kentucky. In 1974 the next generation of coaching legends was just getting started: Dean Smith had established himself at North Carolina but was just beginning his NCAA tournament success, Bobby Knight was only in his third season at Indiana University, and Mike Krzyzewski would not be hired at Duke for another six years. In time, all three—Smith (1982 and 1993), Knight (1976, 1981, and 1987), and Krzyzewski (1991, 1992, 2001, 2010, and 2015)—would combine for 10 national championships, the same number Coach Wooden finished his career with. Along with Wooden, each became a Hall of Fame coach, a legend in the sport, a teacher of the game, an influencer on how the game is played, and a mentor to the next generation of coaches. Yet in 1974, for an aspiring young basketball coach such as Donnie, Coach Wooden stood alone as the epitome of success, at the top of his game and the game of basketball.

With graduation coming in May, he started to look ahead. He applied for teaching and coaching positions, his name Don listed at the top of his résumé. To family and friends, he would always be Donnie, but moving forward in his professional life, people would know him as Don Showalter. The Lone Tree School District hired him to teach and coach for the upcoming school year. For the summer, Don planned to work Buzz Levick's basketball camps at Wartburg and the Southeastern Iowa Hawkeye Basketball Camp with Cal Hickman, but he also started to consider what other summer camp opportunities he could pursue. One such camp was the John Wooden Basketball Fundamentals Camp in Thousand Oaks, California. When Don learned Coach Wooden had a basketball camp, he wondered what it would be like to work it, to be around Coach Wooden. He penned a letter to Wooden his senior year of college inquiring about working his camp.

CHAPTER 5

Lone Tree

A bedroom community 16 miles southeast of Iowa City, Lone Tree is surrounded by farmland. Most of the residents of Lone Tree commute to Iowa City for work, work the land, or support residents through local businesses and services. In the 1970s Lone Tree's population hovered below 1,000, placing the Lions in Iowa's smallest sport-classification level, A. For Donnie, Lone Tree offered an opportunity fresh out of college—a chance to do what he aspired to do: teach and coach.

In the early 1970s the Lone Tree High School athletic programs had fallen on hard times: the football team was winless in 1973 and the basketball squad managed only two victories during the 1973–74 season. Still, Lone Tree supported their athletic teams, win or lose, and Donnie and Vicky felt welcomed in the community. At first, Donnie felt apprehensive about earning respect in the classroom, but that same anxiety did not extend to the basketball court. The summers working basketball camps and the two seasons at Waverly High School had bolstered his confidence.

LIKE SHOWALTER, STEVE BROWER was in his first year at Lone Tree and his first as a head coach. They both had to overcome early roadblocks in their careers, which included getting kids to practice, as many of them had responsibilities on their families' farms that demanded their time. "We had to make accommodations," recalled Brower, who served as Showalter's assistant on the basketball court. "If their families needed them back on the farm, Don and I just had to deal with it."

Both Brower and Showalter set out to establish their presence as coaches, to prove to themselves as much as others that they were capable of holding their respective titles. In his first game as a head coach, Brower found the win column. After losing 19 straight football games, the Lions started the 1974 season with a double-overtime win. "When we won the first game on the road, the community of Lone Tree met us on the outside of town with a procession and followed us back into town," recalled Brower. Donnie's first win would take a little longer.

At the first team meeting prior to the start of the basketball season, Showalter handed out a booklet that included team rules, training guidelines, standards for behavior on and off the court, expectations for the classroom, the team's style of play, information about practice, and a game schedule. One of the expectations, a requirement to trim long hair, did not sit well with some of the players; four of them quit the team, unwilling to adapt to the new regime. While the defections delayed Showalter's chance at his first victory as a head coach, he had to set the tone that he was in charge and things were going to be different.

Showalter knew that the future success of his program depended on his ability to get youth in the community more involved in basketball. He started a youth basketball clinic for 7- to 12-year-olds every Saturday morning during the basketball season. "Don always had a long-term perspective," remembered Brower. "He always had an idea about what he wanted to do, and he was thinking well into the future, even in his first year in coaching." Showalter involved members of the varsity team with helping him teach skills, and he talked Brower and another teacher, Galen Moore, into joining him. Moore coached the eighth grade boys' basketball team and was also in his first year at Lone Tree.

COACH SHOWALTER GLANCED AT the scoreboard one more time before heading into the locker room to address his team. He paused. Then he turned to Steve Brower and said, "We need to get this one." The Lone Tree Lions were winless on the season, nine losses in nine games. For Showalter, it also meant he was winless as a head coach. On paper, that night's game at Wapello did not appear to give the Lions much of a chance at their first win as the Indians entered the contest with a winning record and home-court advantage. But with the game tied at the half, there was a sense of hope among the Lone Tree spectators and the coaching staff. During halftime Showalter instructed them to employ their full-court man-to-man pressure defense to start the second half. The adjustment to full-court pressure seemed to confuse the Indians in the third period as they managed just six points and Lone Tree took at 42–35 lead into the fourth quarter.

In the fourth period, the Lions' 6'4" big man Randy Yakish stepped in front of an oncoming offensive player. He established his ground, put his hands straight up in the air, and waited for contact. The Wapello player ran right through him. Yakish absorbed the contact and allowed the impact to propel him backward and onto the court. Showalter jumped to his feet in jubilation. Yakish had executed the skill of taking a charge perfectly, a technique Showalter had worked on diligently with his team over the past couple months. The play served as an important moment for Showalter as a young coach—the skill he taught in practice had transferred to competition. It was a moment of validation that proved that what he was teaching was being retained.

But Showalter's reaction turned out to be premature; the official whistled Yakish for a blocking foul. While Showalter often kept his emotions in check as a young coach, this moment got the best of him, and he started screaming at the official. Brower sensed his head coach might be taking it too far and left his seat to coax Showalter back down the sideline toward the Lions' bench. The foul on Yakish fired up the Lions, and they stretched their lead to 13 points en route to their first win, 61–49. Yakish finished with a game high of 28 points and Showalter won his first game as a head coach.

OVER THE COURSE OF their first year, a close friendship developed between the Showalters and the Browers. They lived next to one another in the same duplex. Steve's wife, Deb, worked nearby in the Tipton School District as a special education teacher. Vicky had worked in a research lab at the University of Iowa but had recently landed a spot teaching at Kalona Elementary for the upcoming school year.

One day Don invited Steve to a basketball clinic in St. Louis early the next morning. "A couple of coaches are headed over," he said. "The clinic features Bobby Knight from Indiana, Norm Stewart from Missouri, and Ralph Miller is coming from Oregon State."

"Wow, that is quite a lineup, but I think I will have to pass on this one," Steve replied. He just did not share the same enthusiasm for coaching basketball as Don did.

The next morning, the sun had yet to peek above the horizon as a four-door sedan pulled up in front of the Lone Tree duplex. Don stood up from the front steps, where he had been waiting, and strolled toward the car. Through the half-cracked window, the driver, Don King, said, "You must be Don Showalter."

Showalter climbed into the passenger seat and the two Dons began the trip toward St. Louis, Missouri. They exchanged small talk to get better acquainted, but the conversation quickly turned to coaching high school basketball: dialogue about players, teaching skills, game strategy, parents, officials, coaches, upcoming clinics, and summer basketball camps. Showalter asked most of the questions, interested in the elder Don's experience.

By 1975 Don King had more than 20 years of experience as a basketball coach at both the high school and collegiate level. He had built a reputation as a coach who could develop players, and his Cedar Rapids Washington High teams were known for their pressing defense and flex offense. Off the court, King shared his passion for coaching with others. He spoke at basketball clinics and wrote articles for coaches on zone offense and defense. He went on to win 500 games in 37 seasons as a high school coach. For a young coach like Showalter, King modeled an interest in continuing to learn as a coach, reinforcing Showalter's interest in developing his coaching skills.

As they neared Fort Madison, Iowa, the discussion between the two men shifted to the Nike Basketball Clinic in St. Louis: X's and O's talk about Bobby Knight's motion offense and the difference between Norm Stewart's and Ralph Miller's man-to-man pressure defenses. King pulled the sedan into the parking lot at Fort Madison High School and the Dons welcomed two more coaches along for the ride: Jerry Slykhuis, the Fort Madison High School head coach, and his assistant coach.

Slykhuis knew Don King but had never met Showalter. From that weekend, Showalter and Slykhuis became fast friends in coaching, and over the next 40 years their lives intertwined, each offering the other support in his career and together impacting thousands of lives teaching the game of basketball.

While at Lone Tree, Don discovered that after the season ended, opportunities to learn as a coach continued in the summer. He started to attend more coaching clinics, usually within driving distance, and he continued to work summer basketball camps in southeastern Iowa for nearby high schools and colleges. Yet he still longed for an opportunity out in California. When Don never heard back from Coach Wooden in regard to his request to work the John

Wooden Basketball Fundamentals Camp, he wrote Wooden again in the spring of 1975, and then again in the spring of 1976.

The summer also served as a time to build the basketball program. Showalter started a summer basketball camp in Lone Tree. The summer camp, in addition to his Saturday morning clinics, became popular among the youth in Lone Tree and the surrounding area, one of whom was Steve Forbes. Forbes participated in Showalter's camps and then starred for the Lions. He later became one of Lone Tree's more notable alumni, first starting as a community college assistant coach and then climbing the coaching career ladder and landing the head coaching job at Wake Forest University in 2020.

As a new head coach, Showalter did what he thought was best. He employed much of what he had learned playing for Cal Hickman at Mid-Prairie and Buzz Levick at Wartburg, and he leaned on his early coaching experience at Waverly High School under Bud Bergman and his work at summer basketball camps. More than anything, Showalter's energy, and passion for basketball elevated interest for the sport in Lone Tree. As the players got better and their confidence grew, so did their level of respect for the young coach. "The kids at Lone Tree played hard for him," recalled Galen Moore. "They respected him even though we were not winning very many games." Plus, he seemed to have a natural inclination to connect with youth. "He was always able to relate to the kids," recalled Brower. "That is one of the things that stands out to me." Showalter made basketball fun, and parents noticed an improvement in their children's skills; the community was pleased with their new coach.

Both Brower and Moore helped Showalter begin the process of building a basketball program at Lone Tree. But none of the three stuck around long enough to enjoy the fruits of their labor. Brower spent a total of three years there, one more than Showalter, then two more years at Central DeWitt High School in Iowa before embarking on a successful career in commercial real estate. Moore moved to Ames, Iowa, to work in the Ames Community School District. For 33 years he continued to coach at the middle school level in multiple sports. The Lone Tree Lions captured a state football title behind the play of Steve Forbes in 1982 and won a state basketball championship in 1985. Although Showalter, Brower, and Moore cannot claim any credit, all of them would like to think they had a little something to do with it.

With the community of Lone Tree only a short distance from the Wellman-Kalona area, the Showalter family—including both Don's parents, his three younger brothers, and his Uncle Darrel and Aunt Janet—were often in the bleachers when the Lions took the court or the football field. Even though the Lions struggled to win games, the Showalter clan kept showing up.

Don's parents had ingrained the importance of family in him to complement the teachings of the Mennonite church, where family came a close second to God. Still, the lifestyle of a coach can test even those with the best of intentions when it comes to prioritizing family over responsibilities to the team; the stories of broken families and failed marriages dominate the profession. Don recognized how the lifestyle of a coach could interfere with family and a balance of where to spend his time. When his passion took him too far one way and he became too focused on coaching, Vicky would give him a nudge—a reminder that it might be too much. But normally, Don balanced his time and family came first. When he faced a decision that affected the family, such as a new job opportunity, he and Vicky made it together.

In the spring of 1976, Cindy Statler, a high school friend of Vicky's, reached out to her about a job opening for Don in Elkader, Iowa. "She raved about the Elkader area and thought it would be a good environment for us and that we might like it there," recollected

Vicky. Don and Vicky decided that if offered the position, they would take it. The Central Elkader school administration decided to take a chance on Coach Showalter even though he had yet to establish himself as a coach who could win. He finished 8–27 in two seasons at Lone Tree.

CHAPTER 6

Elkader

Showalter sorted through the mail sitting on the counter. When he got to the last letter, a jolt of excitement overcame him. He noticed an envelope displaying the letters UCLA in the top left corner and tore into it. He lifted out a single piece of paper and read the handwritten note to himself.

> *Dear Coach Showalter,*
> *Your kind remarks were deeply appreciated. Thanks! Your letter has been forwarded to Sportsworld who handle all details for my summer camps except the basketball fundamental program. Best wishes.*
> *Sincerely,*
> *John Wooden*

His persistence had paid off. Ever since he had penned the first letter to Coach Wooden in 1974, his senior year in college, he had hoped for an opportunity to work Wooden's camp. Now, in the coming summer of 1977, he would teach the game of basketball in the presence of one of the best teachers of the game. But first he had a new team to coach in a new place.

THE CENTRAL ELKADER WARRIORS opened the 1976–77 basketball season at 4–0. The early success heightened the enthusiasm and

45

increased the expectations among community members that the winning ways of the Warriors would continue under their new coach. For the juniors and seniors, their new coach was unproven. Showalter's accolades as a player were down in southeastern Iowa, and the Elkader newspaper, the *Clayton County Register*, only covered local and regional news. Elkader youth grew up watching the high-paced and exciting play of the Warriors basketball teams led by Coach Merrill Hyde. Under Hyde, the Warriors scored at a blistering pace, including the 108–95 record-breaking victory at the 1972 state tournament against Cal Hickman's Hustlin' Hawks, culminating a season in which they averaged 95.4 points per game. Hyde left Elkader after the 1974 season, winning more games than he lost. But the winning continued: under Hyde's successor, Roger Thomas, the Warriors returned to the state tournament in 1976.

In their fifth game of the season under new coach Showalter, Central Elkader stumbled to conference foe Postville 70–75 in overtime. Just 22 miles northwest of Elkader, the Postville Pirates geographically fit the definition of a rival. Paul Jungblut, the Pirates' head coach, was in his second year of what would be a 25-year tenure with the Pirates, during which he would amass 384 wins. At 6'6" Jungblut's physical presence intensified his competitiveness. But for those who knew him, his good-natured personality and sense of humor made him easy to like and fun to be around. Coaches and youth appreciated his approachability, even if it included a sarcastic remark. Although they battled two to three times each season, often with postseason implications, Showalter found a coaching comrade, a friend, and a mentor in Paul Jungblut.

There is a camaraderie among coaches faced with similar daily commitments and challenges. This fellowship transcends competition, differing personalities, and one's coaching philosophy. There is an understanding of the commitment you must make, often in conflict with family time and the importance of managing multiple roles, all while the paycheck does not reflect the time put in. To coach is to put yourself out there, your work and skills in leading others on display for public observation and critical review. This shared reality creates a common bond among coaches.

After the Postville contest, the Warriors dropped four of their next six games leading into a rematch with the Pirates. Postville led from the tip and shot 52 percent from the field en route to an 81–77 win. Classified as a 2A school by the Iowa High School Athletic Association, Central Elkader lost their first game of the district tournament against the Waukon Indians 44–67 to finish the season at 8–11. After his third season as a head coach, two at Lone Tree and one at Elkader, Showalter had yet to secure a winning season. He knew he needed to win more than he lost to remain the head coach. At Lone Tree, Showalter had found a place to get his feet wet in coaching—a supportive community that recognized his passion for basketball and his commitment to their youth; they embraced the young coach. In Elkader, Showalter arrived in a community with an established passion for basketball. The town filled the gym on Friday evenings, and when the fire marshal refused to allow any more fans into the game, administrators operated a closed-circuit TV in the auditorium for fans to watch. Locals had high expectations for their high school basketball coach, and while Showalter's own enthusiasm for the sport matched or exceeded the community's interest, his competence as a coach would be tested. He needed to continue the tradition Merrill Hyde had established while building his own legacy leading the Warriors.

Showalter started with what he knew: he went to work teaching the fundamental skills of basketball, first with his varsity team and then in the community. Although Merrill Hyde had operated youth programs, Showalter took it to another level. He started a Pee Wee Saturday morning basketball program for youth ages 6 through 12, and in the summer of 1977 he conducted two basketball camps. Future talent for the Warriors participated in the youth programs.

At 25 years of age, Showalter had laid the foundation for his growth as a coach. He had tapped into the passion of Coach Hickman, the discipline of Buzz Levick, and knowledge gleaned from a growing list of coaches he had crossed paths with at coaching clinics and summer camps. With an upcoming trip to Southern California to work John Wooden's basketball camp in the summer of 1977, his confidence and enthusiasm for his role as a coach soared.

BY MIDMORNING THE SOUTHERN California sun started to warm the blacktop parking lots on the campus of Cal Lutheran College. The lots filled with youth; young basketball players, boys in grades 3 through 11, scattered across multiple temporary basketball courts created for the John Wooden Basketball Fundamentals Camp. Don Showalter positioned himself at a basket in preparation for the morning teaching stations. Regardless of where he was—in Elkader, Iowa, or nearly 2,000 miles away in Thousand Oaks, California— Showalter loved to teach the game of basketball and felt confident in his ability to do so.

The repetitive, short (10- to 12-minute) teaching stations challenged a coach to stay focused and provide the same level of energy and quality of instruction to each group. Often a coach's energy might wane after four or five stations. In his first year, and knowing he needed to make a good impression, Showalter had incentive to keep his energy level high. He also heard from other coaches that Coach Wooden walked during the stations and often stopped to observe a coach teaching. If Coach Wooden felt he could add something to the lesson, he jumped right in and started teaching. In the summer of 1977, no other coach in the United States had the instant credibility among basketball coaches of Coach John Wooden. During his 27-year career as a head men's basketball coach, Coach Wooden always considered himself a teacher first and had built a reputation as a master instructor. To have Coach Wooden observe you teaching could be intimidating for any coach working his basketball camp.

As Showalter provided instruction to the new group of campers who had rotated to his teaching station, he noticed Coach Wooden watching him as he taught the proper pivoting techniques to the young campers. Nervous, anxious, and with a sense of urgency, Showalter continued to teach the skill in the best manner he knew how. Afterward, Wooden praised him for a job well-done. Then later in the day, one of the camp directors approached Showalter and told him Wooden was impressed with his teaching station. The recognition from Coach Wooden provided Showalter with a confidence boost.

SHOWALTER RADIATED CONFIDENCE AS he coached his players back in Elkader; he was empowered as a teacher of the game from his two weeks in California. The 1977–78 basketball season proved to be a key turning point in his development as a young coach, but success against rival Postville would have to wait. In their first matchup, the Pirates bested the Warriors 61–53, and then they did it again in their second matchup, 66–57. Showalter fell to 0–4 against Jungblut. In postseason play, Elkader hosted the District 2A tournament and used their home-court advantage to reach the district title game against Wapsie Valley. In the finale, Wapsie Valley shot 62.8 percent from the field, but Central Elkader prevailed 73–66 off the play of 6'3" sophomore Lonnie Meade, who came off the bench in just his fourth varsity game to tally 20 points. At substate, one game away from the state tournament, Elkader fell 58–64 to Waukon to finish the season 13–9—Showalter's first winning season as a head coach. Meade tossed in 14 points, displaying a knack for putting the ball in the basket. His performance in tournament play hinted at exciting things to come in his junior year.

Central Elkader High School (formerly Elkader High Scool) boasted its share of talented athletes over the years, but Jack Dittmer was the greatest. A multisport athlete in the 1940s, Dittmer competed in three sports at the University of Iowa before spending six seasons in the major leagues for the Boston Braves and Detroit Tigers. To place Lonnie Meade in the same conversation as Dittmer would be a stretch in terms of their athletic accolades or what each meant to the Elkader community. Dittmer was a local kid—born, raised, and one of their own. Lonnie arrived as an eighth grader, a transplant from Seattle; he departed before his senior season.

Still, to watch Meade was memorable. He was a special talent, an athlete who blended his natural gifts with a soft shooting touch and an ability to get his own shot. His lanky 6'3" frame sliced through defenders, his shaggy blond hair popped above a crowd of defenders as he leveraged his vertical leaping ability to score near the bucket, and his fingertips lingered on the follow-through of his jump shot, dangling until the ball fell through the bottom of the net.

Lonnie's rise as a basketball star almost never materialized. He grew up playing soccer, a sport with limited opportunities in Iowa in the late 1970s. "I really did not take an interest in basketball until I moved to Elkader," recalled Lonnie. "The entire community was interested in sports, especially basketball. The gyms were packed. After the games everyone would be in the taverns and restaurants talking about the games."

The town's enthusiasm for their high school team, coupled with Showalter's youth programs, hooked Lonnie. As his interest in basketball grew along with his skills and knowledge of the game, he began to excel on the court. For the small-town, rural high school coach, a player with Meade's talent may only come around once in a career, and Showalter knew it. Thus, when the news broke in late summer that Lonnie's father had taken a job in Minnesota, Showalter was disappointed. Lonnie was the difference between a good team and a state title contender. The news hit Lonnie harder. "We moved a lot growing up and I did not want to move," recalled Lonnie. "Everything was what it needed to be for me at that time."

Lonnie stayed behind with his mother so he could stay in Elkader, but midway through the basketball season, she needed to rejoin his father in Minnesota. While losing Lonnie's talents on the court would have had consequences for Showalter's team in the 1978–79 season, Don and Vicky recognized Lonnie had a need to stay in Elkader that went beyond basketball. Through an agreement with Lonnie's parents, he would live with them. And even though Don and Vicky were then adjusting to the challenges of parenthood after the arrival of their first child—daughter Melissa Jo Showalter, born August, 14, 1978—they both felt they were doing the right thing.

In a game on January 20, 1979, the Postville Pirates jumped to an early lead as the Warriors ball handlers struggled against Coach Jungblut's switching defense of man-to-man and trapping zone. After an easy Pirates bucket, one of the Central Elkader guards mishandled the ball for another turnover. Showalter leapt off the bench. He had screwed up. The Warriors were not prepared for the switching defensive scheme Jungblut was throwing at them. Don was getting outcoached. His face flushed redder as he stomped the floor in his loafers, and he barked at the nearest official because he needed someone to yell at.

Before he could take it too far, Wayne Mager, his assistant coach, rose from the bench. At 6'1" his thick, broad-shouldered frame presented a natural presence wherever he went. Without a word, he grabbed Showalter from behind by both arms and pulled him back toward the bench. Despite their troubles with the Pirates defense, the Warriors hung tough and forced Postville into overtime, then a second overtime, before eventually losing 73–68. They stumbled in the second matchup with the Pirates later that season, and Showalter fell to 0–6 against Jungblut.

For eight seasons Wayne Mager served as an assistant coach to Showalter. He fit the persona of a football coach, which he was. His physical size provided him an instant level of respect and authority, especially with youth. Mager's first teaching job was in Elkader, and he never left. In 35 years, he taught social studies and held numerous assistant and head coaching positions. Everyone in Elkader knew Wayne Mager, and every student he coached or taught had a memory of him. He cared about the kids. Both he and Showalter shared a passion for teaching and an unwavering commitment to their roles as coaches. They complemented each other well. Where Showalter enjoyed the preparation, especially as it applied to practice—a meticulous plan, down to every detail—Mager fiddled in the X's and O's and drew up many of the plays during timeouts. Together they formed a system that worked, and in their third season together (1978–79), with Lonnie Meade leading the way, they took another step in building the program.

Using their signature tough man-to-man defense and fast-break, up-tempo style of play, the Warriors captured their second straight district championship, besting Dyersville-Beckman 73–65 in the title game. Meade netted 26 points and 14 rebounds. At substate the Warriors faced a private school, Cedar Rapids Regis. The red-hot Royals were on a nine-game winning streak, a result of their full-court pressing defense. The Warriors, a team that liked to apply pressure, succumbed to it 80–59. The Warriors finished the 1978–79 season at 13–8. Meade led the team in most statistical categories, including points per game (21.1), rebounds per game (12.5), field goal percentage (52 percent), and free-throw percentage (70.5 percent). The *Oelwein Daily Register* named him first-team all-area, and he received honorable mention honors from the *Des Moines Register*. Unfortunately for the Elkader community and Showalter, Lonnie transferred to Fergus Falls High School in Minnesota to rejoin his family for his senior year. He later continued his playing career in college at the University of Northern Iowa on a basketball scholarship.

With the loss of Lonnie Meade, Central Elkader struggled to find their identity early in the 1979–80 season. The guard-heavy Warriors roster included the play of senior Mike Fitzgerald. An athletic 5'11" floor general, Fitz—as he was known by his teammates—utilized his quickness to excel in Showalter's pressure defense, creating havoc for opposing guards. Fitz's running mate in the backcourt was fellow senior John Buckner. A savvy, tenacious defender, the 5'11" Buckner overcame his lack of height with superb leaping ability. Buckner's abrasive manner at times contrasted his unselfish play as he controlled the Warriors offense with his ball-handling skills and his ability to find the open man, leading the team in assists. Fitz and Buckner were the seniors. They were joined on the team by Bob Possehl, a junior, and sophomore Steve Thein.

Possehl was a good athlete, but his natural ability paled in comparison to Fitz or Buckner, which he overcame with a strong basketball IQ and ability to shoot. He loved to shoot the basketball— maybe a little too much, according to his teammates. But because he was good at hitting the open shot or creating his own, Possehl often found the ball in his hands late in the game. At 6'2" he could get his shot off against smaller guards. However, due to the Warriors' lack of size his junior season, he often found a taller defender on him. This did not hinder his productivity, and he led the Warriors in scoring at 17.1 points per game. Only a sophomore, Steve Thein had the talent to fill the shoes of the departed Lonnie Meade. A long 6'5", Thein could run and jump, and he benefited from the fast-paced style the Warriors played. Thein's quiet demeanor meant his talent did the talking; he could handle the ball, giving him the ability to play facing the basket, which Showalter had him do even though they could have used him in the low post.

The Warriors' ability to pressure the ball and force turnovers, in addition to their unselfish play, would be their strength all season. In their fourth game, they faced archrival Postville. The undefeated Pirates were Jungblut's most talented team yet. Postville led from the tip and sailed to a 77–66 win. "We could not beat Postville," recalled Buckner. "We jokingly said they redshirted their players, as they always seemed a bit older than us."

The Warriors finished the regular season at 10–8, then rolled through sectionals and the first game at the district tournament. As they prepared for the district final on Thursday, March 6, 1980, tension in the community brewed over an early February decision by the Central Elkader Community School Board to eliminate Showalter's ninth grade science teaching position (and his coaching position with it). Based on budget cuts and seniority outlined in the master contract for the school district, Showalter's teaching and coaching positions were set for elimination come June. A school board meeting to vote on the matter was scheduled for Monday, March 10. The board meeting had loomed over the excitement of the Warriors' play on the court over the past month, but amid the distraction, the coaches and players did their best to stay focused on basketball. The Tripoli Panthers would require their full attention with their 22–1 record and fifth-place state Class 1A ranking heading into the district title game.

With 12 seconds left and the Warriors leading the Panthers by two, Mike Fitzgerald, a 76 percent foul shooter, stepped to the free-throw line for a one-and-one. With no three-point shot, one make would give the Warriors a three-point lead and likely ice the game.

He missed.

Then he stole the ball. The Panthers fouled him again.

Fitz again clanged the front end of the one-and-one. Tripoli rebounded.

After a timeout, the Panthers found 6'7" Mitch Bergman 18 feet from the basket. He banked a shot at the buzzer to send the game into overtime. The Warriors held a one-point 55–54 lead in overtime with seven seconds left. But when they failed to block out, giving the Panthers two shots and a buzzer-beating put-back, they lost 55–56. "We had the game won," said Buckner. "It still haunts me to this day." After the game, with emotions still high, the competitive Possehl passed Showalter on his way to the locker room and said, "This will not happen next year." Showalter, still stunned, patted Possehl on the back without saying a word. Central Elkader finished 15–9, Showalter's third straight winning season.

With the excitement of the basketball season over, all attention in Elkader turned to the fate of their basketball coach. In this case, Showalter's job status had nothing to do with his performance as a coach or as a teacher; he had built up goodwill among the locals over the past four years, making him a likable figure in the community. Once the announcement of the budget cuts and the elimination of Showalter's teaching position became public information, the Central Elkader Athletic Booster Club started circulating a petition to keep their coach. In a letter to the editor that appeared in the *Clayton County Register* they made a plea for the community to join them in convincing the school board to reconsider their decision.

> The Athletic Boosters of Central Community Schools adopted a motion at their February 13 meeting to protest a decision made by the Central Community School Board to cut from their budget the science position which is currently held by Don Showalter. The boosters give their full support to Mr. Showalter as a teacher and coach in the Central School District and feel that cutting his position would prove to be detrimental to our students...Mr. Showalter gives many extra unpaid hours to programs that

benefit our children, two examples are the Fellowship of Christian Athletes for high school students and the Pee Wee basketball program involving 80–100 boys. The booster club is circulating petitions...to have the school board reconsider their decision and seek alternatives for cuts in other possible areas at their next meeting on March 10[th.]
—*Central Community Athletic Boosters*

At the Central Community School Board meeting on March 10, 1980, the school board rescinded the elimination of the position, citing ambiguous language in Showalter's contract. Whether pressure from the community or confusing contract language pushed the board to reconsider cutting Showalter's position, it turned out to be the right decision, as the upcoming 1980–81 season would be Showalter's best yet.

Possehl benefited from Showalter's arrival during his middle school years. The youth programs and open gyms fueled his interest in basketball. In Showalter, Possehl had a coach who matched his passion for the game. In Possehl, Showalter had a player youth could look up to. Showalter involved his varsity athletes as coaches in summer camps and Saturday morning Pee Wee basketball. Young aspiring players felt a connection to their varsity heroes; they watched them play on Friday night and learned from them on Saturday morning. "You knew the guys who were five to six years older because of camps and Saturday morning basketball," remembered Matt Reimer, a middle schooler in 1981, who later became a college basketball coach. "Then you would see them down at the pool or playing on the blacktops. You just looked up to them."

The Warriors opened the 1980–81 season with a 54–46 win over West Delaware, then trounced North High of West Union 67–40, and followed that with a low-scoring 38–36 victory over Sumner High. "We kind of knew we were going to be pretty good going into my senior year," remembered Possehl. "We played a lot in the summers on the blacktop. A lot of us went to basketball camps. Everyone worked hard to get better."

Undefeated early in the 1980–81 season, their nemesis Postville awaited. After holding on to a one-point lead at the half, the Warriors scored 19 unanswered points in the third period. Possehl tallied 20 points en route to a 56–33 win. With the monkey finally off his back, Showalter and the Warriors beat Postville two more times that season: 76–55 at Postville and 51–46 in the district tournament semifinals.

The Warriors were a complete team. Possehl, the lone senior, was joined in the backcourt by junior John Katschkowsky. The smallest of the five Warriors starters, Katschkowsky could spring off the floor. But his ability to control the ball and run the offense benefited the Warriors most. Together Possehl and Katschkowsky established the pace of play Coach Showalter wanted: up-tempo. The Warriors' size across the frontline gave them an advantage over every team they played. "Brett Nagel was too big for high school basketball," joked Jungblut. "He was 6'6", around 240, and he liked contact." A traditional post player, junior Nagle played with his back to the basket. His physical size magnified his intensity on the court, a rough-and-tough style of play that often put him into early foul trouble. "He could hit the elbow shot and score in the low post," recalled Mager. "But if you were going to guard Brett, watch out for his elbows."

Nagel was the biggest in a trio of boys nicknamed the Triple Towers, which included Steve Thein, the lanky, skilled 6'5" scoring wing player who came on late in tournament play the year before, and 6'6" Doug Watkins, who anchored the block opposite Nagel. Nicknamed Chub—not due to his size but given to him by his family as a baby—Watkins complemented the play of Nagel with his finesse and laid-back style. "I got most of my points off rebounds," remembered Watkins. "Coach did not really want me shooting outside 10 feet."

With their size up front and solid guard play, the Warriors hoped to make a push into the postseason. Yet Showalter knew that talent alone would not get them to state; they needed to learn to work hard each day. "He made us play tough, and he made us play hard," said Possehl. The Warriors kept winning, entering their final regular-season game undefeated at 16–0. However, Oelwein caught them off guard and stole a late season 61–59 win, sending Central Elkader into the district tournament with their first loss.

Unfazed by the defeat, the Warriors rolled through the 1A sectional tournament and their first game at the district tournament to set up a rematch with Tripoli in the district final. After the previous season's overtime loss to the Panthers, Possehl had something to prove. With the game tied and 1:06 left, the Warriors went to their four-corner offense to play for the last shot.

In the early 1980s, basketball coaches often employed a four-corner offense, a stall strategy where the offensive players spread out to dribble, pass, and cut with no intention of scoring. It was a tactic often used by less skilled teams to keep the score low and improve their chance of victory.

With 10 seconds on the clock, Showalter called a timeout and set up the final play for Possehl. From the baseline, Possehl inbounded the ball to Thein at the free-throw line. Then, as designed, Possehl curled off a double screen along the baseline. Thein delivered the ball perfectly to Possehl. In rhythm, without any hesitation, Possehl elevated to his jump shot. This was the moment he had dreamed about and practiced: making the last shot and the crowd roaring. He no longer had to pretend, because the moment was real. He nailed the 19-footer.

The Warriors won the game and the district title 53–51. The shot was a moment of joy and redemption for Possehl, but he and the Warriors were still a step away from their goal: the state tournament.

Showalter and Possehl shared a similar competitive drive, and both had a desire to be the best they could be, Possehl as a player and Showalter as a coach. No one questioned their commitment to the game. Possehl put his time in on the blacktop, in the gym, and at summer camps. Showalter attended coaching clinics and worked camps. "I was in awe of him working the John Wooden camp," said Possehl. "He was very driven." Showalter earned the respect of his players and their parents, who witnessed improvement in their sons' play on the court and their personal growth off it. Most important, Showalter earned the respect of the one person every coach needs in their corner: his athletic director.

In this case that AD was Bob Garms, who carried a sense of confidence that at times bordered on arrogance. He was in charge, and he could be a hard-ass, employing a leadership style often considered abrasive. But Garms cared about the kids and he cared about his role. He wanted to make a difference, and he did for 36 years. Garms is a public figure in Elkader, his legacy tied to his longtime role as head coach of multiple sports and athletic director and 12 years as the city mayor. As mayor Garms organized a community effort to get downtown Elkader listed on the National Register of Historic Places. As an administrator, he developed an active and productive athletic booster club. The club received national recognition for its structure and fundraising ability. On the basketball court, Garms led the transition of the girls' basketball program from a six-player format to the five-player game. Garms preferred the six-player game. "It was easier to coach, because you only had to worry about three kids on one end of the floor and more kids got to play at the same time," described Garms. "It was not as physical as five-on-five. It was a faster game."

As an administrator, Garms was exactly the type of mentor Showalter needed as a young coach—one who had your back. And as Showalter led his team into a substate matchup, Garms, who led his girls team to the state tournament in 1977, knew what an appearance in the state tournament could do for a young coach in terms of confidence and in the eyes of the community. Now only one team stood in the Warriors' way of earning a spot at state: the Rockford Warriors.

Riding a 22-game winning streak, the Rockford Warriors jumped out to an early 17-point lead. After Central Elkader gained their wits, they rallied back to take a 54–53 lead with 2:51 to go in the third period. The back-and-forth affair ended in a tie at 68 at the end of regulation. In the first overtime, Rockford scored a put-back basket with five seconds left to go up two. Then, as he had done all season, Possehl gained control of the ball and dribbled the length of the floor, tossing in a 15-foot runner at the buzzer to send the game into a second overtime. Rockford took the early lead in the second overtime and won 90–85. Possehl finished with 21 points and Thein tossed in 26. Central Elkader ended the season at 21–2, Showalter's best season yet, earning him Coach of the Year honors by the *Oelwein Daily Register*. Possehl earned numerous postseason honors and went on to a four-year playing career at Coe College.

FOR THE SHOWALTERS, THEIR time in Elkader was a coming-of-age period in their young adult lives together. After Melissa, they welcomed their second child—a son, Brent Donald Showalter—on May 6, 1981. They forged close friendships in the Elkader community with other couples to share in faith and leisure, which included Ken and Karen Pittman and Lee and Joyce Probert.

The Showalters, along with these friends and others in the community, created a church, the Grace Evangelical Free Church, a new local Christian congregation in Elkader. At the new church, Don taught Sunday school and both Don and Vicky served on numerous committees. Starting the church deepened the Showalters' ties to the community, demonstrating their commitment to their faith.

The Showalters were busy raising young children, church-planting with friends, and building their careers (Vicky taught kindergarten part-time in Elkader). They still found time for each other, but the distance of Elkader from "city life" was a drawback. It was an hour to Dubuque, and Vicky said, "At times it could feel remote if you wanted to have a theater night or concert night or go out to a nice dinner in the city." Still, they believed they were exactly where they were supposed to be, and with the return of four seniors for the 1980–81 season, the Warriors had their sights set on making a run in the state tournament.

CHAPTER 7

Coach Wooden

Mike Kunstadt glanced at the 16-team playoff bracket for the 1973 Texas State 4A Boys' basketball Tournament. A young coach, Kunstadt felt anxious about his first playoff experience and wondered if he could get some advice on preparing his team for the playoffs. "I thought of Coach John Wooden," recalled Kunstadt. "I don't know what I was thinking; I was just a young, green coach. I called the UCLA basketball office, and Coach Wooden answered the phone."

Coach Wooden and his 1972–73 UCLA Bruins were in the midst of an undefeated season and defending their sixth straight national championship. Wooden led the conversation. He shared with Kunstadt the essence of his Pyramid of Success, a concept Kunstadt had no knowledge of at the time. The Pyramid of Success is a visual diagram, a pyramid featuring fourteen blocks, and each block features a characteristic and trait that Wooden used as a teacher to help others strive for success, which he defined thus: "Success is a peace of mind attained only through self-satisfaction in knowing you made the effort to do the best of which you're capable." Coach Wooden's Pyramid of Success, in time, became almost as iconic as Coach Wooden himself, a leadership philosophy and model for future generations in all professional fields. But in the early 1970s, knowledge of the Pyramid of Success, beyond Coach Wooden's players, was only beginning with the release of Coach Wooden's book *They Call Me Coach* in 1972.

Wooden's message to Kunstadt, as stated in Greg Hayes's book *Camp with Coach Wooden*, was: "Fully prepare your team, make sure the players prepare themselves, and hopefully the outcome will be favorable. But if not, have peace that you did your best, that you did all you could."

Kunstadt shared the message with his team and his Tigers advanced to the final four at the state tournament. Grateful for Wooden's time, Kunstadt followed up with the UCLA coach. "I sent him a thank-you note for taking the time to share his wisdom with me," said Kunstadt. "Then I read in *Sports Illustrated* that he had basketball camps. We were not allowed to have basketball camps in Texas at that time. I called Coach Wooden again and asked him if I could work his camp."

In the summer of 1973, Kunstadt worked his first John Wooden basketball camp. He returned for 18 straight summers. In Texas Kunstadt developed his own legacy in basketball, first as a successful prep coach for 20 seasons, then as an entrepreneur, starting Great American Sports Inc., an organization that through a variety of services provides talent evaluation and exposure for prep basketball players in the state of Texas. Kunstadt helped grow the roster of out-of-state coaches at Wooden's camp. In the summer of 1977—the same year Showalter first arrived at Cal Lutheran—two coaches from Texas, Larry Brown and Dave Meyers, also made the trip. Kunstadt, Brown and Meyers all became an important part of Showalter's growing network of basketball coaches, the start of lifelong friendships built on a love for teaching the game of basketball.

THE CLOCK ON THE wall showed well past last call as Larry Brown crumpled the napkins covered in basketball plays and stuffed them into his pockets. The camp coaches ambled back toward the dormitory, their pockets full of notes to review later, drills and set plays to use with their teams back home. "L. B., you going to make it?" joked one of the coaches. Four late nights in a row filled with stories and conversation on basketball strategy, after long days of coaching, had sapped Brown's energy. He knew he needed to dig deep for the last morning session of camp, just a few hours away. "That last Friday, I had to be at the front of the lines when Coach Wooden led the campers through morning drills," said Brown. "I had not had much sleep at all, and man, I said to myself, 'I need to bring it today.' I was doing everything I could to keep myself motivated."

Long days and short nights served as Brown's summer routine. One summer he worked nine different summer basketball camps. Larry Brown is known as a basketball lifer, a junkie; he needs the game. Not to be confused with the other Larry Brown, the longtime college and NBA coach, L. B. has experienced just about everything one can as a basketball coach. His career spans Friday night high school contests, junior college games in the middle of nowhere, Division I athletics in front of sellout crowds, and international travel as a professional coach. Along the way, L. B. built a vast network of coaching friends, including Don Showalter.

In 1977 Dave Meyers worked his first camp. The head coach at MacArthur High School in Irving, Texas, Meyers started as a camp counselor his first week with Showalter, helping the camp run smoothly, with tasks such as the daily wake-up call, dormitory supervision, and the movement of campers between activities. Meyers and Showalter moved into a coaching role for the second week. Early in the second week, Meyers's team competed against Showalter's squad. Late in the second half, one of Showalter's players made a poor play. Visibly upset, Showalter threw his hands in the air and blurted, "Oh, jeepers!" "That was about as frustrated as he would get," recalled Meyers, chuckling. "I can still hear him saying that to this day. I thought it was some type of midwestern thing."

The Wooden camp brought coaches together like kids at a traditional summer camp: they came as strangers, shared experiences, and left as friends. The bond forged ongoing correspondence throughout the year, basketball conversation and words of encouragement. For those who returned each year, the rapport strengthened.

Coach Wooden took pride in how the camp operated, and he actively involved himself each day, following a consistent routine. He arrived for breakfast at 6:55 each morning to eat with the camp coaches. He taught the early morning drills, and then during the midmorning skill workstations, led by the hired camp coaches, Wooden went on a daily five-mile walk. As he walked, Wooden observed how the youth were being coached. At lunch he joined the camp coaches in the Cal Lutheran cafeteria. After lunch he conducted the early afternoon instructional clinic, which often included a motivational message from a guest speaker (usually one of his former players); and when the campers broke for their afternoon free time, he headed home for the day, as the camp continued to operate well into the evening.

For Wooden, hosting a basketball camp proved to be lucrative endeavor, and there were rumors that his profits after four weeks of basketball camp surpassed his annual salary at any point during his career. But money never drove Wooden's passion for teaching the game. Following his retirement from UCLA, the John Wooden Basketball Fundamentals Camp provided Wooden a place to continue to teach the game he loved and to influence others. For Showalter, Wooden's influence on him as a mentor and a friend became more personal.

DON SHOWALTER LOADED ANOTHER pancake on his tray as Dave Meyers slid in line behind him. "Hungry, Coach?" blurted Dave sarcastically.

"Just filling up for another big day at camp," Don said, smiling.

Dave started to load up his tray. Don spared Meyers a clever remark; instead he glanced toward the table where Coach Wooden usually sat.

"Dave, there are still a couple of seats at Coach's table," said Don. "Let's grab them."

Dave and Don scurried in the direction of Coach Wooden's table. An opportunity to sit, listen, and be in Wooden's presence over a plate of pancakes jolted them like a strong cup of coffee. At the breakfast table or on the basketball court, Wooden was the center of attention. Coaches asked questions to siphon knowledge from the great coach, a tip or hint they could apply with their own teams. And the breakfast table offered this type of forum.

To ask a question in this setting required thought, as a camp coach might only have one opportunity within the week to ask a question. Dave Meyers took an opportunity to ask the question marinating in his mind when Wooden paused during the table conversation. With confidence, Meyers proceeded, "Coach Wooden, if there were one coaching principle at the top of your list, what would it be?"

"Dave, nobody has ever asked me that question before," replied Wooden. Coach Wooden went on to explain the concept of transfer: the skills and strategies your players take from the practice floor to the competitive arena. Coach Wooden then looked at Meyers and gave him a challenge: "Dave, tell me tomorrow what changes you make in practice today that will transfer to your camp game this evening."

Dave now had a directive, a charge from Wooden to teach better. He knew he had to be on his toes. As they left the table, Don looked at Dave and snickered, "Boy, you have done it now, Dave."

The opportunity to work alongside Coach Wooden, to work under the legend teaching the game of basketball, could leave a coach awestruck. Wooden's notoriety and success put him on a pedestal;

no one was more revered as a basketball coach. Wooden's presence influenced each coach to do better. "He expected you to be positive with the kids," recalled Brown. "He had a high standard."

It seemed that the great Hall of Fame coach appreciated being a coach among coaches. He enjoyed the company of the coaches working his camp. He took an interest in them, who they were and where they coached. In return, coaches felt more comfortable interacting with the legend, always grounded in the reality that they were in the company of greatness.

The freeway traffic on the 101 between Thousand Oaks and Encino did little to impede Brad Barbarick's progress on his drive to pick up Coach Wooden from his condo, it was well before the morning rush hour. A former camper, Barbarick worked the Wooden camp, first as a counselor and then as head counselor during his college years. When offered a coaching position at the camp after his college graduation, he said no. "The job of the head counselor was to pick Coach Wooden up every morning and have him at the camp before the campers started at 7:30," said Barbarick. "I wanted the opportunity to continue picking up Coach Wooden and have those one-on-one conversations."

In time, Barbarick combined his experiences at John Wooden camps with other opportunities and built a thirty-plus-year career as a successful small college basketball coach in the Pacific Northwest. For now, Barbarick's focus centered on coordinating a timely and safe commute for Coach Wooden. Other coaches often joined Barbarick on his drive; Showalter was a regular companion. As Barbarick maneuvered through the residential streets back toward the 101 with Coach Wooden in the passenger seat, he and Showalter waited patiently; it always seemed best to let Wooden speak first. Wooden put them as ease, and a casual conversation about baseball ensued. He often talked baseball, golf, his family, current events, and the Bible. Wooden lived in the moment.

Showalter and the other coaches treasured their opportunity to be around Coach Wooden, but they first had to overcome their admiration. "My first year, I am sitting in the dormitory lobby, the only coach not from California, and Coach Wooden walks in," recalled Kunstadt. "It was almost like God had appeared. That was the first time I had seen him in person." Once the wonderment wore off and it became apparent that Wooden enjoyed their company, coaches sought opportunities to be in Wooden's presence, which is why Don often joined Wooden on his daily commute. What Showalter did not realize, at the time, though, was just how influential the great basketball coach would be on his coaching career and in his personal life.

For basketball coaches from the 1970s into the early '80s, Wooden stood alone as a coach, the pinnacle of success on the court. Upon retirement in 1975, after winning his 10th championship, Wooden's legacy was intact; he could have enjoyed his later years out of the public eye. Instead he continued to lead others through speaking engagements, book writing, and his summer basketball camps. Wooden became a mentor to the next generation, a man whose principles, forever etched in his Pyramid of Success, came to life through his generosity and genuineness as a person. In Wooden's presence one could feel at ease. He made you feel important. "He took an interest in me. He actually enjoyed our company," recalled Dave Meyers. "That meant so much to guys like Don and me. Here is this man with so much wisdom and knowledge of the sport. He wanted to mentor us and enjoyed it."

At his core, Wooden was a teacher. Even with his accomplishments and his notoriety, Wooden shared a commonality with many of the coaches working his camp; however, he seemed to connect more closely with a few coaches, including Don Showalter. An authenticity radiated from Showalter, and his fellow coaches working the camp noticed. "He was always a guy who wanted to learn. And he did not mind sharing his ideas, either," remembered Kunstadt. "Sometimes coaches want to learn but they don't want to share. He was always willing to share. You could tell then that he was hard-working and intent on learning."

Showalter gravitated toward Wooden's style and approach, and Wooden likely felt Showalter's genuineness in how he taught the game and in his willingness to learn. Or maybe Wooden felt a kinship to Showalter's modest Midwest upbringing, a similarity they shared. Whatever the reason, Wooden took a liking to the young coach from Iowa. A mentor-mentee relationship developed, and Showalter picked up key aspects of Wooden's coaching style, such as how to make the game simple, *how* to teach as opposed to *what* to teach, how to interact with athletes, and the importance of preparation.

Over the next several years, Wooden became a part of Showalter's conscience, the coach on his shoulder, constantly reminding him: "What would Wooden do? How would Coach Wooden handle this situation?" Wooden's presence in his mind served as guidance, a proven way to teach and coach. Yet Showalter knew who he was. He lived his values and coached by them. He did not need to copy Wooden's style. However, as a mentor, through his example and the manner in which he lived his life, Wooden gave Showalter confidence that he too could stay true to his values and find success as a coach. More important, because Wooden's humbleness superseded his greatness as a coach, Showalter gained an example of how one could handle success with humility, an important attribute that over time became how others described Showalter.

For Showalter, his knowledge of the game grew exponentially each year at Wooden's camp, and each summer he continued to make new connections in the game and learn of new opportunities. One friendship in particular from the Wooden camp, a young teacher-coach from Southern California named Wayne Carlson, connected him with a new experience, another basketball camp just up the road. Showalter had no idea then just how far the new camp would take him.

WAYNE CARLSON TAUGHT U.S. History and coached basketball for 30 years at El Dorado High School in Placentia, California. In addition to the John Wooden camp, Carlson started coaching each summer at the Snow Valley Basketball School at Westmont College in Santa Barbara, California. He spent 41 summers at Snow Valley, eventually serving as camp director in 1984 and then part owner from 2001 to 2016.

When he told Showalter about the camp, Don had some questions. "How does it compare to this camp?" he asked.

"It's totally different than the Wooden camp," said Wayne. "I mean, you are not around John Wooden every day, but it's a great teaching camp. You should come work it. I can put you in touch with Herb Livsey. He runs it."

Without hesitation, Showalter replied, "That would be great."

Back home in Elkader, Showalter, through Carlson, contacted Herb Livsey, who shared with him an overview of the Snow Valley Basketball School, the daily schedule, and the emphasis on teaching. Showalter told Livsey he was interested and wanted to work the camp, but as Showalter hung up the phone, he wondered if he could add another camp to his already busy summer schedule. The previous summer he had stayed in Southern California an extra week to work the Los Angeles Lakers' basketball camp under Coach Paul Westhead. Then he added a long weekend working the John Wooden Encounter, an adult fantasy camp on the Pepperdine campus. Plus, he had just spent two weeks overseas at a camp in Tolworth, England. With the school year just a couple weeks away, he shifted his focus to the upcoming basketball season. The Warriors, with their Triple Towers, were state tournament hopefuls.

Anticipation for the 1981–82 boys' basketball season in Elkader hinged on the return of four seniors: Nagle, Watkins, and Thein in the frontcourt and John Katschkowsky in the backcourt. All four players had earned significant minutes the previous season, but Thein was the star. He developed into a player to watch in northeast Iowa, a college prospect, and their go-to player when they needed a bucket. His height and leaping ability had given him a natural edge on the court since his sophomore season. In Showalter's system, his basketball skills steadily improved each year to match his athletic gifts; he also matured mentally.

During his sophomore season, Thein tended to be a bit of a whiner. In one practice, he complained too much and Showalter threw him out. "He sent me down to the locker room, and I sat in the locker room for what felt like an hour," said Thein. "I was petrified. I thought, *Is he going to kick me off the team?*" When Showalter came into the locker room, he let Thein know that the attitude and behavior he displayed would not be tolerated. "He did not yell at me," said Thein. "He calmly asked me why I was acting this way and if I was going to keep doing it. He wanted my thoughts. It was a good lesson."

Now a senior, Thein helped the Warriors to a 7–0 start. The Warriors entertained the fans with their fast-paced style of play, and Thein usually added a dunk or two to bring the crowd to their feet. Thein became the most accomplished player Showalter coached during his time in Elkader, finishing his career with 1,040 points and earning third-team all-state Class 1A honors and a full-ride athletic scholarship to Augustana University, an NCAA D-2 school in South Dakota.

In his sixth season, Showalter's players understood his expectations on the court: you played hard by always giving your best effort; you played by the rules; and you respected the game, the officials, and your opponent. High standards extended off the court as well. "Coach Show demanded we do things the right way," remembered Nagel. "You were to be a gentleman. He demanded that you got a haircut and that you did not wear a headband. You wore a suit to ballgames. And he had high expectations in the classroom."

The Warriors fell 62–60 to West Central from Maynard before the holiday break for their first loss of the season, and they suffered a second defeat to Decorah High by three, 74–71 after the break. The Warriors did not lose another game in the regular season, including a convincing 50–36 victory over their rival, Postville, giving Showalter four straight over Jungblut.

The Warriors entered tournament play at 16–2 and quickly won three straight to set up a meeting with Postville in the opening round of districts. The Warriors got the Pirates for a third time, winning 61–49 in a close contest behind Thein's 30 points, including one of his signature slams at the right moment to give the Warriors all the momentum they needed. After a 19-point victory over La Porte City in the district semifinals, the Mason City Newman Knights stood in their way of a state tournament berth.

With 12 straight wins coming into the game, Central Elkader was playing their best basketball of the season. The Knights employed a box and one defensive strategy on Thein, placing one defender on him while the other four defenders played a zone defense. Nagel stepped up and had one of his best games, pouring in 23 points and securing 14 rebounds. Thein, closely guarded all game, added 20 points, with 10 coming from the foul line. In a tight game throughout, the Warriors pulled away in the fourth period for a 76–67 victory and a berth in the State 1A tournament.

The trip to Des Moines for the state tournament would be Central Elkader's first since the 1976 season and Showalter's first as a head coach. With their size, confidence, and team play, Showalter and the Warriors felt they could make a run for the state title. They matched up well with their first opponent, Cardinal Stritch from

Keokuk, Iowa. Unfortunately, things did not go the Warriors' way. Right before the tournament, guard Jim Moyna got tonsillitis. Then in the first quarter, the foul-prone Nagel got stuck with three fouls and Watkins went down with a knee injury. Central Elkader's loss of both big men gave the advantage to Cardinal Stritch, and the Lions took a 33–25 lead into halftime and extended it to 49–33 at the end of the third period. The Warriors never caught up, falling 65–56. Central Elkader finished the 1981–82 season at 22–3. The talent level subsided temporarily, and the Warriors slipped to 6–12 in the 1982–83 season. They returned to their winning ways in 1983–84, tying for second place in the conference before bowing out in the first game at districts to finish 10–9.

DON HURRIED ACROSS THE street and strolled into Pedretti's Bakery. The bakery, on the corner of Bridge and Main Streets in downtown Elkader, served as his Saturday morning breakfast stop for doughnut holes before Pee Wee basketball. As Don pulled open the door to leave, he heard the familiar voice of a booster club member from the corner table. "Hey, Coach Show," the man said. "I heard the Mid-Prairie job is open."

Don turned toward the booster as he kept walking, half his body already out the front door. He smiled and replied, "I heard that it was." He kept his stride and added, "I need to get to Pee Wee basketball. See you later."

Showalter knew about the Mid-Prairie job opening. He encouraged his assistant Wayne Mager to apply for it. When Showalter graduated from Wartburg in 1974, he interviewed for the head job at his alma mater; Cal Hickman had departed for the job in Blue Springs, Missouri. At the time, going back to Mid-Prairie appealed to Don. The school meant a lot to him and Vicky. They had many wonderful memories there, and they would be closer to their families again. The success of the 1970 Mid-Prairie basketball team still resonated positively in the community. Plus, Donnie came back each summer to work Hickman's camps, so the high school players knew him and respected him. It would be a comfortable move—too comfortable, and he was not ready for the job.

In 1974 Mid-Prairie passed on hiring their hometown son, and the excitement of coaching his hometown team waned with each passing year. Don started to believe it would be best not to go back. They would remember him as a player and might have unrealistic expectations.

When the Mid-Prairie administration struggled to fill the position, they reached out to Showalter in late June 1984 to gauge his interest. The teaching contract included an elementary physical education position for Don, and to make the decision more appealing, they now had a kindergarten teaching position open for Vicky. The opportunity for both Don and Vicky became too good to pass up. In making the decision, they leaned on their faith and kept the focus on what was best for the family. "There was a job for both of us," said Vicky. "In the end we felt that both our children would benefit from being around grandparents and our extended family. That sold us on the opportunity."

Showalter accepted the position. After eight seasons, Showalter left Elkader with a 108–63 record. His departure came as a surprise. "I still remember it," recalled Reimer, then a rising sophomore. "He called us all in and told us he was leaving." He did not leave the cupboard bare. His replacement, Mike Billings, found success in his third season. The 1986–87 Central Elkader squad lost only one game: the state championship final to Pocahontas High, on a three-point shot with eight seconds to go to. The second-place finish was the highest ever for a Warriors team. While the credit goes to the athletes and Coach Billings for the second-place finish, the players came up in Showalter's youth programs and witnessed the 1982 state tournament team. "By the time Coach Billings had taken over, our love of the game had already been instilled in us," said Reimer, a senior point guard on the 1987 team. "We were fundamentally sound, we knew how to play the game, and we were not going to beat ourselves. That had already been drilled into us by Coach Show."

Any pride Showalter felt regarding the 1987 team's success likely paled in comparison to the influence he had on the players he coached, an impact they recalled years later. "He was one of the most influential people in my life in terms of how things turned out for me. He was constantly talking about the future after high school and college," recalled Lonnie Meade. "At the time, I was not sure I was going to make it to college. He cared about you, and it was not always about basketball."

If anyone felt hurt by the announcement of Showalter's departure, they realized he was going home. If anything, they were going to miss him. "I cannot really say anything bad about Don Showalter. He is sincere and caring. He was kind to his players and kids," said Garms. "Don was approachable. He would listen to ideas. Everything he has done is above and beyond and more. He was an extremely effective coach and a tremendous role model."

Don Showalter's experience in Elkader prepared him well for the new opportunity that awaited him back home at Mid-Prairie. But before he began his new position, he worked his first Snow Valley Basketball Camp in the summer of 1984. Showalter was 10 years into his coaching career, but the journey was just beginning.

CHAPTER 8

Snow Valley

Don Showalter backed the gray Dodge Ram conversion van out of the driveway. It was packed for a family summer adventure, with camping gear, clothes, and summer essentials such as bug spray and swimming goggles, and a milk crate full of books, markers, crayons, and other road supplies for the kids.

Don steered the van west. They always drove straight through the night, stopping only for gas, maybe a snack, and for Don a Pepsi, his beverage of choice. The 1,800-mile trip from Wellman to Thousand Oaks, California, included one overnight stop; after 20 hours of driving, the Showalters got off the road to relax and enjoy the evening at a roadside motel with a swimming pool. The next morning, they finished the last six hours of the drive, arriving in time for Don to check into the John Wooden Basketball Fundamentals Camp. For the next few weeks, the Showalters' summer vacation looked nothing like the summer vacations their friends back home were taking. Melissa and Brent did not know any different. This is what they did each summer, and they looked forward to it, especially since they had made new friends. "The Kunstadts had two daughters similar in age to Brent and Melissa. The Meyers had one daughter about Melissa's age," remembered Vicky. "The kids had instant friends. Year after year we saw each other."

Each family stayed together in the dorms and ate meals in the cafeteria with the campers and the coaching staff. While their fathers coached, the kids swam in the campus swimming pool, played games, and visited local tourist attractions. Coach Wooden welcomed coaches bringing their families; he encouraged it and enjoyed entertaining the children, usually interacting with them during meals in the cafeteria. "My kids were elementary school age, and he would entertain them. He would put both of them in his lap and talk to them," recalled Kunstadt. "He would talk like *Sesame Street* characters. Because of all their years going with me to camp, my children got to know him like a grandfather." Vicky remembered how Wooden doted on Brent and Melissa, stopping and talking to them. "Our little kiddos had no idea how important he was," said Vicky. "He just seemed like an ordinary person to them."

Coach Wooden embraced his grandfatherly role. He watched the children grow up each summer. He became a part of their lives, sending them birthday cards and later graduation cards. A photo collage of annual snapshots of Coach Wooden, Don, Vicky, Melissa, and Brent hangs in the Showalter family home in Iowa; it is a conversation piece for visitors.

The return trip from California offered the commonalties of a traditional summer vacation; Vicky made sure of that. "Every year I would plan our route coming back. We would hit most of the national parks. One year we went all the way to Seattle up the coast," Vicky recalled. "We camped—that was the only way we could afford it." Thus, a more traditional summer family vacation ensued on the trip home: cooking over the camp stove, roasting marshmallows, making s'mores, and tent camping in KOA campgrounds. Before they left California, they often spent a couple days at Disneyland, pitching a tent in the campground by the amusement park. The summers gave the Showalter kids a lot of experiences; they grew up traveling, and it was a normal part of their life. "I have pretty fond memories of the annual summer trip," recalled Melissa. "I would say my brother may not have as fond of memories of the actual camping part."

"I remember camping at the campground near Disneyland and just how hot it was and how uncomfortable it was," said Brent. "But I think Melissa and I knew at the time it was special and, as we got a little older, what a great opportunity that was, and we probably appreciated more what Mom and Dad sacrificed to take us on all those trips."

Summer travel for the Showalters extended twice to Alaska and even overseas, to England, Scotland, and Switzerland. For Don and Vicky, including their children in travel aligned with their family values, and for Don it provided a balance between family and his passion for coaching. Showalter knew he was getting better as a coach; working the Wooden camp recharged him, drove him to want more. The more places he worked, the more he learned and the more connections he made, which led to new opportunities and new connections. It snowballed, and the Snow Valley Basketball School would be the biggest snowball of them all.

DON SHOWALTER LOOKED OVER his notes one more time. In a few minutes, he would lead his first instructional clinic at the Snow Valley Basketball School. He had prepared, but he felt nervous. Showalter knew the eyes of Herb Livsey would watch his every move: how he spoke to the kids, how he taught the skill, and how he led them through the drill. Livsey's observational approach bordered on a little overbearing. He sat close enough to hear, often in a metal folding chair, his body hunched over a yellow legal pad. His eyes penetrated the action before him while he scribbled notes. He never lost focus and he never said a word. Livsey was evaluating the coach on his ability to teach the game of basketball, and he did this by observing the youth being taught: their body language, the energy they displayed, and how they responded to instructions from the coach.

Herb Livsey spent a life in hoops. A trained educator, Livsey began his career as a high school teacher and coach. In 1969 he moved to Orange Coast College (OCC) in California to serve as the head men's basketball coach and teach English. He worked in that dual role until 1976 and continued to teach English until 1997. In 1998 he became an NBA scout, first with the Portland Trailblazers, then with the Atlanta Hawks, and finally with the Denver Nuggets. And for 40 years, from 1961 to 2001, Livsey operated one of the top instructional basketball camps in the United States: the Snow Valley Basketball School.

Herb Livsey cofounded the Snow Valley Basketball School with Chuck Walker; both taught high school in Winnemuca, Nevada. The idea for the Snow Valley Basketball School originated in the late 1950s in eastern New Hampshire, at Camp Graylag, a traditional boys' summer camp run by the Cousy family. A professional sports star and member of the Basketball Hall of Fame, Bob Cousy was a renowned ball handler and playmaker, leading the Boston Celtics to six NBA championships. At the end of the traditional camp, Cousy organized a fundamentals basketball camp and asked Livsey, a counselor at the camp, if he would like to stay and work it. "Cousy said he would pay me 25 dollars," recalled Livsey. "Here I was a 19-year-old kid on the camp staff, and Bob put me in charge of 16-year-old kids.... I remember he watched over my shoulder so I would be okay."

In 1961, in a parking lot at the Snow Valley Mountain Resort in Running Springs, California, Livsey and Walker ran the first Snow Valley camp, focused on a full day of teaching fundamental basketball skills. The camp morphed over time into an indoor/outdoor summer basketball camp at Westmont College in Santa Barbara. What separates Snow Valley from other basketball camps are the instructional clinics—structured sessions focused on teaching fundamental basketball skills. And Showalter, for the first time—in front of Livsey—was running an instructional clinic as the lead clinician.

The instructional clinics drive the camp schedule. The morning clinics concentrate on defense, with afternoon sessions centered on offensive concepts. In addition to the clinics, each day of camp includes a team practice and an evening game. When Showalter finished his instructional clinic he glanced toward Livsey, looking for some type of feedback. Herb offered no response. Undeterred, Showalter sought Livsey's advice. "He was always asking questions," stated Livsey. "He had a lot of questions. I could tell he loved the game, he loved teaching it, and he loved seeing those kids getting better." While Livsey's assessment of Don's ability to lead a clinic may have been clear to Herb, he did not communicate this to Showalter; it was not until Showalter started picking up more instructional clinics that he knew he must be meeting Livsey's expectations. Livsey was finicky in assigning lead clinicians and took great care in selecting the right coaches.

Showalter embraced the Snow Valley Way. The pressure to meet Livsey's standard of teaching at Snow Valley helped Showalter improve as a teacher of the game. A meticulous note-taker, Don recorded what he was learning at Snow Valley: new basketball terminology and teaching methods. Snow Valley became a powerful mechanism for Showalter to gauge his development as a teacher of the game. And although Showalter did not know it at the time, he was exactly the type of coach Livsey wanted: one who could teach the game, was willing to share his insight, and was open to accepting advice and strategies from other coaches.

Livsey strived to find the best teachers of the game to run the instructional clinics, regardless of the coaches' national reputations— as long as they valued teaching the game. For Livsey, the skill to teach was paramount to the success of the camp, but he understood that coaches were still learning. Livsey recruited coaches working in high schools, small colleges, and overseas. If he was watching a game and liked the way the coach ran his team, he invited them to work camp. Other coaches, such as Showalter, came on a recommendation. Livsey also sought out a few "big-name" coaches, such as the legendary Pete Newell.

Newell's teams at the University of California dominated college basketball from the late 1950s into the early 1960s, winning the national championship in 1961. Coach Newell is one of only three coaches to win the National Invitation Tournament (NIT), an NCAA championship, and an Olympic gold medal. Livsey often thought of what it would be like if he could get Newell to teach the defense at Snow Valley. Then one summer, Pete Newell's grandson enrolled in Snow Valley. Livsey, familiar with where Newell lived, drove to Rancho Santa Fe, California, knocked on Newell's door, and sold him on the idea of coming to Snow Valley.

The list of coaches Livsey pursued and hired to work Snow Valley is long. One year he invited NBA coach Dick Motta to teach the defense at Snow Valley. Motta, who first led Grace High School in Idaho to a state title in 1959, eventually worked his way to the NBA, winning a title in 1978 and finishing his career as one of the all-time winningest coaches in NBA history. Motta had a certain method he used to teach the defense; he called it Cutthroat. Cutthroat is a four-on-four live scrimmage situation used to develop both offensive and defensive skills. Three basic rules govern the drill: catch and square, move after a pass, and thank the passer when you score. Coaches can modify the rules of Cutthroat to adapt to their coaching philosophies.

With Motta's influence, Cutthroat became a staple of the Snow Valley Camp. Coaches working Snow Valley, including Showalter, took the drill back to their own communities. Showalter found Cutthroat to be exactly the type of drill that fit his coaching style, allowing him to adjust to what his team needed; it helped him realize that *how* he taught a drill was more important than what type of drill he used.

Motta's Cutthroat is just one basketball drill that gained traction at Snow Valley. Others include Box Drills, a series of drills designed to practice the proper footwork associated with the offensive skills of basketball, and Oiler Shooting Drills, conditioning and shooting drills that push players to practice at game speed. The teaching of Cutthroat, Box Drills, and Oiler Shooting Drills occurs at every level of basketball, in gymnasiums all over the world.

Showalter's development and career as a coach also followed the growth of summer basketball in the United States: he worked camps to develop his skills as a coach, and he used summer camps to build the basketball programs at each of his coaching stops.

Throughout the 1970s local summer sport camps were sprouting up in rural communities and urban areas alike. As participation numbers in basketball camps increased and revenues soared, others wanted in the game. During the 1980s, universities and colleges added overnight and day camps. The main purpose was to increase revenue for athletic programs and coaches' salaries. In the early stages, colleges used their summer camps to bring in prospective student-athletes for tryouts and to spend time with the coaching staff and current collegiate players working the camp.

In the early 1990s, summer basketball shifted again. Driven by collegiate recruiting, regional showcase tournaments proliferated, attracting teams and top talent from all over the country. For the high school athlete with college aspirations, participating on a travel team became a necessity to secure a college scholarship. Funded by registration fees from the participants or financial support from sponsors, travel teams pool athletes from different school districts and communities. The coach conducts practices and often schedules competitions.

With the growth in travel teams, more colleges started to offer team camps, where high school teams could attend a camp together. This shift coincided with a reduction in restrictions set forth by the state high school associations on how much time high school coaches could work with their athletes in the off-season. Each state governs off-season guidelines in a different manner. When Showalter coached at Lone Tree and Central Elkader, the state of Iowa only allowed him to work with his athletes over a 10-day period in the summer. Thus, high school coaches encouraged their athletes to attend local instructional camps, where coaches could sign up to work the camp and have access to work with their players. When Showalter took the Mid-Prairie job, the restrictions lessened and coaches were free to work with athletes for the entire summer. With this change, coaches backed away from working the collegiate camps; they exerted more control by keeping their team together and attending team camps or running a local camp, consisting of their high school team roster.

Livsey adapted to the changes. During its peak, Snow Valley had four consecutive weeks of camp with more than 300 kids per week. Livsey reduced the number of sessions back to two a summer. At the height of Snow Valley's popularity in the late 1980s and early 1990s, there were two independently owned camps in the United States considered the finest for fundamental skill development: Snow Valley on the West Coast and the Five-Star Basketball Camps on the East Coast. Five-Star, founded in 1966 by Howard Garfinkel and Will Klein, became the proving ground for future Hall of Fame coaches and close to 500 future NBA players.

Both Five-Star and Snow Valley started as fundamental skill camps driven by passionate individual teachers of the game in Livsey and Garfinkel. Both camps affected the teaching of basketball. Yet each evolved, finding its own niche in the history of the game. Garfinkel is referred to as the godfather of summer recruiting and summer basketball, and Five-Star became the place where the most talented players went to hone their skills and be seen by college coaches. Snow Valley never attracted the talent of Five-Star, but Livsey's quest to teach the fundamentals created a following of

coaches who shared his passion—coaches such as Don Showalter—
who spread the Snow Valley Way across the country, implementing
the Snow Valley concepts in camps and with their teams.

In Livsey, as with Coach Wooden, Showalter had a mentor to
foster his development as a coach. Through Livsey's intense and
hyperfocused approach, Showalter learned the importance of setting
high expectations. Whereas Wooden elicited adherence to standards
based on his credibility as a Hall of Fame coach, Livsey had to fight
for his standards each day. He established a perfectionist tone, and
either out of fear or the will to please him, coaches complied.

Showalter's first-year experience at Snow Valley caused his
confidence to surge; he was inspired by new knowledge and
stimulated by new relationships with others in basketball that could
lead to new opportunities. Showalter learned the more he pursued
opportunities, the more experiences he acquired. Penning the letter
to Coach Wooden as a senior in college had taught Showalter an
important lesson that he never forgot: In order to get opportunities
in basketball (or in life), you have to ask for them. No one is going
to find a rural high school basketball coach in southeastern Iowa.

Thus, when he heard about the Amateur Basketball Association
of the United States of America (ABAUSA), later renamed USA
Basketball, he wrote a letter to the executive director, Bill Wall. Wall
served as executive director of the ABAUSA from 1974 to 1992
and helped lead the transition of NBA players into the Olympics,
culminating in the 1992 Olympic Dream Team. Wall responded to
Showalter with a letter stating they did not have any opportunities
for him at the time—but Showalter had planted the seed.

CHAPTER 9

Mid-Prairie

The miles stretched out in front of them until at last the familiar sights of Wellman-Kalona came into view. Don and Vicky were home again.

There are three communities that make up the Mid-Prairie School District, all with a rich agricultural history: Wellman, Kalona, and West Chester. Wellman, home to Maplecrest Turkey Farms—for decades a leading producer of turkey in the US and a major employer in the region, including Donnie's grandfather—at one time dubbed itself "Thanksgiving Town." Farmers in Kalona, now known as the Quilt Capital of Iowa, built a grain mill in 1880, establishing the town as a center of commerce in the region. West Chester served as an important shipping and trading point on the famed Chicago and Rock Island Railroad, though the growth of corporate farming and abandonment of the railroad caused the population of West Chester to decline significantly. The trio of communities had a combined population of less than 4,000 residents, a small pool from which to develop basketball talent. The challenge was set.

THE MID-PRAIRIE FANS TRADED barbs with the Washington faithful as the 1985 2A District Championship Game tightened between the Demons and the Golden Hawks. Washington held an eight-point lead at the half, but Mid-Prairie roared back, knotting the score at 34 going into the fourth quarter. The stingy Golden Hawks defense shut down senior scoring guard Larry Fishback. With only one field goal on 11 attempts, Fishback, the Southeast 7 Conference Player of the Year, had struggled. Yet his play throughout the season had earned him the respect of his teammates and trust with the coaching staff; the ball would be in his hands at the end of the game.

The Demons held a one-point advantage late in the fourth quarter. Mid-Prairie swung the ball around the perimeter and found Todd Bontrager with 1:50 on the clock. Bontrager, consistent all season, tossed in a midrange jumper to give Mid-Prairie a one-point edge. For the next 1:46, neither team scored. Then with four seconds left, the Demons got the ball to Fishback. It was Larry's game to win or lose. When Fishback's shot rimmed out, the Mid-Prairie fans stormed the court; their team was one win away from the state tournament! "Fishback slumped to the floor," remembered Ross Anderson, an assistant coach with the Demons. "He was devastated because he played so hard." The season ended for the Demons, but their unprecedented run of success was just starting.

The community of Washington rests 16 miles south of Wellman-Kalona and maintains a consistent population of approximately 7,000. With an agricultural heritage, Washington boasts the world's oldest continuously operating cinema (since 1897) and is considered the Barn Quilt Capital of Iowa. All three communities reside in Washington county, with Washington serving as the county seat.

Through 1984, Iowa separated high schools into three classification levels: 1A, 2A, and 3A, with 3A being the largest. With only three levels, enrollment discrepancies developed between schools within the same level. This was the case for Mid-Prairie when competing against their rival, Washington, as the Demons had a larger talent pool of potential student-athletes to draw from. In the 1984–85 season, Iowa added a smaller, fourth classification level: A. Both Washington and Mid-Prairie continued to compete in 2A until the 1992–93 season, when the classification system shifted again, renaming and aligning the four levels to: 1A, 2A, 3A, and 4A. With this alteration, Washington High bumped up to 3A and Mid-Prairie remained in 2A. For the rest of Showalter's tenure at Mid-Prairie, the Golden Hawks played Washington at most once in the regular season, but all postseason encounters ended after the 1991–92 season. The Demons competed in the Southeast 7 Conference and the Golden Hawks competed in the Eastern Iowa Hawkeye Conference, but county bragging rights were at stake; youth in the Wellman-Kalona area grew up with a disdain for the Demons.

Showalter's adversary on the Demons sideline was Washington head coach Dave Tremmel. From 1976 to 1995, Tremmel led the Demons to 14 conference championships and 8 state tournament appearances, including an undefeated state title run in 1986. Tremmel coached hard, using a militaristic approach that kept him in charge, commanding respect and attention with his sharp tongue. "If he chewed on somebody, which he did, they expected that and that's just the way he was," remembered Ross Anderson. "He was very demanding of his players and me. He expected us to commit to basketball."

Tremmel pushed kids mentally and physically beyond what many had experienced before. "He was intimidating," remembered Tony Wilson, a Demons player from 1988 to 1990. "He had high expectations, and we all tried to live up to them." Under Tremmel it was his way or the highway; players did not want to disappoint their coach or feel his wrath if they did. A few never made it through the season. "I remember we were at Burlington in my first year, and one of our starters was not doing what Dave wanted him to do in the first half," recalled Steve Roland, an assistant coach at Washington from 1976 to 1980. "Dave lit into him at halftime, I mean blistered him, and did not start him but played him in the second half. He ended up quitting that night—came in and threw his stuff at Tremmel's feet."

Roland worked closely with Tremmel during his four years at Washington, before continuing his own career as an educator and coach in Iowa for 40 years. "Tremmel was a good teacher, good at breaking down the different components of the game," recalled Roland. "But he was super competitive, a motivator, and some people liked him and some did not." For Buddy Boulton, a point guard for the Demons from 1988 to 1990, Tremmel provided the motivation he needed to succeed. "I liked him. He was hard, he was tough, but he was fair," recalled Boulton. "I was a kid at that time who needed that—to excel, to get the most out of myself."

Off the court, it was common to catch Tremmel enjoying a smoke before a game, at halftime, and in his office at school, between teaching physical education classes. Tremmel played as he coached: hard. He was known to go scout a high school game and then enjoy libations into the early morning hours, while betting on games of pool. An avid gambler, Tremmel's competitive nature spilled into his leisurely pursuits. "After two weeks of summer basketball camp, Tremmel liked to take us golfing," recalled Roland. "But he wanted to bet on everything, on every hole: longest putt, longest drive, and closest to the pin. I did not come back with too much money after two weeks of working camp."

Tremmel's style contrasted Showalters' on and off the court, but the two coaches shared a mutual respect for each other, a coaching friendship built on a passion for teaching the game and sharing it with others. On the court, they engaged in a competitive rivalry, each striving for county bragging rights and, at times, one spoiling a chance for the other to continue in postseason play.

Leading up to his big shot in the district championship, Todd Bontrager provided senior leadership to a junior-heavy Mid-Prairie roster in Showalter's first season back at Mid-Prairie. A product of the southeastern Iowa basketball camps since third grade, Bontrager was already familiar with the Showalter name and knew his new coach from the summers he spent attending camp. Bontrager, a three-point marksman, could also beat you off the dribble, not with his quickness but with his ability to read the defense, outsmarting his defender for open looks at the basket.

Bontrager's running mates featured two 5'11" tough-minded guards in juniors Lonnie Yoder and Pat Woodburn, in addition to a skilled big man, junior Brian Bender. A 6'4", smooth-playing forward, Bender was a threat to score with his back to the basket or facing up, where he often nailed the open jump shot. Bender also liked to mix it up; he played his best when challenged, a trait he shared with Woodburn. A well-conditioned shooting guard and natural leader, Woodburn played with a high motor. Bontrager often led the team in scoring, but both Bender and Woodburn challenged him for game honors. With most of the scoring distributed among those three, Lonnie Yoder fulfilled his role as a traditional point guard. He kept the team together as a coach on the floor—a savvy, scrappy, pass-first guard.

The team found ways to win, but it took the full regular-season schedule before Mid-Prairie gelled as a unit. It took them less time to adjust to their new coach. Coming home, Showalter had instant credibility, as many people in the community had fond memories of the 1970 state tournament team. However, this did not resonate as much with his players, many of whom had never seen him play. "We found out about his playing success at Mid-Prairie later on," shared Yoder. "We respected him as a coach first. I remember our first day. We had an early-morning practice before school and then a practice after school. We got together in the locker room and were like, 'Why is this guy coaching us? He should be coaching in college.' You could just tell he knew so much, just the way he taught things."

With a berth at the state tournament on the line, Mid-Prairie raced out to an early 16–12 lead against West Liberty at substate. But the Comets responded with a 13-point run to take a 33–24 lead into the half. The Golden Hawks never caught up, losing 63–50, ending their season at 14–9. In the locker room, as reported by the *Washington Evening Journal*, Showalter consoled his team and gave his four juniors a message for next year: "And now you fellas know what it takes to get here. There were only 16 teams that made it this far. The ball is on your fingertips; give it a whirl."

The move back to Wellman-Kalona in the summer of 1984 allowed Donnie and Vicky to reunite with family. And there was the excitement of new opportunities, as Vicky returned to teaching kindergarten full-time and Don had, for the first time, a full-time position teaching physical education; he would also serve as assistant football coach at the high school, a position he had not held since Lone Tree. Showalter's experiences in Elkader had given him confidence, but he was still learning as a coach.

THE FIRST PRACTICE OF the 1985–86 basketball season could not have come soon enough. This was their year, and they were ready to get going. Showalter returned to a veteran group. He had determined athletes with a competitive drive to win who also enjoyed competing together. Woodburn and Yoder had been best friends since the third grade, when Woodburn's family moved to Kalona to open a restaurant. Woody, as he was called by his friends and teammates, remembered how united the team was, how they treated each other as equals even when not all athletes on the team had access to the same privileges: "We all knew some people had money and some people did not have money, but yet we felt like we were the same."

The Golden Hawks returned a fourth starter in Neill Griffith, a 6'4" senior five-man who had multiple games with double-digit rebounds. The starting lineup featured one junior, Don's younger brother Dennis Showalter. To coach his own brother opened up Showalter to criticism. "There were a couple of parents who thought he was playing favorites with me starting. But I just remember him being harder on me than anybody else," shared Dennis. "It never bothered me."

For Dennis, occasional ridicule from jealous teammates occurred. "He caught a lot of flak from some of the other guys in our class: 'You're only playing because you're Donnie's brother' and 'I should be starting over you'—that type of stuff," remembered Woodburn. "But that was not the case at all. I never noticed him getting any favoritism. Coach Show put him in the lineup our senior year not because he was his brother but because he deserved it…he fit right in."

Fortunately for Don, Dennis's play on the court dampened any criticism. A 6'1" lefty, Dennis provided perimeter shooting on the wing, and with his ball-handling skills he could relieve Yoder or Woodburn in the backcourt. Plus, Dennis's athleticism suited Don's style of play: a full-court 1-2-1-1 zone press and man-for-man full-court pressure. The 1985–86 Golden Hawks helped Showalter establish his fast-paced, pressing style of play for future Golden Hawks teams. But for this team in particular, it went beyond the basic execution of the press and any havoc it may have caused for the opposing offense; the fast-paced, intense style of play fit the personalities of the players executing it, especially Woodburn. "Pat had one speed," shared Yoder. "He played as hard in practice as he did in the games. He could go and go and never get tired."

Woodburn also had a temper, aggravated by his hypercompetitive nature. "Pat played like his head was on fire," recalled Dave Schlabaugh, an assistant coach at Mid-Prairie during Woodburn's prep career.

At times, Woodburn's fervor could get out of control. "One practice, I was hot. I remember being angry," said Woodburn. "I chucked the ball against the wall, and Coach Show came right over and put a stop to it." Showalter knew he needed to curtail Woodburn's outbursts and channel his intensity. At the same time,

Woodburn's unequivocal drive to win was innate; it was a trait Showalter nurtured in other players through drills and motivation.

Mid-Prairie opened the season with blowout victories over Wilton High and Mount Vernon. Their archrival the Washington Demons awaited in the third matchup. The 1985 district championship loss to Mid-Prairie stunned Washington so much it had pushed the Demons to hone their game in the off-season. In case they needed more motivation, Tremmel had the score of the district championship loss, 42–41, printed on the right pant leg of their practice shorts. The skilled, senior-laden Demons featured an imposing front line of 6'6", 6'7", and 6'6". In his 10th season, this was Tremmel's best team. The Demons led the entire game for a 59–50 win.

Mid-Prairie dominated their next three opponents, routing West Branch, Durant, and Sigourney. Their pressing style of play wore out opponents. "We played up-tempo and pressed all over the place," recalled Yoder. The Sigourney victory placed the Golden Hawks in a championship matchup against Washington for the four-team midseason Mid-Prairie Tournament title. Neither the Demons nor the Golden Hawks had lost since their previous meeting.

Beyond the obvious physical size differences between the Demons and Golden Hawks, the two teams were a contrast in style of play. The Demons orchestrated a deliberate half-court game aimed at getting high-percentage shots around the basket; it was an approach to match their size. The slower pace allowed Tremmel to keep his starters in the game longer; he only played five to seven players per game. The Golden Hawks liked to force the pace of the game and get the opposing team to shoot a quicker, low-quality shot. It was a pace that allowed Showalter to go deeper into his bench. Tremmel's success and drive to create a competitive program gave Showalter a program to measure his against. It was a similar scenario to what he had faced with Paul Jungblut and the Postville Pirates early in his career when building the Central Elkader program—a rivalry that made him a better coach.

The Demons mopped the floor with the Golden Hawks in the second matchup for a 65–45 victory. This second Washington loss was the final loss of the 1985–86 regular season for the Golden Hawks; they won the next 12 leading into the district tournament, going undefeated, 14–0, in their conference for the first time in more than a decade. Rolling into postseason play with 12 straight wins could set any team up for a letdown, but Showalter's 1986 team was too stubborn and competitive to let that happen.

The Golden Hawks were playing their best basketball down the stretch. With the shift in districts for the 1985–86 season, Mid-Prairie would not play Washington in the postseason unless they made it to Des Moines. After winning the district championship 73–71 over Cedar Rapids Regis, excitement brewed in Wellman and Kalona with aspirations of a Golden Hawks trip to the state tournament. Would the 14-year drought end?

Next up was Vinton High. The Blue Jays came into substate undefeated at 21–0. They used a solid half-court game, built around the size of their front line, which towered over opponents at 6'6", 6'6", and 6'5". Yet Vinton did not possess the talent Mid-Prairie did in their backcourt, giving the Golden Hawks confidence they could overcome the height inequality. They started the game strong, taking a 6–2 lead on a Bender jumper. Then in an unfortunate moment, Bender went down with a knee injury. He continued to play but was limited, and the Blue Jays exploded for a 22–9 second quarter to take and keep the lead for good, winning 69–59. The dream ended for Woodburn and his teammates. "I think we deserved to play in Des Moines," said Woodburn. "It's a thorn in my side. It really is. It still sickens me today." Woodburn earned fifth-team all-state honors and appeared in two postseason regional All-Star games. Mid-Prairie finished 19–3. The 1986 Golden Hawks left their place in the Mid-Prairie history books, with a second straight district championship and an undefeated conference record.

Washington, on the other hand, went unscathed, 25–0, en route to a state 2A title. Tremmel never subbed in the title game, even when two starters picked up two fouls in the first quarter. The undefeated season captured the Washington community, and hundreds met the team in West Chester on their return from Des Moines; people lined the streets with lawn chairs. Washington athletic director Doug Dunlap was quoted as saying, "This is the biggest celebration this town has seen in some time. No doubt about it, this is the highlight of athletic history at Washington." The players on the 1986 Demons were heroes, celebrities for the next wave of youth. The county rivalry between Washington and Mid-Prairie would continue, but now Tremmel had one thing Showalter did not: a state title.

GERRY BEELER BLEW HIS whistle, and 10 boys ages 12 to 13 stopped. "Halftime," hollered Beeler above the din of the large drum fans positioned in front of the exits to circulate the hot, stale, late June air. The gym—next to Assembly Hall, the home arena of the Indiana Hoosiers—offered no air-conditioning, bathing the youth and the coaches in their own perspiration.

As the youth took turns at the drinking fountain, Beeler noticed an imposing figure—the head men's basketball coach at Indiana University, Bobby Knight—walk toward the court. Knight, who by the summer of 1986 had two of his three NCAA national championships, had been watching the play on the court. He walked across the gym toward a coach working on an adjacent court. Knight, almost a foot taller than the coach he was approaching, dug into his pockets and pulled out some cash; he handed the money to the coach and pointed toward the exit. Knight sent him home.

At the Bob Knight Basketball Camp, coaches officiated and coached the evening games simultaneously while moving up and down the court. This particular coach failed to meet Knight's expectations; he didn't work hard enough. Showalter forewarned Beeler about Coach Knight's standards. A first-time head varsity boys' basketball coach at Iowa Valley High School, Beeler rode with Showalter, whom he had never met, from Iowa to Bloomington. "Show had previous experience with the camp, and on the way out he shared how structured and disciplined it was. How they expected you to teach the skills and they monitored what you did," said Beeler. Beeler and Showalter met Knight's expectations and returned for the next four summers. Ten years later, in 1996, Beeler became the principal at Mid-Prairie High School, where he supervised and worked alongside his athletic director, Don Showalter, for the next 17 years.

Some summers, Showalter worked up to 10 weeks of summer basketball camps, including the John Wooden Basketball Fundamentals Camp, the Snow Valley Basketball School, and the Southeastern Iowa Hawkeye Basketball Camp. In addition, Showalter worked a number of other camps but not necessarily every summer, including the Roy Williams Basketball Camp at the University of Kansas; the University of Iowa Basketball Camps, first with Lute Olson and then under Tom Davis; and at camps ran by Iowa State University. Showalter dabbled in other camps associated with different organizations, such as Nike, where he coached at the Nike All-America Camp and the Nike Skills Camp, an instructional-based camp for the top 40 to 50 high school players in the United States. He taught basketball to future NBA players at the NBA Players Association Top 100 Camp and instructed youth in fundamental basketball skills at camps featuring future NBA players, such as the Kobe Bryant Nike Skills Academy, the Nike LeBron James Camp, and the Magic Johnson Camp.

Showalter served as a camp coach for the esteemed B/C All Stars Basketball Camp, an invitation-only camp that served as a recruiting showcase for the top high school talent, that over the years featured future NBA legends Magic Johnson, Larry Bird, Charles Barkley, and many more. He worked the Pete Newell Big Man Camp, a top instructional camp for collegiate and professional post players. At the Big Man Camp, Showalter worked with elite talent, but maybe more important, he garnered knowledge on teaching post play from Hall of Famer Pete Newell.

Summer basketball camps serve as a training ground for basketball coaches, with national, regional, and local camps helping coaches learn how to better teach the game. For coaches working camp outside their home states or a thousand miles away, the experience can lead to new connections in the sport. This network becomes the source of information, where a coach goes to have conversations about basketball, coaching jobs, and life. Showalter advanced his career working basketball camps. He became a better teacher of the game and expanded his coaching network. Yet he did not stop there; he invested time and energy into professional organizations for coaches, especially an organization right in his backyard, the Iowa Basketball Coaches Association (IBCA).

THE 75-YEAR-OLD JOHN WOODEN was back in the Midwest but not in his hometown of Martinsville, Indiana. Instead he stood in front of several hundred coaches at the 1986 Iowa Basketball Coaches Association annual coaching clinic in Des Moines. When asked why he was speaking at a basketball clinic in Iowa, Wooden responded, "Because my good friend Don Showalter invited me."

Coach Wooden headlined the IBCA Annual Clinic, along with Hubie Brown, the head coach of the New York Knicks at the time (who later became a well-known broadcaster for the NBA on CBS and then on TNT). Other renowned basketball coaches spoke in

Des Moines over the years, including Vivian Stringer, John Calipari, Bob Huggins, Bob Knight, Kelvin Sampson, and Morgan Wooten. In 1995 the clinic drew 1,417 coaches to hear a speaker lineup that included Roy Williams, the head men's basketball coach at the University of Kansas.

The success of the annual coaching clinic and the growth in membership numbers over the years did not happen by chance. Since its inception in 1969, the IBCA has empowered Iowa coaches to serve on the board of directors and in different leadership positions. Cal Hickman, Don's high school coach, served as the first IBCA president. Don Logan, a football and basketball coach in the Benton Community School District, joined the IBCA in 1977 and was elected to the board of directors in 1978; in 1983 he became the executive secretary. "I had four goals for the IBCA," said Logan. "One, increase our exposure in the state first, then regionally, and then nationally; second, I wanted Iowa coaches to know they were as good as anyone in the nation; third, I wanted Iowa kids to believe they could play at a higher level; and lastly, help coaches expand their knowledge, technique, and skills as a coach."

Due to his enthusiasm for the role, his fellow board members gave him the freedom to grow the association, and for the next 39 years and counting, he achieved each of his four goals, but not single-handedly. "Don Showalter was a young coach and got on our board in the early 1980s," recalled Logan. "He was one of the people I really tapped into for his energy and his vision. Don and I played off each other fairly well. We are both organizers. We both like to plan, and we both like to think things through."

Working alongside other coaches on the board of directors and within the membership, Logan and Showalter collaborated to establish the annual Academic All-State Teams; the McDonald's Midwest Classic, a game matching up the best seniors from Iowa against the best seniors from Michigan; and the Dr. Pepper All-Star Series, a multiday event featuring seniors from Iowa playing in a four-team tournament representing the north, south, east, and west regions of the state. Showalter's involvement with the IBCA on the board of directors, including his tenure as president of the board, expanded his coaching network in a different way: he got to know basketball coaches across the state of Iowa, and they got to know him. Showalter's experience with the IBCA helped him develop his voice as a leader among coaches. His experiences in the game and knowledge of the game now gave him wisdom to pass along to younger coaches. The mentee had become a mentor, and he started getting more opportunities to share his knowledge with others.

SHOWALTER FLIPPED OVER THE name tag hanging below his neck to display his name and the title of the event: NABC National Convention, 1986 Final Four. In a few moments he would give a presentation on practice planning to coaches attending the National Association of Basketball Coaches (NABC) annual convention in Dallas, Texas. To speak at the NABC convention was quite an honor for Showalter. In basketball coaching, the NABC convention at the Final Four is the mecca for basketball coaches at all levels, where coaches go for professional growth and to promote themselves for future job opportunities. The Final Four captured all of Showalter's basketball needs, a plethora of information from convention speakers on topics related to strategy and philosophy, along with an opportunity to have conversations with coaches at every level of competition.

Showalter's presentation at the 1986 convention was a success. Others recognized he had something to share, including the NABC leadership, and they offered Showalter a position on the NABC High School Committee, where they tasked him with securing a high school speaker for the convention. He eventually became the chair of the committee, helping to organize roundtable sessions on hot topics and trends facing high school coaches, including annual sessions on rule changes. Showalter's work with the NABC led to other committee assignments under the umbrella of the National Federation of State High Schools (NFHS), including both their rules and publication committees. He was becoming a recognizable figure in high school basketball.

IN THE 1986–87 SEASON, Dennis was the only returning starter. A savvy player, Dennis led the team in scoring his senior season at 20.6 points a game. That included 28 points against Tipton in a late-season win and a 30-point performance, with six threes, in a season finale loss to Cedar Rapids LaSalle at the district tournament, ending Mid-Prairie's season at 16–4. Because Dennis could play, he earned first-team all-conference honors and the team named him MVP. Because Dennis was the best player, Don pushed him harder and Dennis felt it. "Dennis always joked that Donnie was harder on him," laughed Vicky. In reality, Showalter was always a little harder on all his best players; in this case one just happened to be his brother.

Dennis shared a love of basketball with Donnie, and he enjoyed playing for him. "I never remember any tension with my brother," recalled Dennis. "He was hard on us, but he always had a calm, instructional presence about him. I always had this view of him that he knew what he was doing and he was a good coach." Dennis did not share the same passion for coaching; after attending Coe College, where he played basketball for two seasons, he completed medical school at the University of Iowa and started a family medicine practice in Minnesota.

Coaching Dennis provided Don an opportunity to spend time with his brother—time previously reserved for holidays and family gatherings due to the 16-year age gap between the two. The potential awkwardness in coaching your brother never seemed to faze Don. If he felt any apprehension, his mother, Iva, eased his initial concerns. "Donnie did ask me [about coaching Dennis]," remembered Iva. "Donnie had been gone for 10 years, and I felt that Donnie was very mature about it." Dennis would be the last of five Showalter brothers to grace the hardwood for the Mid-Prairie Golden Hawks. Dean, two years older than Dennis and three classes ahead, missed playing for Donnie by one year, graduating in 1984. "I wondered what [playing for Donnie] would have been like," recalled Dean. "It would have been fun for me. In my three years, we won more than we lost but never made it deep in the postseason." A well-rounded student, Dean earned an economics degree while playing football at Coe College. He later pursued graduate work and became a faculty member at Texas State University, San Marcos, teaching finance and economics.

The number of years between the two sets of brothers was significant. "Donnie and Doug were almost like uncles," recalled Dean. "Dennis and I were close." That left Dave as the middle child, six years younger than Doug and six years older than Dean. "Everyone knew my older two brothers and my younger two brothers," joked Dave. "But everyone was like, 'Who are you?'"

While Don and Doug would lead the Golden Hawks to the state basketball tournament in Des Moines, Dave did not find as much success on the basketball court. Instead, he shined on the baseball diamond and football field, and as a state long jump champion. Arguably the most athletically gifted of the five brothers, Dave was an NCAA Division III football All-American for the Coe College Kohawks—a defensive back good enough to earn an NFL tryout. He graduated with a business degree and became a supply chain purchaser for a wide range of products, including sweatshirts, tea, and olive oil.

Donald and Iva raised a close-knit family, even if all the brothers were not necessarily close in age. "There was hardly a game my family missed," recalled Dave. Wherever the boys played, an entourage of Showalters followed—grandparents, parents, aunts, uncles, cousins, nephews, nieces, and siblings. Occasionally, someone could not make it because of work or another obligation, but Donald Showalter hardly ever missed a game; he was steadfast in being at every event, even when Don started coaching. "I traveled with Donnie's parents to many games, and often just with Donald," recalled Vicky. "Donald would travel to all home and away games when Donnie was coaching." With the support of his family, Don continued to build the Mid-Prairie program going into his fourth season.

Going into the 1987–88 season, senior Jason Dumont had little to prove in terms of his role and value to the Mid-Prairie Golden Hawks. The 6'5", 195-pound forward was coming off a junior season in which he averaged 17.8 points per game and was named first-team all-conference. Yet it was Dumont's talents on the football field as a defensive end that had collegiate recruiters drooling, including at the University of Iowa. He picked the Hawkeyes, making a verbal commitment in early December.

Dumont excelled in football, but he loved basketball, debunking the label often applied when a football player of Dumont's size laces up a pair of high-tops: a bruiser who uses his size and muscle to intimidate, hiding his lack of the finer skills of the game. Dumont could intimidate and he could bang in the block to gain an edge, but due to the focus on fundamental skill development in the Golden Hawks program, Dumont developed the efficiency of an athlete seasoned in the proper footwork and how to use one's body to gain position for easy buckets. He controlled the glass, often finishing a game with a double-double, leading the team in both rebounds and points. A coachable athlete, Dumont raised the intensity level of play each day in practice. "Dumont competed his butt off," recalled longtime Mid-Prairie assistant basketball coach Chris Kern. "He would do anything you asked him to." Dumont met and exceeded

Showalter's expectations, standards he laid out in a binder given to each player before the season.

Ryan Schlabaugh sat with his teammates in the Mid-Prairie locker room prior to the first practice of the 1987–88 season with an open half-inch-thick three-ring binder draped across his lap. Like a prayer session in Sunday school, each member of the Golden Hawks bowed their heads and read along as Showalter recited a long paragraph on bench behavior: "Every man on the bench is important to his team and must assume a positive attitude at all times.... All players will stand and applaud the player coming out of the game.... The use of profanity or any type of 'snide remark' to an official or opponent is strictly forbidden."

As a junior guard, Ryan Schlabaugh knew he had a spot on the team, but if there was any chance at getting court time in a varsity game, he had to be one of the 15 players who suited up for the game. "None of us were guaranteed a spot on that bench. You had to earn your spot every week," recalled Schlabaugh. "Every week [Coach Show] would say, 'Here are the 15 that are going to suit up,' and you just hoped your name was one of the 15."

With their full attention, Showalter continued with some basic rules, like no towel snapping and no horseplay. As Showalter dismissed them to the practice floor, Schlabaugh stood up and put the binder in his gym locker. He would look at it again later that evening—they all would. The binder contained Coach John Wooden's Pyramid of Success, which Showalter used to teach and reinforce key aspects of the Mid-Prairie program throughout the season, and copies of pages titled Game Goals, designed as fill-in-the-blank activities. At the top was space to document the game and date, followed by a numbered list, with blank spaces to fill in up to five goals. "Before every game he would have you write down one or two goals you wanted to accomplish," remembered Dumont. "Then after the game, you had to check the box: Did you or didn't you?"

The binder grew thicker throughout the season, an accumulation of goal sheets, stat sheets, newspaper clippings (Showalter made copies of the local articles from the *Washington Evening Journal*, *Kalona News*, and occasionally the *Iowa City Press* or the *Des Moines Register* when they covered the Golden Hawks), and performance sheets, a plus/minus statistical system used to evaluate individual performances on different elements of the game. By the end of the season, the binder provided a detailed snapshot of each athlete's season—a memory book the whereabouts of which many Golden Hawks players know immediately, even decades later. "I would have never had those stats and newspaper clippings," said Bryan Tobin, a point guard from 1991 to 1992. "It's nice to be able to relive your junior and senior year with Coach."

For the players on the 1987–88 team, the binder shared evidence of a successful season. After a 1–3 start that included two 14-point losses, Mid-Prairie routed conference foe Clear Creek 74–52 to improve to 2–2. Next up, the Golden Hawks hosted the Solon Spartans. The talent in the growing bedroom community of Solon, just 12 miles north of Iowa City, seemed to get better each year, and the contests between the two schools, home or away, always took on an extra level of intensity. Ranked seventh and undefeated, Solon took a one-point lead into the first quarter break. Sensing his team needed a little spark, Showalter pushed his squad in the timeout, his voice elevated and his word choice sharper than usual. "He rarely used profanity," recalled Dumont. "But when he did, you knew he meant it."

The Golden Hawks owned the second quarter and pulled out in front for a 31–27 halftime lead. The teams played leapfrog on the scoreboard in the second half, ending the fourth period in a tie. One of Dumont's pregame goals for that night might have been to secure a double-double as he finished with 12 points and 12 rebounds, but the late game heroics in the overtime period went to his teammate

Joe Floss. With four seconds on the clock, Floss secured a rebound and was fouled. He hit the front end of a one-and-one free throw to break the tie at 63 and seal a one-point victory at 64–63.

Mid-Prairie finished the regular season at 14–4 heading into the district tournament. After disposing of Louisa-Muscatine 81–54, the Washington Demons awaited in the district final—the only matchup of the season between the county rivals. After their undefeated state championship season in 1986, Tremmel's Demons had returned to state in 1987, and they were poised to do it again in 1988, with only four losses. As usual, the Washington High gym was standing room only. Mid-Prairie struck first, taking an 11–4 lead, but it was all Demons after that. They had too much firepower, including 6'9" big man Matt Fish. Fish, a better-than-average center in high school, later blossomed in college at the University of North Carolina Wilmington and went on to a professional playing career, including three seasons in the NBA. The Demons won 82–59. Senior point guard Tom Miller had a career night for Mid-Prairie in his final high school game, scoring 23 points. Dumont added 22. The Golden Hawks finished 15–5.

After four seasons, Showalter was 64–21 at his high school alma mater; his knowledge of the game continued to grow and his connections in basketball expanded.

CHAPTER 10

The Program

Senior guard Kirk Bailey lost control of the ball after a defender bumped him. Showalter slapped his hands together in the direction of Bailey, hollering "Get back! Get back!" while his eyes fixated on the official, Jim Buitendorp. As the Golden Hawks retreated on defense, Buitendorp, who officiated Mid-Prairie games for more than two decades, jogged by Showalter and said, "Coach, you have to sit down." Then he glanced at Chris Kern, the lead Mid-Prairie assistant coach, and added, "Chris, keep him on the bench!" The IHSAA required coaches to remain seated during play on the court, except to cheer a good play or call a timeout. The rule became known as the Seat Belt Rule.

Showalter sat down as Bailey and his teammates dropped back to a man-to-man defense. When the ball handler switched hands and made a move toward the basket, Bailey redeemed himself and stripped him. As he took two dribbles to start a breakaway layup, a whistle blew. The official called Bailey for a foul. Showalter, still steaming from the previous call, started to rise from the bench, but this time Kern, on his right side, shifted his lower body while grabbing Showalter's right arm, pushing him down the bench in the direction of Pat Woodburn. Woodburn, by then an assistant coach with his former team, pushed Showalter back in the direction of Kern, tugging at the coach's left arm. Every time Don tried to get up, his two assistants brought him back down again.

Chris Kern, the son of a banker, grew up a Golden Hawk. He was an avid sports fan, and his first taste of basketball was as a Kalona elementary school student watching Don lead Hickman's Hustlin' Hawks to the 1970 state tournament. "I really idolized him as a kid," recalled Kern. "Donnie was the golden boy of that basketball team." Kern prepped in basketball and football, but with a 5'7" solid, athletic build, he excelled in the physicality of football, taking his talents to Coe College in the fall of 1980. After graduating with a degree in criminal justice administration, Kern joined Showalter's staff as an assistant coach in the 1986–87 season. Pulled to coaching, he pursued a second degree in education and eventually landed a position in the Mid-Prairie School District, teaching physical education and health.

Kern fulfilled the traditional role of an assistant coach in practice: helping with breakdown drills and point guard play, and running the scout team through the opponent's offensive sets. During games, he communicated with officials, statisticians, and the public address announcer; offered Showalter suggestions on offensive and defensive strategy; and recommended when a player might need a substitution. Off the court, during the season he watched film, supervised the team managers, and engaged in conversations with Showalter about the players on the team. "[Showalter] gave me a lot of responsibilities," reflected Kern. "He wanted me to state my opinion on how I felt on things. Sometimes he would listen and sometimes he did not. My role as an assistant was to support him on whatever he did."

For 26 years Kern lived it. In the off-season, he opened the gym for free play, ran summer league, coordinated summer camps, and coached travel teams made up of current and future Golden Hawks players. He connected with kids and was known for his passionate, enthusiastic style that often played out in short temper flare-ups. "Coach Kern was fiery. He would just throw his emotions out there," remembered Tom Hill, a varsity player for the Golden Hawks from 1991 to 1992. "There were times his face would get so red because he'd be yelling and screaming."

To some, this was an endearing and memorable quality. "Us guys would try to poke him," chuckled Hill. "Poke the bear a little bit and get him going." Players knew Kern cared, even if they were on the back end of one of his tirades. "He was very instrumental to the success of my group when I was there," recalled Jake Fisher, a standout guard from 1996 to 1997.

Kern provided the perfect complement to Showalter. "It was Batman and Robin," recalled Brian Tobin. Whereas Kern vocally pushed players to elicit a change in behavior, Showalter tended to be calmer. There were strong expectations, and the players knew what they were. Showalter and Kern found that sweet spot in their coaching relationship, supporting each other's strengths and closing gaps for each other's weaknesses. It was a friendship nurtured on a commitment to building the Mid-Prairie program. And whereas Showalter stretched his coaching opportunities beyond the border of southeastern Iowa to see where they might take him, Kern kept his coaching aspirations closer to home, creating a dynamic and unspoken mutual agreement that benefited the Mid-Prairie basketball program.

The energy for building a program rests with the head coach, but the implementation of that energy lies in that coach's ability to empower assistant coaches to be a part of the process—a synergy among the coaching staff to fulfill the vision of the head coach. As Showalter improved his coaching skills and expanded his connections in the game, he offered his athletes more in terms of better teaching and opportunities beyond Wellman-Kalona, such as All-Star games, international camps, and postgraduation connections. And Kern took on more responsibility, tasks that grew his confidence and stature in the program and created more scenarios for athletes to hone their game. Kern shared in Showalter's vision, and together they built and sustained a dominant boys' basketball program in southeastern Iowa. They had some help along the way.

A loss to Washington in the 1988 district tournament kept Mid-Prairie out of the state tournament for the 16th straight season, their last appearance in 1972. One of the stalwarts of that 1972 season was sharpshooting junior Delwyn "Bud" Bender. Like Showalter, Bender was a farm kid, and he was passionate about basketball. When he finished milking cows, he shot baskets. The practice paid off. Bud graduated in 1973 as Mid-Prairie's second all-time leading scorer with 867 points, a mark later crossed by seven future Golden Hawks players, six of them coached by Showalter. After high school, Bud went to work at a local gas station with his brother for 24 years, and when his brother sold out, he stayed on at Kalona Tire as a mechanic.

In his spare time, Bud volunteered to coach with his former team. His laid-back style balanced Kern's intensity in practice, where he served in a supporting role, working with athletes on shooting technique and basic fundamental skills. His credibility as a coach, at first, connected to his ability as a shooter, was eventually replaced by his approachable, good-natured personality. Players enjoyed being around Bud and respected what he added to the program. "He was very soft-spoken and did not say a lot—but when he did, you listened," recalled Matt Larsen, the tallest Golden Hawk on the roster from 1990 to 1993, at 6'7".

Bender attended practices and sat on the bench during games. He charted statistics and communicated with the score table regarding the number of timeouts and personal fouls. Off the court Bender served as a positive voice for the basketball program in the community. He knew everyone in town and talked hoops with patrons who visited the gas station and later Kalona Tire. His loyalty to the Golden Hawks was exemplary. Showalter found other assistant coaches throughout the years, former Golden Hawks players, to assist in building the program.

The son of a home contractor, Dave Schlabaugh grew up in Kalona. Like Kern and Bender, he watched Don Showalter lead the Golden Hawks to the 1970 state tournament. Schlabaugh yearned to follow in Showalter's footsteps, which he did, first as a two-year varsity player for the Golden Hawks in 1978–80 and later as a coach, joining Showalter's staff for the 1984–85 season. "I probably got a break as a young coach to get in [Showalter's] shadow a little bit," shared Schlabaugh. "He allowed me, at a young age, to work and get to know a lot of people. It really set me up to have a good career in coaching."

Driven to be a head coach, Schlabaugh pursued opportunities that kept him in and out of the Mid-Prairie program for the next 24 years, but he always had a role and made his impact: as a bench coach, working summer camps, coaching Mid-Prairie athletes on travel teams, and providing individual player development. His pursuit of a head coaching position led him first to Williamsburg High School in Williamsburg, Iowa, for seven seasons as head coach and then to the position of head coach at Cornell College in Mount Vernon, Iowa.

Showalter, going into his fifth season at Mid-Prairie in 1988–89, had already established the groundwork for the future of the program. "When Donnie came back to Mid-Prairie, you could see the change," remembered John Boyse, a former Golden Hawk, whose two sons, Todd and Brad, played for Donnie. "It just took on a whole new meaning. The best thing about it is right away he started Saturday morning youth basketball."

This was important for younger kids who wanted to become Golden Hawks and play for Showalter later on. "I was not a very good basketball player in the seventh or eighth grades, not that I was a great basketball player later in my career," recalled Ryan Schlabaugh, Dave's nephew. "But I improved because I wanted to and because I wanted to be a part of the program." The 5'10" Schlabaugh improved to become a starting point guard his senior season, dropping a season high 30 points in a game against Clear Creek. Schlabaugh's experience as a youth in Wellman-Kalona explains the importance of quality youth sport programs. "Show always did it from the ground up," remembered Dave Schlabaugh. "A kid who was a fourth grader starting off in the summer camp or youth leagues aspired to be a Mid-Prairie player and knew what the style was going to be."

The success of a feeder program is communication and oversight by the head coach, in addition to hiring middle school coaches who can teach the fundamentals and strategic skills necessary for the athletes' development. In Tony Evans, Showalter found a coach capable of teaching both, and more important, a coach who bought in to the philosophy of the varsity program. "Don got the program on the same page all the way through," said Evans. "We [middle school coaches] learned the style of play he expected, and that trickled down to the feeder programs. I went to his practices to see how things were done, and I worked the summer camps." A 1979 graduate of Mid-Prairie, Evans coached middle school for 18 seasons. Showalter kept close tabs on the middle school program. But he didn't micromanage; he let Evans coach. "I had a lot of respect for Don because of the way he acted," said Evans. "He gave you trust and he did not give you a reason not to trust him."

In Showalter's second year back, the Mid-Prairie School District hired Steve Hollan to teach fifth grade and coach the ninth grade boys' basketball team. "He brought me in early on and worked with me. Helped me understand what his philosophy was and helped me move forward," remembered Hollan. For the next 27 years, Hollan worked first with Showalter as an assistant basketball coach for 12 seasons and then as the head track-and-field coach, reporting to his athletic director.

Showalter knew his program would be better if his coaches were prepared. "He worked very hard with all the coaches—it did not matter what level they were on—to really train them, teach them," remembered Hollan. "He spends and invests time in making sure practices are done properly. Not only does Don know what he wants done for practice, but every coach knows what he wants done for practice as well."

Showalter never lost sight of what basketball meant to him and what the game provided for him growing up. He continued to share his energy and passion for basketball through his youth programs and his work with the feeder programs. "I was always impressed with the energy and passion he put in with the younger kids," said Gerry Beeler, a longtime Mid-Prairie High School principal. "When you hire at the school, sometimes you get people so overly focused on the varsity and that record that they lose sight of the whole package, so to speak. [Show] would lose a tough game [Friday with the varsity], one that could have gone either way, and as down as he might have been, he did not show it in front of the kids. And the next day [with the youth program] he gave it over to the kids—he was right back out there."

Going into his 15th season as a head coach in 1988–89, Showalter never felt more confident. The pieces were coming together in his coaching career. He knew how to run a basketball program. His ability as a teacher continued to improve through his work at basketball camps, and he could pick up the phone and call hundreds of coaches across the country and have a conversation about basketball. Everything lined up for another winning season. Would this be the year the Golden Hawks made it back to Des Moines for the state tournament?

If a student at Mid-Prairie high school came out for basketball, they made the team—no one got cut. Yet Showalter never promised playing time, and he leveled with each player about his opportunity, encouraging some athletes to consider a supporting role as a team manager. For juniors and seniors who saw limited action on varsity, Showalter scheduled varsity reserve games with larger high schools' subvarsity teams in the Iowa City area. "My junior and senior year there were 20-some kids out; four or five never saw the court," remembered Jason Dumont. "They ran every damn sprint we ran. They ran every damn drill we did. They never complained."

Early-season practice sessions ran upward of three hours then tapered down throughout the season. A strong emphasis on individual skill development filled the early portion of the daily schedule—dribbling, footwork, shooting, and passing—followed by game-based drills such as Cutthroat, rebounding, screening, full-court fast-break drills, and pressing drills. A student manager operated the score clock to time the drills, and the quick pace of practice kept athletes on the move between drills and within each drill. "He was very detailed with every practice…down to the minute," recalled Hollan. "He knew if something was not going right, and he could be flexible on the practice plan…scrap this and work on something else."

Practice finished with team strategy: offensive sets, defensive schemes, out-of-bounds plays, in-game scenarios, and conditioning. "It was an up-tempo practice and then conditioning," recalled Bud Bender. "He would line them up and have them do Killers. A Killer involved sprinting from the baseline to the first free-throw line extended, touching the line, and sprinting back to the baseline. Then half-court and back, followed by three-quarters court and back. A Killer finished with a full-court sprint, baseline to baseline, and back."

The intensity and structure of practice gave the Golden Hawks a physical and mental edge, although some may not have recognized it at the time. "I remember doing passing drills…a step-around bounce pass or whatever, and I was like, 'Dude, this is dumb,'" said

Kirk Bailey. Bailey later realized the importance of fundamentals when he went into law enforcement and got involved with SWAT. "The SWAT stuff is really like a sport, where you have to have the fundamentals," said Bailey. "If you can do the small things right, big things will come. That is one of the things that carried over from practices with Coach Show."

The Golden Hawks finished the 1988–89 regular season at 9–9. The Demons, yet again, proved to be too much in the postseason, beating them 78–69 in the district tournament final. The Golden Hawks finished 11–10 overall. Washington secured their fourth consecutive trip to the state tournament and continued to have the upper hand over Mid-Prairie when it came to postseason play. Getting the Golden Hawks back to the state tournament continued to elude Showalter, but he had reason to be optimistic for the coming season: he had a star in Kelby Bender who could take them there.

CHAPTER 11

Golden Hawks

The temperature in the Washington Demon gymnasium continued to rise as the clock ticked away the last 30 seconds of pregame warm-ups. Washington patrons and Mid-Prairie faithful crowded into every available bleacher seat on Friday, March 2, 1990. Spectators sat on top of one another, falling into the aisles, standing in the stairwells and doorframes, along the baseline wall and tucked into the back corners behind the bleachers.

The Golden Hawks entered the district final game at 11–9. The Demons, ranked No. 4 in Class 2A, were 18–2 and were led by three seniors: Steve Brown, the Demons' all-time leading scorer; Tony Wilson; and Buddy Boulton. All three earned all-state honors in 1990, with Steve Brown named 2A first-team all-state. Brown, the 6'4" lefty post, could score inside or out, hitting floaters, going to the basket, or getting to the free-throw line. A talented baseball player, the 6'2" Wilson hid his athleticism behind a silky-smooth jump shot. Point guard Boulton harassed opposing teams' guards on defense and orchestrated Tremmel's offense as a tough-minded, heady player who seldom got rattled.

Mid-Prairie countered with 6'3" junior Kelby Bender. After a strong sophomore season, Bender became the go-to player for Mid-Prairie during his junior campaign. He stood out. First, he had a physical advantage with his length and long arms; second, he had a knack for the game from hours honing his talents on the outdoor

114

playgrounds and in pickup games with older players; and third, he had the ability to score. "He had that same Larry Bird mentality that you could not stop his midrange game," recalled Tobin. "You knew exactly what he could offer, and no team could stop him. He would get his 15 to 30 points a game."

Bender was the most talented player Showalter had coached since Lonnie Meade at Central Elkader. Like Meade, Bender demonstrated an ability to score that separated him from this teammates and the competition. Unlike Meade, who played freely and loosely, Bender was buttoned-up; he played with efficiency, moving with a sense of control and balance. He grew up in Wellman-Kalona and always wanted to be a Golden Hawk. "My parents remember me saying in fourth grade...I wanted to be the best basketball player at Mid-Prairie," remembered Bender.

The Golden Hawks took an early 10–2 lead. "They were beating the tar out of us," recalled Boulton. "They were in control." Then Bryan Tobin hit his second three-point shot to up the lead to 13–2. Tobin anchored the Golden Hawks offensive, usually dishing out assists to the more proficient scorers, but he made the most of his opportunities, and tonight his shooting was exactly what Mid-Prairie needed. Always the smallest player on the court at 5'5", Tobin was accustomed to comments about his stature; rumors persist that a radio announcer once stated on-air, "He's not 5'5" in his mom's high heels." Tobin developed a tough mindset to overcome his height limitations. "Being from a small town, all the kids played together from third grade through high school," shared Tobin. "You got it handed to you plenty of times. You had to grow up tough, bullheaded, and stubborn."

Showalter elevated Tobin to a starting role at point guard five games into his junior season. Tonight, in an elimination game, he led the Golden Hawks to a first-half lead of 35–27. The Demons went on a four-point run to start the third period and then tied the game for the first time at 46 on two free throws by Brown early in the fourth quarter. Brown scored again to break a three-minute drought by both teams and give the Demons a 48–46 lead with 4:32 remaining.

The Golden Hawks and Demons traded possessions for the next two minutes, with Mid-Prairie edging out front by three, 52–49. Boulton brought the Demons back and with 1:40 left nailed a three-point shot, tying the game at 52. On the Golden Hawks' next possession, Bender responded with a jumper to put Mid-Prairie back out front by two. But Brown had the hot hand, and the senior, not wanting this to be his last game, knotted the score again at 54 with a short jumper.

With 40 seconds on the clock and the game tied, Mid-Prairie put the ball and the game in the hands of Bender. A good ball handler, Bender drove the ball across half-court and two Demons converged on him. The trap worked, as Boulton stripped the ball from Bender and raced ahead for an uncontested layup. The Demons, now up two, inadvertently fouled senior Ryan Swartzendruber on the next possession. Swartzendruber calmly hit both free throws to tie it back up at 56.

Tremmel wanted the ball in Boulton's hands. With eight seconds on the clock and the game tied, Boulton faced Tobin, one-on-one. Dribbling, he faked, leaning his body to the right, then accelerated to his left toward the middle of the lane, gaining a slight step on Tobin, enough of an edge to draw a foul as Tobin attempted to cut him off.

Two seconds remained on the clock. Boulton got set for his first of a one-on-one attempt. One make to break the tie.

Boulton's free throw rimmed in. Washington led by one, 57–56.

Boulton's second attempt bounced out and Mid-Prairie chased down the rebound as time expired. Washington went on to beat Mount Vernon 58–44 in substate for a return trip to Des Moines, their fifth straight. The Golden Hawks finished 11–10.

The final game, even in a loss, meant something to Showalter. He knew how good the Demons were and had been the last few years. His young squad competed and earned a shot to win. "This is one of the biggest games of my career," he said when interviewed after the game. "We executed our game plan to a *T*. I just couldn't ask for anything more from these guys." Showalter had six straight winning seasons in his first six years back at Mid-Prairie, but it had been 19 years since a Mid-Prairie team won 20 or more games in a season. The 1990–91 team was equipped to reach that goal.

NOTHING CLICKED FOR RISING senior Bryan Tobin on this mid-June summer night. He turned the ball over, he shot too much and made too few, and he got beaten off the dribble. When the buzzer signaled the end of the summer league game, Tobin headed for the showers. A minute into the shower, naked and wet, Tobin turned to see Kern and Showalter walking toward him. Kern, his face red, pointed a finger at him and blurted, "You were drinking! You were drinking!" as Tobin did his best to cover up.

"Bryan, were you drinking last night?" asked Showalter.

"Yes, I was, Coach."

"I want you to realize what you put on the line last night because of what you have coming up your senior year. Even though you were not caught drinking, we heard about it," said Showalter. "If this would have been during the school year, you could have jeopardized yourself and the team. You would have been suspended and had to sit out half your senior season."

"Yes, Coach. I got it," said Tobin as he moved closer to a nearby towel. Showalter and Kern turned and left. "That really opened my eyes. He just put it into perspective," remembered Tobin. "I took an ass-chewing bare-naked." Tobin straightened out his off-the-court social activities, making a commitment to his senior season.

The team knew they were going to be good. "We were really hungry…we wanted to get over that hump," Bender stated. "We put in a lot of time.… Our goal was the state tournament."

The Golden Hawks checked all the boxes required to make a run in 1990–91. "We had size, quickness, playmakers, and shooters," shared Tobin. "We could press, push, and run and gun." While Tobin handled the playmaking duties and Bender occupied one wing, junior Josh Bailey ran the opposite wing. At 6'3" Bailey gave the Golden Hawks another threat to complement the all-stater Bender. Like Bender, Bailey contributed in multiple ways: scoring, rebounding, and handling the ball. He also became a stopper on defense, a benefit of his size and athleticism.

Josh Bailey is a cousin of Kirk Bailey and his younger brother Jorey, an up-and-coming Golden Hawk. "We call ourselves double cousins," explained Josh. "My mom and dad met at [Kirk's] mom and dad's wedding. My mom is [Kirk's] mom's sister and my dad is [Kirks'] dad's brother. So we have all the same relatives on both sides."

In the low post, Showalter had a big man in 6'7" Matt Larsen, who moved in prior to the start of his sophomore season. A back-to-the-basket type player at 180 pounds, Larsen's height throughout his youth gave him a distinct advantage but also limited his skill development. "I didn't have to work on my skills," recalled Larsen. "So I didn't." Larsen also struggled to mind authority. Showalter's program helped Larsen mature on and off the court to become a starter his junior year, and Showalter became an important adult in his life. "He was sort of that father figure where you would not listen to anyone else, but you would listen to him," said Larsen. "When I got in trouble, they did not send me to the principal. They sent me to Showalter. He would just look at me and say, 'Hey, what's going on? What are you doing?' And that's all it took."

Showalter could see the potential in Larsen—a soft touch, an ability to pass the ball, and Larsen could run; he just needed to work on his game. Showalter pushed him, and Larsen improved. This was Showalter's best team in 17 years as a high school coach; top to bottom, the roster went deep. Mid-Prairie blew teams out, and 10 to 12 players saw action in each game. The team oozed togetherness. They generally liked one another, or at least enough to come together for a common goal and play for Coach Showalter. "We could not wait to be a part of the team, and we were absolutely confident we were going to bring back the state title," recalled Bailey.

Showalter nurtured their sense of purpose and the team's chemistry. "We knew why we were coming to practice and we knew what we were working for," remembered team captain Bender. And players fulfilled their roles, such as the 6'1" Todd Boyse, a hard-nosed banger who never found the shooting touch of his father, John, one of Mid-Prairie's all-time leading scorers, but contributed as a defensive-minded enforcer and rebounder. "He was very good at getting people to accept their role and know what they brought to the team," shared Bender. "Everyone did bring something to our team that year." For Showalter, that included his cousin Craig.

Coaching Craig would be different than coaching his brother Dennis, but Showalter took the same approach and let Craig know that he would be harder on him than the other players. Craig added another inside presence for opposing teams to contend with. A tall, lanky 6'5" four-man, he worked on the opposite block of Larsen, doing a lot of dirty work on the boards and setting up shooters Bender and Bailey for open looks. His likable, humble personality forged friendships with his teammates while his dedication and determination on the court endeared him to the coaching staff.

Mid-Prairie opened the 1990–91 season with six straight wins, setting up a home contest against the Washington Demons. Both Showalter, in his 7th season, and Tremmel, in his 16th, had established their basketball programs, and both programs ignited interest in their communities, making basketball the sport to play for youth growing up. "I was a much better baseball player, but that was not the allure," described Bailey. "It was basketball."

The programs presented a magnetism built on the success of the players before them: "We wanted to be just like them," said Bender. "We wanted to play like that. Win games. Have close battles. Be victorious at the end." Players in each program wanted to play for Tremmel, the most successful high school coach: "At that time in my life, [Tremmel] was the greatest coach I knew," shared Boulton. "I wanted to be in his program." And the fascination of playing before packed gymnasiums intrigued them: "The way the gym was every Tuesday and Friday night, it was insane," recalled Wilson. "I wanted to eventually be in that position where 2,000 people were coming out to watch me and my friends play."

The similarities between Showalter and Tremmel hid behind their more visible differences. "[Tremmel] swore a lot, and the kids expected that from him and they did not get upset when he did that, because they knew that was his way of making them better," remembered Ross Anderson. "Showalter knew how to get through to his players in a different way than Dave did it—less abrasive." The differences were also visible to their players. "Coach Show and Tremmel were night-and-day-different people. They were brought up differently, thought differently, but had the same goals for bringing the best out of every player," shared Tobin. "I am not sure I could have played for [Tremmel]. I am a small guy. I don't have much of a butt—I am not sure how many ass-chewings I could have took." There might have been some ass-chewings in the Demons' next practice; Tobin and his teammates had the better team in 1991, earning Showalter a midseason win over Tremmel, 51–41, to keep the Golden Hawks undefeated at 7–0.

KELBY BENDER TOSSED THE ball from the high block, right elbow to Matt Larsen perfectly positioned on the opposite low block. A black practice jersey, a teammate, rotated over to contend Larsen, but Matt had the advantage and powered himself toward the hoop, extending his right hand, with the ball, above the rim. Then letting the ball roll off his fingertips toward the rim. The ball slipped off the back rim—rolling out.

"Timeout!" hollered Showalter. "Give me the ball." Showalter snapped a chest pass in the direction of Larsen and shouted, "Dunk it!"

Larsen grabbed the ball and executed a two-handed dunk. "No! Matt," exclaimed Showalter. "Dunk it!" Larsen proceeded to dunk the ball again. Then again, seven more times. The practice scrimmage continued, and in similar fashion, Bender lobbed a short pass to Larsen in the low block. Larsen drop-stepped and finger-rolled the ball again, this time into the basket.

"Timeout! Damn it, Matt! Dunk the damn ball!"

Showalter had Larsen repeat the drill. Everyone watched as Larsen drop-stepped and dunked with two hands seven more times. "Matt, do you know what a dunk does for our crowd? What it does to an opposing team?" shouted Showalter. "Bring it to another level and dunk the ball!"

In the next game, Larsen had a breakaway, wide-open run at the basket. He exploded, rising to the rim with the ball secured in both hands. As he reached to stuff the ball in, it bounced off the back of the rim straight up into the air. Larsen grabbed the rim and hung on a little too long. He missed the dunk and got whistled for a technical. Showalter leapt off the bench before his assistants could corral him. "That's what I'm talking about, Matt!" Larsen took a giant step in his development as a player with that missed dunk. He would get a chance to redeem the miss when the Golden Hawks needed it most.

THE WASHINGTON DEMONS LED the Golden Hawks 21–12 in the first quarter. The undefeated, second-ranked Mid-Prairie team was two wins away from state. The Demons, 16–3, were seeking their sixth straight district championship, with aspirations of a sixth straight trip to Des Moines. But the Golden Hawks were the better team this year, and were favored to win. If they needed any motivation, many of the players still carried the one-point loss in the 1990 district final with them. The neutral site, at Iowa City West High, still brought fans in droves. "I remember warming up and doing a layup and almost stepping on people on the baseline," recalled junior reserve guard Tom Hill. "It just seemed like there were people standing on top of us as we warmed up."

Down 19–12 at the end of the first quarter, Mid-Prairie needed a spark, and they got one. The last time Matt Larsen had attempted a dunk, it ended in a miss and technical foul, so when Larsen had Otis Penelton, the 6'8" transfer from Saginaw, Michigan, beat going to the basket in the second quarter of an elimination game, none of the Golden Hawks would have questioned another finger roll from their 6'7" center. But Larsen took his game to another level. He finished with a two-handed slam, his first ever in a game. The Mid-Prairie crowd went into a frenzy, contributing to a 13–0 Golden Hawks run to take the lead. "It was deafeningly loud," recalled Josh Bailey. "You could barely hear each other talk, or even hear yourself think."

Mid-Prairie never relinquished the lead. When the Demons cut the lead to one at 57–56 late in the fourth quarter, senior Bender took over, draining two back-to-back 17-footers to help Mid-Prairie pull ahead and win 66–63. Bender finished with 15 points. Larsen finished with 19 points and 8 rebounds. Sophomore big man 6'4" Kris Griffith scored 26 points and snagged 13 rebounds for the Demons, hinting at things to come for Washington in the next couple years. Penelton finished with 20 points. The elation of a win over Washington in the postseason again after five straight losses propelled Mid-Prairie to a 65–55 district championship win over West Liberty. Showalter's best team was one victory from Des Moines. The Wellman-Kalona community was ready to relive the glory days with him.

Undefeated at 21–0 going into their substate game, the Golden Hawks felt confident. "We might have been a little arrogant," remembered Larsen. Mid-Prairie earned their swagger with their dominant play in the regular season and resilience in the district tournament, but the Knights of Davenport Assumption, a private Catholic school, deserved their respect. The Knights came into the game at 14–7, but due to Iowa's classification system for private schools at the time, the Knights played schools with larger enrollments (3A or 4A) in the regular season and then dropped down to the 2A classification level for postseason play.

Unaccustomed to the physicality of competing against bigger high schools, Mid-Prairie struggled in a rougher, more physical substate game, trailing 41–29 at half time. In the second half, the Golden Hawks hit five three-pointers in the fourth period, three from Tobin and one each from Bender and Bailey, but the Knights pulled away for a 72–68 win, earning a trip to Des Moines and the 2A state tournament.

The 21 wins set a school record for victories in a season that stood for 31 years. The 1990–91 Mid-Prairie Golden Hawks became a team generations of players talked about for years to come. "People can argue it all day long," said Tobin. "But our team, that year, will always come up in conversation [about which was the best team]." Kelby Bender finished his career with 1,031 points, earning multiple postseason honors. He took his talents first to Iowa Lakes Community College and then to St. Ambrose College, a National Association of Intercollegiate Athletics (NAIA) school in Davenport, Iowa. Bender later returned to southeast Iowa as a teacher and coach, joining Showalter on the bench as an assistant.

The 1990–91 team was a special group, and Showalter, in 17 seasons as a head high school coach, knew to have a team like this did not happen often, which made the loss more difficult to bear. However, with senior starters Bailey and Larsen returning, Showalter had a lot to look forward to in the 1991–92 season: another talented group with aspirations of a trip to the state tournament and a chance at a state title.

The Iowa City West gymnasium hosted, for the second year in a row, a district final game between the Washington Demons and the Mid-Prairie Golden Hawks. Josh Bailey and Matt Larsen stepped up to lead the Golden Hawks to a 19–2 record coming into the district final. For his play, Bailey earned second-team all-state from the Iowa Newspaper Association and team MVP honors, and Larsen earned honorable all-state honors from the Iowa Newspaper Association.

They'd also added a transfer from Iowa Mennonite School (IMS), senior guard Josh Rediger, who averaged 14 points a game and led the conference in three-pointers made his senior year. Throughout the season Mid-Prairie demonstrated a continuation of their previous season's success. They extended their winning streak in Eastern Iowa Hawkeye Conference play to 34 straight games, carried a ranking in the state polls all season, and captured the conference championship for a second year in a row, Showalter's third such title since returning to Mid-Prairie.

With Showalter's battles against Tremmel over the past seven seasons in postseason play, it was fitting that the two would square off once again, for the final time in the postseason. The IHSAA reclassified Washington as a 3A school beginning in the 1992–93 season, ending the postseason rivalry. They continued to play a nonconference game in the regular season, but after the 1995 season, Tremmel left Washington to pursue his dream of college coaching, taking the reins of Iowa Wesleyan College. The IHSAA Hall of Fame coach never found the longevity, nor the success, he had at

Washington High. Washington High won nine straight conference championships under Tremmel, made eight state tournament appearances, and won a state title in 1986, the school's only state championship in boys' basketball. With limited success at the college level, Tremmel returned to the high school ranks, where he continued to coach at multiple high schools, before finishing his career where it all started, at Sigourney High, his alma mater, retiring after the 2015 season.

In the 1991–92 season, both Showalter and Tremmel had their sights set on the state tournament, and standing in the way for the Golden Hawks in the district final was one of the most talented players ever to wear a Demons uniform: junior Kris Griffith. He dressed all four years, starting his final three seasons to become the Demons' second all-time leading scorer with 1,166 points. Griffith's natural size at 6'5" and 240 pounds gave him a distinct advantage, and he enhanced his genetic gifts with his agility and great footwork. "I could get where I wanted to have a close-range shot," said Griffith. And he rarely missed, kissing the ball off the glass with a soft touch. "Big Griff was a specimen," remembered Tobin, who competed against Griffith the year before. "A lefty, and smooth."

Griffith scored 15 points in the district final, but his teammate senior guard Todd Watson stole the show, and the ball when Mid-Prairie needed it most. Watson, who usually came off the bench, started in the district final and tossed in a game high 20 points. In the game's waning minutes, with the Demons holding a four-point lead, Watson picked off an ill-timed Golden Hawks pass; his teammates picked off two more passes, and the Demons made 10 of 12 free throws to ice the game, winning 55–49.

In two seasons the Golden Hawks won 40 games with only 4 losses; an energy surrounded the program. "After the games, no matter what the game, kids would storm the floor and almost treat us like we were pro athletes or college athletes, high-fiving us," recalled Bailey. Even reserve guard Tom Hill held celebrity status. "These little kids had no idea who I am. They could really not care if I was a benchwarmer or not; they gave me a high-five or pat on the back."

Basketball continued to be the sport of interest for youth in Wellman-Kalona, and juniors and seniors continued to go out for the team even when their chances of playing were slim to none. The climate Showalter created in the basketball program attracted them. First, they won a lot of games; second, the community came out to support the team, filling the bleachers at home games; third, swag: "We had excellent things for our kids, and they knew that," stated Chris Kern. "Sometimes you might get a few kids out because they liked that gear."

Beyond the perks of being on the Mid-Prairie Golden Hawks roster, Showalter had a way to make everyone feel valued and like part of the team. "We suited 15 in a game, but 19 on the team. No one dropped out," remembered Craig Showalter, a starter on the 1991 team. Craig Showalter grew up following his cousin's coaching career. He had a good feel for Don the coach and the person, giving him a unique perspective on who Coach Showalter was and how he coached.

While Craig started on the 1991 team, Tom Hill saw most games from the pine. "His expectations for me as the third-string point guard were the same as the first-string point guard," remembered Hill, who grew up on a farm like Showalter, working for his father. "I never felt like I was on a different level [with my classmates] when I played basketball. Show would tell me good things, and he was hard on me too. I never felt he gave up on me. He rode me as hard as the starters."

Showalter created a pipeline for his varsity program and could gauge his upcoming varsity season by the talent pool of middle school athletes; he knew most of the kids from their time in his youth programs, including their personalities, skill sets, and work ethic. Also, by the time they were in middle school, many were starting to develop physically into the athletes they would become. This was a great situation to be in as a coach, except it was not quite that simple. Usually a student attending middle school in a school district will continue on and attend the high school in the same district, unless their family moves or they decide to attend a private school. For families in the Wellman-Kalona area, IMS provided a private school option.

Beginning in the 1972–73 season, IMS agreed to compete in interscholastic sports, a change that allowed IMS to recruit and retain students, including Dwight Gingerich. A standout athlete in the mid-1970s, Gingerich returned to coach IMS prior to the 1981–82 season. Forty years later, in 2022, Gingerich still leads the boys' basketball team (the school rebranded as the Hillcrest Academy before the 2018–19 season). Gingerich embodied the faith-based teachings and values of IMS and instilled them in leading his team. As a teacher-coach, and later as a principal-coach, Gingerich's value to IMS became inestimable; he was the face of the school. With graduating class sizes between 50 and 60 students, IMS competed at the 1A classification level. Under Gingerich, they made consistent postseason runs, making 12 state tournament appearances and capturing a state 1A championship in 1992.

Although not all of IMS's students came from the Mid-Prairie Middle School, many did, pulling potential roster talent away from Showalter's Golden Hawks. For example, both Mike and Jason Hershberger finished their careers in the top three for points scored in IMS history. Aaron Swartzendruber averaged 26.6 points a game his senior year, scoring 46 points in one game—an IMS school record. He played four seasons for Kansas State University, from 1994 to 1998. There were others over the years, including Jace

Bailey, the brother of Josh Bailey, who scored 1,122 career points for Coach Gingerich in four seasons from 1996 to 2000.

The decision to attend IMS is a family decision made by all those involved, and one supported by longtime Mid-Prairie School District superintendent Mark Schneider. "I value choice and the parents' right to choose whatever fits their family best. And I support any decision they make," said Schneider. "I am sure there are people that say, 'Wow, think of the basketball program we could have had if all those kids could have stayed together.' [IMS has] experienced success and we've experienced success. We should just be happy that we have a community where students have a wide variety of options."

Not everyone shares Schneider's sentiment: "We lost some good athletes to IMS. We would play with them through eighth grade and then they would go out to IMS," recalled Danny Jirsa, a Golden Hawk with Showalter in 1970 and a father of three children who went through the Mid-Prairie School District. "We did not all care for the IMS kids."

Showalter understood the family expectation that a son or daughter would attend IMS; the family pull was strong. Other youth were less predictable: "There were times when a kid got to seventh and eighth grade and you did not know where they would go," remembered Kern. "We would work with those kids at basketball camps and we thought they were going to be Mid-Prairie kids, and at the last minute they went to IMS. That hurt."

For Showalter, IMS and the presence of Gingerich created an interesting dynamic—a scenario in which Showalter might feel swayed to use his influence to convince kids to attend Mid-Prairie, recruit his own district's middle school. Showalter and Kern never took this approach, at least not directly. "We were trying to do everything we could," said Kern, in speaking about building relationships with up-and-coming players. "But we never bad-mouthed IMS to any kids or said anything bad about Dwight."

Showalter and Gingerich shared a mutual respect for one another; they knew they had to share kids. "Sometimes we had kids that could go either way, either Mid-Prairie or IMS," said Gingerich. "When that happened Don and I would have a conversation, and we always respected the family's decision in that regard." Even if Showalter and Gingerich played fair and did what was best for the kids, a parent or group of parents could get in the way, focused only on what was best for their kid, recruiting youth to switch schools to build a better team around their son. Everything a community needed for an intense rivalry between two schools existed—proximity of location, two successful basketball programs, two well-respected coaches, the sharing of local talent, and loyalty to family and faith—except one thing: Mid-Prairie and IMS did not compete against one another in games that counted.

The last regular-season game between the two schools occurred in 1984 in a Christmas tournament. Prior to that, IMS lost to Mid-Prairie in a sectional championship game in 1974, when both schools competed at the 1A level. IMS, a smaller school, always competed in a different conference, and when Iowa added a fourth classification level in 1985, the chances of the two schools playing in the postseason disappeared. Instead, the rivalry between the two schools brewed in conversations away from the court, with in-season, on-the-court competitions resigned to preseason Jamborees (in the late 1980s and early 1990s) and preseason scrimmages, where no fans attended or scores were kept. For 28 seasons Showalter and Gingerich shared athletes in southeastern Iowa. Both coaches found long-term success. Gingerich won his 700th career game as a head coach at Hillcrest (formerly IMS) in 2021.

The basketball talent in southeastern Iowa in the early 1990s matched the growth of talent across the state of Iowa—a result of a variety of factors, likely including the work of the Iowa Basketball Coaches Association (IBCA). Don Logan, executive director of the IBCA—with the assistance of IBCA member coaches such as Showalter and Gingerich—helped to establish more opportunities and exposure for Iowa basketball players. Thus, when a traveling team from Russia stopped in Iowa to play some basketball games, the IBCA jumped on it and Showalter would coach his first team, made up of Iowa players, in international competition—18 years before going for gold with USA Basketball.

CHAPTER 12

Snow Valley Iowa

Showalter sketched out the action before him, drawing arrows representing the movement of players and dotted lines detailing the path of the ball. Sitting 10 rows off the court above the baseline, Showalter occupied Section C in Carver-Hawkeye Arena all to himself. Dr. Tom Davis, the head men's basketball coach at the University of Iowa, orchestrated the action on the court. Showalter watched, pausing only to record on his notepad the movement and teaching points of Coach Davis's flex offense. The flex offense is a patterned offense that focuses on continued movement using a series of screens and cuts, including the flex cut, where an offensive player receives a screen from a player in the corner and reads the defender while making a cut toward the basket. Showalter started running the flex offense at Elkader and continued using it in his early years at Mid-Prairie. He liked how it used cutters and ball reversals. By observing Coach Davis, Showalter learned how a master teacher helped his players better execute the offense.

With the University of Iowa in his backyard, Showalter took advantage of learning from the coaches leading the Hawkeyes men's basketball program, such as Lute Olson, who coached the Hawkeyes from 1974 to 1983, guiding them to the 1980 Final Four. Showalter picked up how to organize a practice and establish a defensive emphasis from Olson, observing his 1-1-3 zone defense. Olson departed for the University of Arizona in 1983, where he finished his career with more than 700 victories. Showalter tapped into George Raveling's techniques in mentally preparing his players to play. Raveling, who followed Olson, led the Hawkeyes from 1983 to 1986 and is best known for his contributions to the game of basketball and coaching, serving in positions and on committees with the National Association of Basketball Coaches (NABC), the NCAA, Nike, and USA Basketball.

Now, in late October 1990, on a Saturday morning, Showalter listened to Dr. Tom Davis, or Dr. Tom, a title he earned by completing doctoral work at the University of Maryland while serving as an assistant coach, and due to the fact that he looked like a professor. Davis won 598 games in 32 seasons as a head collegiate basketball coach. In addition to his flex offense, Dr. Tom nurtured Showalter's love of the press and fast break with a 1-2-1-1 full-court press. Much of what Don learned from Davis, and the Hawkeyes coaches before him, was reflected in the on-court success of his Mid-Prairie teams and those he later coached in international competition.

In the spring of 1991, a Russian Junior National Team from Stavropol, Russia, visited their sister city, Des Moines, Iowa. The Stavropol team, with an average roster height of 6'6", completed an eight-city tour, including a stop in Washington, Iowa, to compete against a roster of southeastern Iowa athletes. Tremmel and Showalter coached the team, filling the roster with Mid-Prairie, IMS, and Washington players, along with a sophomore from Winfield–Mount Union named Jess Settles, who later went on to star for the Iowa Hawkeyes.

On home soil, the Iowa team overcame a 12-point halftime deficit to win 110–108 in double overtime. The experience of playing for the pride of your country and coaching a roster of United States athletes (all from Iowa) in international competition was a first for Showalter. Within a few months, in the summer of 1991, through the IBCA, he would lead another team of select Iowa players in international competition, this time to Melbourne, Australia. The roster included recent Mid-Prairie graduate Kelby Bender and Iowa's 1991 Mr. Basketball, Fred Hoiberg. Showalter, along with Jerry Slykhuis, coached the team, and Don Logan from the IBCA joined them on the trip. The Iowa Select team rolled to an 8–0 record, averaging 127 points a game.

The following summer, in 1992, Showalter and Al Rabenold, the head basketball coach at Montezuma High School, took a select Amateur Athletic Union (AAU) team from Iowa to Russia. The team of Iowa basketball All-Stars won three and lost three on their two-week trip. The new international experiences increased Showalter's basketball network to coaches overseas, new acquaintances, and new opportunities. However, one overseas break had already come his way a few years earlier, from an old acquaintance, in 1986.

STEVE BONTRAGER NEVER FORGOT Donnie Showalter, the basketball player he idolized growing up on a farm just a couple cornfields over from the Showalter place. The former collegiate All-American became a shooting instructor in the Tulsa community, working out future professional players such as Wayman Tisdale, a three-time All-American at the University of Oklahoma. Bontrager was a professional player in England in the mid-1980s, and the organization he played for tasked him with organizing a basketball camp. "We could bring in five American coaches," said Bontrager. "I brought Donnie and Dwight [Gingerich] over."

The instructional skills camp also doubled as a coaches' clinic. Showalter quickly hit it off with Englishman Mike Vear, an accountant with a basketball habit. Vear's three sons drove his coaching interests in basketball, and he became an important part of Showalter's growing network of international basketball friends. Showalter became a coach to Vear's three sons. "He made time to ask us how we were enjoying camp," remembered James Vear. "He also took the time to give me and my brothers feedback about what we needed to do to become better." All three Vear boys became coaches or teachers of the game, and Showalter continued to be a part of their lives.

In the first day at the England camp, a local radio station approached Showalter and another coach standing next to him, Bruce Kreutzer. "I was just standing there with Don, and one of the local radio stations came up to us," said Kreutzer, an American coach. "We did a 15- to 20-minute radio interview together and we just hit it off and remained really good friends since that time."

Kreutzer is a basketball lifer. "When people ask me what I do for a living," laughed Kreutzer, "I tell them I wear T-shirts and sneakers." He paid his dues, cutting his teeth first as a junior varsity high school coach and working his way up the coaching ladder to the collegiate level, the D league, before becoming a player-development coach in the NBA, first with the Charlotte Hornets and later with the Orlando Magic. Showalter and Kreutzer bonded first over basketball, then travel. One summer, Kreutzer and Showalter worked two weeks of basketball camp in Switzerland. Vicky joined Don for the trip and Kreutzer's wife, Nancy, joined him. "Vicky and Nancy ventured out on their own while we were working the camp," recalled Kreutzer. "Then the girls would go down and wait at the train station, and then as soon as we were done, we would hustle to the train station and get on the train and go sightsee."

That same summer, at the conclusion of the camp, the two couples spent three days together being tourists. Showalter liked to be prepared whether on the court getting ready for a game traveling in a foreign country. He carried a guidebook that listed hotels, restaurants, and a great deal of other information.

"Don, what does your guidebook say about where we should stay?" asked Kreutzer sarcastically, poking fun at Don's preparedness while at the same time hoping Don would have the name of a place to spend the night.

"There is a place with a view of the castle," responded Don, thumbing through the book.

"Well, that place you picked in Zermatt worked out well, with the two adjoining rooms. Let's try it."

Checked in, the two couples opened the door to the hotel room. Bruce walked across the room to the window and pulled open the shutters. As advertised in Don's guidebook, a view of the Neuschwanstein Castle in Schwangau, Germany, filled the window. Basketball brought the two couples together, but travel gave them shared non-basketball memories. Both Don and Bruce understood the role their wives played in their passion for the sport, neither one taking it for granted. "It's a commitment from the spouse," said Kreutzer. "I think that made the bond stronger [with the Showalters]—since we all went through the same experience."

The Showalters' international travel increased over the years, but the trips always included basketball. "A coaching friend was running a camp, and so we went," said Vicky. "I cannot remember when we traveled that it did not involve basketball." That is how they made it work on two public school teachers' salaries: Don worked a couple weeks of camp to help pay for the trip. In terms of their marriage, basketball was something Don did; traveling became something Don and Vicky did together. They used basketball as the vehicle to make it happen, and as their kids got older, they included them; these experiences exposed Melissa and Brent to a world outside of Iowa. While Dad worked camp, Mom took the kids to see the sights. "I think the travel really shaped who I am and what I enjoy doing," shared Melissa. "And how I think of others today."

Don Showalter's experiences now extended beyond the United States, exposing him to how the international game is played and what other opportunities might be overseas for him. Showalter's pursuit of getting better as a coach and meeting new people in the game continued to open up more opportunities for him in basketball. As he worked to improve his craft, he and his good friend Jerry Slykhuis made a decision that improved both the fundamental basketball skills of youth in Iowa and the ability of Iowa coaches to teach the game.

HERB LIVSEY, A LIFELONG educator, commanded the room, trading the attention of youth at his basketball camp for a room full of coaches. Showalter invited Livsey to speak at the IBCA Annual Clinic in the fall of 1992. As always, Livsey provided a detailed, well-thought-out message, but his presence in Iowa went beyond giving a presentation; Livsey was there to promote the Snow Valley Basketball School.

One of the Iowa coaches in attendance that day was Jerry Slykhuis. Showalter and Slykhuis had been good friends since sharing a car with Don King en route to St. Louis for a coaching clinic in the mid-1970s. By the fall of 1992, Slykhuis had taken the reins of the boys' basketball program at Cedar Falls High School. Slykhuis found longevity coaching at one high school, staying at Cedar Falls High School for 35 years. He finished his high school basketball coaching career with 531 career wins, and the Iowa High School Athletic Association inducted him into its Hall of Fame in 2009.

Showalter got Slykhuis involved in Snow Valley California in the summer of 1990. Like Showalter, Slykhuis embraced Snow Valley's focus on player development. Both felt the camp could find success in the Midwest, so they approached Livsey about operating a Snow Valley camp in Iowa. Livsey agreed.

In the summer of 1993, Snow Valley Iowa hosted one week of camp with 80 kids, all from either Wellman-Kalona or Cedar Falls. Snow Valley Iowa grew to two weeks in 1996 and eventually five sessions. After a few summers of five sessions, it was reduced back to four. In 2019, the 26th summer of the camp in Iowa, more than 1,400 youths would attend the camp across four different sessions.

As codirectors of the camp, Showalter and Slykhuis shared duties. "Don was the one who brought the coaches in and organized the clinics, the teaching sessions," said Logan. "Jerry was the organizer." Slykhuis was responsible for coordinating the facilities, including the campus dormitories and food service. Beyond that, neither one seemed to know exactly what the other one was doing or exactly what their role was; they just got the job done.

In California, Livsey believed his camp was only as good as the staff he hired to work it. Showalter and Slykhuis wasted no time following his lead. "Show is one of those guys that hires the right people, surrounds himself with people that are passionate about what they do, and it works," said Kreutzer. They hired Chris Kern. Although Kern had never worked Snow Valley in California, his familiarity with Showalter made his presence at the camp a logical fit. As camp enrollment began to grow, Showalter reached out to another Mid-Prairie connection in Dave Schlabaugh. Schlabaugh started as a camp coach but soon became Slykhuis's confidant and moved into an administrative role, working behind the scenes with Slykhuis and Wartburg College to ensure all camp facilities and food service were on schedule throughout the week. The Wartburg College men's basketball staff had limited involvement in the camp until Dick Peth was hired as the head men's basketball coach in 1997 and became a key liaison between the camp and the college.

They talked Ken Spielbauer into working the camp. Like Schlabaugh, Spielbauer started as a camp coach and later moved into a director's position. A standout athlete at Guttenberg High School, Spielbauer remembered Showalter coaching at Central Elkader, a high school just 30 miles up the road. "I remember when I was in high school and our school would not let us in the gym," recalled

Spielbauer. "His school would. So we would go up there and play at Central Elkader." Spielbauer landed a teaching-coaching position in Wapello, Iowa, as the head boys' basketball coach in 1984, and stayed for 35 seasons, winning 418 games. The Snow Valley Iowa Basketball School "really put Don and Jerry on the map in Iowa," shared Logan. Bringing Snow Valley to Iowa increased Showalter's influence and impact on coaches in the state of Iowa and beyond. But in the fall of 1993, his guidance was needed at home.

THE POLICE REPORTED THAT on Sunday, October 3, 1993, Douglas Showalter was ejected from the backseat of the vehicle he was riding in, sustaining a traumatic head injury. The two-vehicle crash included his spouse, Judy (Vicky's younger sister), and their three children: Annie (13), Chad (12), and Josh (4). Judy was not injured. Annie was treated and released at the scene. Both Chad and Josh were taken to the hospital and treated; they fully recovered. Doug survived but was never the same; he had permanent short-term memory loss.

Prior to the accident, after graduating from Coe College, Doug—who had always enjoyed farm work—returned to work on the family farm, working the land for his grandfather Monroe. In the mid-1970s his father, Donald, learned he had diabetes when a scratch on his arm was slow to heal. For the next 16 years, Donald managed his health while working at Yoder Feeds, and he and Iva stayed on the farm. Then in 1991, when Donald started dialysis, they moved to Kalona. Doug continued to work on the farm.

For a few years after the accident, Doug and Judy continued to manage the farm together, but the accident had changed all their lives. Doug's kids lost a part of their father they knew. Judy lost a part of her husband she loved. In 1998 Judy and Doug divorced. She moved with the kids to Kalona, and Doug moved in with Donald and Iva, also in Kalona. The extended Showalter and Bauer families offered continued support for Doug, Judy, and their kids. Don, as an uncle first and later as Chad and Josh's basketball coach, became an important source of support in their lives.

During the season prior to Doug's accident, 1992–93, Don suffered his first losing campaign (9–12) at Mid-Prairie. And he would follow it up with another one (10–14) in 1993–94. But those would comprise but a short blip in Mid-Prairie's run of success.

CHAPTER 13

AD

Don Showalter arrived at the school, sat down at his desk, and grabbed the *Iowa City Press-Citizen*. Splashed across the front page was the headline: MID-PRAIRIE HIGH SUSPENDS 24 PLAYERS. He read the article, but he already knew the content; he had been living the story for the past few days. Alone in his office, Showalter contemplated what to do next. High school kids dabbling in drugs and alcohol was nothing new. But the Wellman-Kalona community had never experienced anything like this incident.

During fall homecoming activities, students and student-athletes partied, drinking alcohol and smoking marijuana. After local law enforcement broke up the party, they notified the parents and the Mid-Prairie School administrators. The student-athletes in violation included 24 members of the football team and athletes from other sports. The school district had a policy on alcohol and drug use: any student-athlete caught drinking or using drugs was in violation of the training rules. "My stepson was one of those involved in the 'drug incident' with the football team," recalled Jaynie Bontrager, who later worked with Showalter at the high school. "We got the phone call about 11:30 at night from Show stating we needed to come to the high school to visit." Showalter shared with parents that night that their child faced suspension as part of the district's policy. The suspensions sent a message, but school administrators felt like

140

they needed to do more; drug use was a growing concern among parents and school officials.

Showalter had assumed the role of athletic director prior to the 1987–88 school year, reducing his teaching schedule to two days a week and eliminating any other coaching duties besides head boys' basketball coach. As he reflected on all that had happened in the last few days he, like other school administrators, hoped to keep the media attention to a minimum, but with the suspension of so many football players in midseason, he knew the spotlight on Mid-Prairie would only get brighter in the next few days.

One solution discussed by school officials involved the implementation of an athlete drug-testing program. A Supreme Court ruling on June 26, 1995, allowed public schools to implement random drug testing for student-athletes not suspected of drug use, stating drug testing did not violate their Fourth Amendment rights. If Mid-Prairie implemented drug testing, they would be the first school in the state of Iowa to do so.

Not everyone agreed with the school district's drug-testing idea, which created tension in the community that played out in the local newspapers and would increase attendance at upcoming school board meetings. The drug-testing policy never came to fruition. The school district, in consultation with their attorney, determined drug testing would violate Iowa state law. But the incident in mid-October 1995 did lead to the creation of the Good Conduct Policy, a solution to better educate youth on drug and alcohol use and health-related consequences of abusing substances and its potential impact on their extracurricular eligibility.

The AD in a small school fulfills a hands-on role. "We had a standing deal that we would change out the backboards for the district tournament," shared John Boyse, an alum, parent, and booster club member. "We did it on stepladders. He and I would switch them out." Showalter built up trust within the community. He led an effort to double the capacity of the gym by removing the stage on one side and installing new bleachers. He expanded membership in the Mid-Prairie Athletic Boosters club to raise money for all athletic programs. They trusted him. "We gave him a lot of control of where the money needed to be spent," said Boyse.

Still, Don's role as the athletic director and head boys' basketball coach placed him in a position where others might question where the money was going. The school district allowed head coaches to raise their own funds and keep it in their sports program. For the boys' basketball team members, fundraising became part of their basketball experience. "We had to go pull turkeys out of cages on a semi truck. The worst fundraiser," remembered Ryan Schlabaugh, a 1989 grad. "We did not get paid at all. The money went back into the program, but we always had the best stuff: the ability to purchase good shoes and the best practice equipment."

With all the basketball events Showalter organized—weekend tournaments, camps, summer leagues, and youth clinics—the boys' basketball program benefited from better uniforms, more apparel, and nicer team meals on the road than some of the other sports programs. It was a situation that could create jealousy with the head coaches Showalter supervised in his role as AD. "The perception might be that boys' basketball received more than girls' basketball," shared retired Mid-Prairie principal Gerry Beeler. "He never seemed to favor one team or the other. He had such a good reputation that when they ran a tournament, they would make unbelievable money."

Showalter's role as AD and basketball coach also provided him some advantages when it came to managing the Mid-Prairie gymnasium. Opposing coaches, athletes, and officials all felt the gym ran hot, accusing Showalter, in a form of gamesmanship, of turning up the thermostat to wear opponents down. "It was always so damn hot there. I swore he did that on purpose," laughed Solon coach Brad Randall. "Every time we went there, I always asked him if he was going to turn the heat down. I was completely drenched by the time the national anthem was over."

Showalter did not shy away from gamesmanship if he thought it might give his team an edge. "Don was always pushing the envelope," recalled superintendent Mark Schneider. "He was always looking for a better way in which they could perform as a team or as an individual." He rode the officials during the game to gain a call here and there, but he did it in a respectful way as not to detract from the game itself. "He did not have any hostility when he was barking at you," shared Chuck Liston, who officiated high school sports in Iowa for 53 years, including 32 seasons as a basketball official. "It was just a conversation piece." Jim Buitendorp, who also officiated a couple Golden Hawks games each year, had the same experience. "I could make a call, and he would argue about it," recalled Buitendorp. "But after the game, win or lose, he would not hold a grudge."

The dual role of athletic director and coach forced Showalter to keep things in perspective, deciding when to wear his "coaching hat" and when to put on his "AD hat." He navigated these roles by being approachable. "He was always available," recalled Beeler. "He was easy to get along with, wanted to do what was best, and he would hear what you had to say." His approachability helped him connect with students and his athletes. "It was not uncommon to walk by his office and see a student-athlete visiting with him, and not just basketball players," remembered Steve Hollan.

The young athletes benefited from his commitment. The 1994–95 team overachieved to finish 17–5, a preview of what would come next. A talented group of underclassman was coming up, including a rising sophomore named Randy Jirsa. Randy was the son of Dan

Jirsa, Showalter's teammate in high school. After high school, Dan had married and raised his family in the same community in which he grew up, driving a road grader for Washington County for 30 years. Randy, his second of three children, at just seven years old, took a liking to basketball, participating in Showalter's youth programs. Randy would be unlike any other athlete Showalter coached at Mid-Prairie.

CHAPTER 14

State

Prior to the 1995–96 season, Showalter flirted with a teaching and coaching position at Linn-Mar High School in Marion, Iowa. He spent a day visiting the school with Vicky, Melissa, and Brent and did a teaching demonstration for a physical education class. Showalter considered the job, then turned it down. "It would have involved moving Melissa in her senior year of high school," said Vicky. "It just did not work with the family, and family has always been a priority." Linn-Mar High School made nine state tournament appearances and captured three 4A state titles between 1996 to 2012.

Showalter listened to overtures from a couple NCAA D-3 schools in Iowa over the years. In one situation he lacked a master's degree, and in another scenario the position felt unstable because the school turned over coaches at a high rate. In each case, Showalter chose to stay at Mid-Prairie. In his 12th season at Mid-Prairie, a state tournament appearance continued to escape him. Going into the 1995–96 season, it had been 26 years since Don's 1970 team finished second at state and 24 years since the 1972 squad finished fourth. The Golden Hawks' last substate appearance was a heartbreaking loss to Davenport Assumption in 1991.

With his 1995–96 squad, Showalter had physical size and talent at key positions. The roster included 6'3" senior banger Andrew Wiles, who scored often in the low block on high-low lob passes; 6'4" junior Jorey Bailey (Kirk's younger brother), an athletic four-man who complemented Wiles's style with a finesse approach, garnering him court time facing the basket and posting up; 6'1" junior point guard Jake Fisher, who quarterbacked the football *and* basketball team, a floor general and playmaker; 6'1" junior Caleb Yoder, a tenacious defender who outhustled the competition and his teammates, earning him playing time in multiple positions on the court; and 6'3" sophomore Randy Jirsa, a lanky, long-armed wing who could dunk in traffic, score off the dribble, shoot the pull-up jumper, and hit the deep three. The question that lingered: Could they come together as a team?

CALEB YODER FELL BACKWARD. The force of the offensive player running into him sent him sprawling to the hardwood. Showalter, calm, watched and waited for the call. The block-charge call, one of the more difficult calls for an official, could go either way. Showalter learned to expect either call, while always applauding the effort of his players. After the whistle, the official bounced both hands off his hips, indicating a blocking foul on Yoder. In reaction to the call, Showalter leaned forward to shift his body in preparation to stand up; at the same time, he threw his elbows back, hitting Chris Kern in the arm or shoulder. Kern learned to anticipate Showalter's reaction, but that did not mean he always avoided the physical contact on the bench, leaving Kern with the occasional bruise the next day. "It actually hurt," remembered Kern. "I would say, 'Damn it, Show.' He always apologized."

The Golden Hawks went on to win the game, and the next three games, to up their record to 7–0 going into a nonconference tilt with county rival Washington. In their first seven games, the Golden Hawks were better than everyone they played, even if clicking as a team was still a few weeks off. The Demons had talent too, and they played together—a little better at this point in the season, embarrassing the Golden Hawks 102–60.

Golden Hawks players knew to expect a tougher practice session with Showalter after a loss. "When he first came back to Mid-Prairie, he was called Donnie Discipline," remembered Kelby Bender. A teacher first, Showalter did not shy away from his role as a motivator. "He can be very authoritarian," said Kern. "He would not degrade a kid, but he could be very much an in-your-face kind of coach. At the same time, he knew which kids could respond to that and which ones could not. He knew when to back off."

Showing resiliency, Mid-Prairie rebounded from the 42-point setback to win nine straight, upping their record to 16–1, with an 85–81 victory over Solon to clinch the Eastern Iowa Hawkeye Conference championship. The winning streak gave them confidence and masked some dissension on the team. Showalter believed in starting upperclassmen first, but the best players needed to play, and Jirsa logged plenty of minutes, coming off the bench to lead the team in scoring. There was some resentment over the sophomore getting so much playing time, but this was not the first time Showalter had dealt with such jealousy. Jirsa gave them the best chance to win. He had to play.

Mid-Prairie would face two conference foes—the West Liberty Comets and the Mt. Vernon Mustangs—in the final two games of the regular season. The Comets beat the Golden Hawks 67–56. In the next game, the Mustangs squeezed out a 10-point win, 61–51, dropping Mid-Prairie to 16–3. Showalter and his staff needed to bring the team together if they were going to make a run at Des Moines for the first time in 24 seasons. Mid-Prairie recovered to win three straight games and the district championship.

For the fourth time since returning to Mid-Prairie, Showalter found himself one game away from Des Moines. This time Pella Christian High School presented the substate matchup. The Eagles were looking for their fourth state tournament appearance and their first under head basketball coach Larry Hessing; their previous three championships had come in 1990, 1992, and 1993. (Pella Christian would become a formidable program under Hessing; in 27 seasons, Hessing would win 456 games, leading the Eagles to 12 state tournament appearances.)

With 50 seconds remaining and the game tied at 62, Mid-Prairie played for the final shot. Showalter elected not to call a timeout and run a play they had already practiced, but when an errant pass bounced off an Eagles player along the sideline with three seconds left, he called one. The game came down to the final play, and Randy Jirsa, the sophomore, would get the final shot to try to win it.

Showalter had Jake Fisher inbound the ball. Hessing instructed his tallest player to pressure the inbound passer as he had done all game. Fisher's instructions were to get the ball to Jirsa. The message in the timeout was clear, and the significance of the moment was emotional. Tensions were high. "There was conversation in the huddle—'Don't throw the ball away, don't throw the ball away,'" recalled Fisher. As the huddle broke, Kern—the often fiery, emotional assistant—offered a calm voice when Fisher needed it most. "Kern grabbed me by the back of my jersey, leaned across my shoulder, and said, 'Jake, make a good pass,'" recalled Fisher, emotional in remembering the moment. "He was really good about [sending a positive message]."

Kern then looked for Jirsa. He yanked Jirsa's jersey. "Kern grabbed me and he just shook me," recalled Jirsa. "He told me, 'Jirsa, you got to swish it. You got to swish it.'"

Fisher prepared to inbound the ball. Everyone on the Mid-Prairie bench and the Pella Christian bench was standing—the Iowa Seat Belt Rule be damned. Fisher slapped the ball. Jirsa broke. Fisher faked one direction, first with the ball, then gave a slight head nod upward. The defender leaned just enough for Fisher to pass the ball to a breaking Jirsa, coming off a double screen—a perfect pass.

The clock was ticking down.

Jirsa took one dribble to his left, planted his right foot, and rose into a jump shot 14 feet from the hoop. Every eyeball in the gym was on Jirsa and the ball in that moment. Jirsa elevated maybe a little higher than usual—more than enough to release the ball with no chance of a deflection. The ball backspun toward the basket. The season for both teams hung on Jirsa's final shot. So did Mid-Prairie's chances of ending a 24-year state tournament drought.

Swish. The Golden Hawks were state-bound!

The elation of making the state tournament did not override the Golden Hawks' focus heading to state. "We came down here with the idea that we were playing Friday night [in the title game]. We weren't coming down here with the idea it was a vacation," stated Showalter after the Golden Hawks beat a talented Aplington-Parkersburg team 62–55 in the first round.

In the semifinals, the Golden Hawks fell 68–65 to Westwood High of Sloan in a tight contest with multiple lead changes, in which Mid-Prairie guard Casey Christner missed a leaning three-pointer at the buzzer to tie it. Emotionally Mid-Prairie had nothing left, and it showed in the consolation final against Wapsie Valley, a 41-point loss to end their season at 21–5.

The 1995–96 season served as a turning point for Showalter; he had led the Golden Hawks back to state. This was his second trip to the state tournament as a coach, as he had taken the Central Elkader Warriors to state in 1982. With Bailey and Fisher returning, along with Jirsa, expectations for the Golden Hawks went beyond *making* state—they wanted a state championship the next year.

THE STREETS AROUND CONTINENTAL Airlines Arena flowed with spectators and basketball coaches for the 1996 NCAA Final Four in East Rutherford, New Jersey. Among the crowd roamed the Mid-Prairie Mafia, a nicknamed bestowed on the Mid-Prairie basketball coaching staff by Tom Kummer, a longtime assistant coach at Cedar

Rapids Washington, in reference to their presence at the Final Four each year. The entire staff came to the Final Four each year; Chris Kern, Bud Bender, Tony Evans, and Dave Schlabaugh were the regulars, and other coaches on the staff throughout the years joined them.

At first glance it was an odd bunch, a jack-of-all-trades group with day jobs in education, automobiles, farming, and sales. Each was moonlighting as a coach, strolling the streets, eating in restaurants, and rubbing elbows with career coaches—college and professional coaches gathered for camaraderie, education, and networking. At the same time, they fit right in. Coaches come from all walks of life, and each and every coach at the Final Four has a backstory that connects him to the others—similarities that make it a small fraternity.

Showalter organized the Final Four trip. The trip did not include tickets to the games, but Don coordinated an opportunity through the National Association of Basketball Coaches to have the Mid-Prairie staff work the coaching convention. The Mid-Prairie Mafia ran the hospitality room and coordinated the raffle prize giveaways for the Nike-sponsored coaches' party, a party for college coaches unable to afford or acquire a Final Four ticket. They also assisted with the high school coaches' clinic, roundtable meeting, and rules session. For their service, the NABC comped their hotel rooms. Like college students on a spring break trip, they bunked up together in one or two rooms, with coaches sleeping on the floor. It was a memorable bonding experience for the staff, and the gesture by Showalter demonstrated he valued them and their contributions to the program.

THE KIDS CHASED THE loose candy like they were at a parade. Except they were in a gym, crawling behind the bleachers, under the home and visiting team's bench, and on the score table. When they weren't chasing candy, they watched where the coach might throw it next.

Brad Randall ran the pregame show at Solon High School home games. The head boys' basketball coach liked to throw out candy before tip-off—just one of his many antics that frustrated opposing coaches and fans. He got on officials and bantered back and forth with opposing coaches, including Showalter. "When the ball went up, there were no friends. That was just how it was supposed to be," said Randall. "The kids were intense and the coaches were intense. Once it was over, it was over."

Behind the showman was a passionate and competent coach. Like Showalter, Randall prepped at the school where he now coached (and would coach for 21 seasons, winning 368 games and making four state tournaments, including a state championship in 2009). When Randall became the head coach of the Spartans in 1993, to him Mid-Prairie was the standard. "[Show] was the measuring stick for a small-school basketball program," said Randall. "That was the program you wanted to become. When you defeated Mid-Prairie, it was an accomplishment."

Under Randall the Solon Spartans proved to be a formidable conference rival for the Golden Hawks. In this mid-December contest, the two teams battled through the first half, but it would be the Spartans that found their range beyond the arc, making 11 of 13 threes to pull away late for a 79–68 win, dumping Mid-Prairie for their first loss of the 1996–97 season.

After the Solon loss, the Golden Hawks faced Washington with an opportunity to avenge the previous year's 41-point blowout. "[Showalter] went up to an extra level [of intensity] when we played Washington," said Jirsa. Late in the fourth quarter, with the clock winding down, Jirsa had a breakaway dunk that could have sealed the win. "I dribbled it perfectly to dunk it, and for some reason when I snapped the rim, the ball ended up shooting up into the ceiling and I missed the dunk," recalled Jirsa, laughing. "[Showalter] chewed my ass in front of everybody. We went into overtime and we came back and won. I hit a deep three to kick off overtime and mellowed him down a bit."

Jirsa played with a swagger. He liked to win, and he took pleasure at others' expense. Jirsa's haughtiness was authentic; he was stubborn, and he challenged Showalter in ways the coach had not experienced before. He walked the edge of not being obedient, and he tested the rules off the court. "We all kind of broke the rules. A lot of people smoked cigarettes, some people smoked dope, and some people drank," recalled Jirsa. "It was fuckin' Wellman, Iowa; there was not much to do." Jirsa enjoyed the social aspects of high school life and got caught up in the drug and alcohol culture, which came to a head with the aforementioned suspension of 24 football players and fall sport athletes in the fall of 1995. Jirsa, then a sophomore, served a suspension for his involvement, missing the rest of the cross-country season.

He kept his nose clean for the rest of his high school career, or at least he never got caught. At a 2A high school, Jirsa was a superstar—the most talented player Showalter had ever coached in his 22 seasons. Jirsa could do it all: dribble, pass, shoot, score, rebound, defend, run, and jump; plus he competed and he challenged his teammates to play hard. Selected as a player to watch by *USA Today* in his junior year, Jirsa had a lot to live up to. And he did not disappoint.

Showalter pushed Jirsa. He always believed the best players needed to be pushed the hardest. "He expected a lot because he provided us with a lot of his knowledge and his skill set," remembered Jirsa. "He would let you know if you were not doing what you should be doing or holding up your end of the bargain, and he didn't give a fuck who you were." Jirsa was coachable, he liked to play hard, and he liked to win. He finished his career as the school's all-time leading scorer with 1,433 points.

With only the Solon blemish on their record, Jirsa and his teammates felt confident going into their matchup with West Liberty and living up to their high expectations for the season. "There was an expectation that we would do well after our junior year, and for the most part we lived up to that," recalled Jorey Bailey. "[At times] we maybe thought too highly of ourselves.... We just thought it would come to us, instead of us just going out and making it happen."

They stumbled against the West Liberty Comets 58–51, giving them two conference losses. "The league was a grind," said Randall. "It was balanced, and most anyone could beat anyone on a given night." The Eastern Iowa Hawkeye Conference has a long history in southeastern Iowa. Beginning in the 1963–64 season, seven original members spent 42 years battling for conference championships: Durant, Mid-Prairie, Mount Vernon, Solon, West Branch, West Liberty, and Wilton. Five other area schools spent time in the conference, including Regina (Iowa City) and Tipton. The conference disbanded after the 2007–08 season. In boys' basketball, Mid-Prairie had the most state tournament qualifying teams over 42 years: six. The parity in the league made Showalter a better coach, as coaches such as Brad Randall challenged him to be better.

Unable to bounce back from their defeat to the Comets, the Golden Hawks found themselves playing less aggressively in their matchup with the Mount Vernon Mustangs, getting to the free-throw line only 4 times compared to 18 for Mount Vernon, to fall 76–70. "There isn't much difference between ourselves, Mount Vernon, Solon, and West Liberty," said Showalter following the game, when interviewed by the *Kalona News*. "Everybody still needs to play everybody else a second time around."

After their third overall defeat and their third in conference, the Golden Hawks won 10 straight games and rolled through districts to set up a matchup with the North Cedar High School Knights for a berth in the Class 2A state tournament. Mid-Prairie played to their strengths against the Knights, using an inside and outside attack, pushing their lead to 11, to go into the half up 36–25. Jirsa got hot in the second half, hitting four three-pointers and scoring 21 points after the break to seal the Golden Hawks' return trip to Des Moines. "Last year, I think the kids felt they had what it took to make it [to state]," stated Showalter after the North Cedar victory. "But this year, I think they feel they have what it takes to win it."

GOING INTO THE FIRST-ROUND matchup with Prairie City Monroe (PCM), Mid-Prairie carried a 14-game winning streak; their confidence in each other, their coach, and themselves was at an all-time high. "We went into every game expecting to win, and win big," said Fisher. "We had that confidence level that we were better than our opponent." It was not as if the players were taking PCM lightly; they knew the Mustangs had competed against 11 Class 3A teams during the season and featured two skilled 6'5" post players. "We're aware that they are better than their record [14–7] might indicate," said Showalter a couple days prior to the state matchup. "They did something right in order to make the tournament. We're definitely not taking them lightly."

Yet the Golden Hawks, the favored team, forgot to pack their jump shots for the trip to Des Moines, struggling to find the bottom of the net, making only 5 of their first 20 attempts in the contest. The Mustangs focused their defensive efforts on Jirsa, holding him to 12 points on 4-of-17 shooting. In contrast, PCM was hot, making six of their first eight shots to secure the lead and never relinquish it, winning 73–53. It was PCM's night. "They beat us to every loose ball," said Fisher following the game. "They wanted it more than we did."

Fisher and his teammates wanted it too; they just lost focus. "Because of our success, we may have gotten away from some of the things that make you successful," recalled Fisher. "There was a little more standing around, a little more focus on individual play and newspaper headlines."

In reflection, the 1995–96 and the 1996–97 teams accomplished what no other Mid-Prairie teams had done before: back-to-back state tournaments and 41 wins in two seasons. The quest for a third trip back to state in the 1997–98 season would fall on Jirsa, the only returning starter.

IN THE 1997–98 SEASON, Jirsa averaged 24.3 points per game and the Golden Hawks won the EIHC championship. They lost to Durant 71–66 in overtime in the district championship to end their season at 17–5. End-of-season accolades rained down on Jirsa like on no Mid-Prairie player before him. He earned first-team all-state honors from the *Des Moines Register*, Iowa Newspaper Association, and IBCA; earned first-team all-area from the *Iowa City Press-Citizen*; and received a Dr. Pepper All-Star Game Selection.

Jirsa took his game to the collegiate level at Upper Iowa University, an NCAA D-2 school, but his stay was short. "Randy went to college and went the wrong way," said his father, Dan. "He played for a bit and then he quit and started working." He dabbled in the temptations away from the court too much. "I got into drugs. That kind of ruined me as far as having a goal," said Jirsa. "I think they destroyed my dreams and goals. Drugs really take a toll on a person if you can't come out of it—some people really get lost."

Jirsa came out of it. He earned a college degree and now manages a construction business while growing a business of his own. He got married and is raising a family, and he even built a basketball court in his home. "You got to have goals in your life—milestones you want to reach," said Jirsa. "I have goals and meet milestones now."

In 22 seasons as a head coach, Showalter continued to reach milestones. He coached talented high school players such as Jirsa,

Bender, and Meade. He molded top Iowa high school players to play as a team in All-Star games, against a touring Russian team, and on international trips to Australia and Russia. He wondered what it would be like to coach the best high school players—not just in Iowa but in the United States. Then he got his chance, sooner than he expected.

CHAPTER 15

All-American

Nobody could stop the 19-year-old kid from Germany, Dirk Nowitzki; he dominated the USA Basketball Junior National Select Team. The USA squad featured five future NBA players, but future Dallas Maverick and 14-time NBA All-Star Nowitzki was too much. He scored 33 points and grabbed 14 rebounds as the International Select Team prevailed 104–99 in the 1998 Nike Hoop Summit game in San Antonio, Texas.

The Nike Hoop Summit game, organized by USA Basketball, started in 1995 as part of USA Basketball's efforts to offer more competition for younger players. Showalter received an invitation to coach the Hoop Summit team from Milt Newton. Newton, a starter on the 1988 Kansas Jayhawks national championship men's basketball team, worked for USA Basketball as an assistant director. Showalter and Newton met at a Nike clinic, and they stayed in touch, with Showalter offering to volunteer as a coach whenever Newton needed one. Since Showalter first wrote to Bill Wall in the late 1980s, his interest in USA Basketball had never waned. Now, more than a decade later, he was coaching a team of All-Stars from across the United States against international competition, against a future NBA MVP in Nowitzki.

The loss to the International Select Team did not deter USA Basketball from asking Showalter to coach again in June 1998 at the USA Basketball Men's Youth Development Festival. The event, held in Colorado Springs, featured the top 43 high school players in the United States spread evenly across four teams: North, South, East, and West. The teams played in a mini-Olympics type of tournament, starting in pool play and ending with a medal round. The Youth Development Festival continued for the next eight summers, and Showalter stayed involved, serving on the Cadet and Youth Committee, later renamed the Developmental National Team Committee. The committee focused on evaluating talent for the Festival competitions, which included future NBA superstars LeBron James, Carmelo Anthony, Chris Paul, and many more.

The Hoop Summit game and the Youth Development Festival in 1998 fulfilled Showalter's goal to coach elite high school basketball talent. The opportunities were created by his deliberate pursuit of new experiences in the game that came his way because he put himself in a position to get them by actively approaching, connecting with, and developing relationships with others. This came naturally to him and fit his personality: "Don was forever, through his coaching career, volunteering whenever and wherever he could. He loves to be busy," Vicky stated. "He is a very extroverted person. He is social. That energizes him."

ROY WILLIAMS, THE UNIVERSITY of Kansas men's basketball coach, was among the college basketball coaches in attendance at the 1998 USA Basketball Men's Youth Development Festival. Showalter's North team included Williams's prize recruit, rising senior Kirk Hinrich. Hinrich started three seasons for the Jayhawks, leading them to back-to-back Final Fours in 2002 and 2003 before spending 13 seasons in the NBA.

During a break between games, Showalter noticed Coach Williams sitting courtside. Showalter had worked the Jayhawks' summer basketball camp for a few years and had had conversations with Coach Williams before.

"Coach Williams," said Showalter as he extended his hand to the Jayhawks coach. The two coaches exchanged pleasantries and a few words about Hinrich.

"Coach, I really enjoyed how your teams ran the secondary break this past season," stated Showalter.

Coach Williams briefly shared his thoughts on the Jayhawks' secondary break, and a short conversation ensued. With the action on the court ready to resume, their interaction ended.

Back in Wellman a week after the festival, Showalter wrote Coach Williams a short note stating it was nice to see him again and reiterating a couple key points about their conversation. Showalter used this same approach when he met new coaches. At a minimum, the initial interaction and follow-up note served as an ice-breaker the next time he saw the coach at a basketball event; he did not need to reintroduce himself. Oftentimes the initial exchange led to future conversations about the technical aspects of basketball, and occasionally Showalter developed a professional or even personal relationship with the coaches he met, speaking regularly with them on the phone or at basketball events. Each new connection may or may not lead to an opportunity like a camp or a clinic, but sometimes it did.

Showalter's approach to building a professional network of colleagues in basketball followed tried-and-true methods for developing new contacts and opportunities in any professional field; he followed what worked. Showalter's passion for basketball and his authenticity toward learning allowed him to build lasting relationships with coaches at all levels. His deliberate method for building connections led to more opportunities, and his mastery of the handwritten note opened doors when an opportunity piqued his interest. In the spring of 1998, after coaching the Hoop Summit game, Showalter attended the 1998 McDonald's All-American Game in Norfolk, Virginia, and wondered what it would take to get an opportunity to lead the East or West team.

SHOWALTER GLANCED AT THE opposing team, the East squad, lined up for the national anthem—a roster that included Jason Williams, a future National College Player of the Year at Duke and second overall pick in the 2002 NBA Draft. On his squad, the West team featured Carlos Boozer, an All-American Duke star who would go on to become a two-time NBA All-Star; Jonathan Bender, who would be the fifth overall pick by the Toronto Raptors in the 1999 NBA Draft; and Nick Collison, who would play 15 seasons in the NBA for the Oklahoma City Thunder after being a first-team All-American for the Kansas Jayhawks.

The moment seemed unreal for Showalter. He was here to coach because he was a proven high school coach; he had earned this opportunity. But other coaches in the state of Iowa had earned it too. What made Showalter stand out—besides his 25 years of coaching experience, his work with professional organizations, and the connections he had made from working basketball camps across the United States—was that he knew you got opportunities if you asked for them.

The first McDonald's game occurred in 1977, and Showalter attended his first in 1986, in Detroit. He went to watch elite talent and learn as a coach but also to enjoy the game as a fan. All the top coaches attended the game, so one year Showalter brought an old, bladder-filled laced leather basketball with him and got the top coaches to sign it: Dean Smith; John Wooden; Morgan Wootten from DeMatha High School, who served as the chair of the All-American Game Selection Committee; and Bill Guthridge, who assisted Dean Smith and later replaced him as the head coach at North Carolina.

The McDonald's All-American Game rotates between different states across the country each year. The coaches for the East and West teams must be high school coaches in the state in which the game is played. With the game coming to Ames, Iowa, in 1999, Showalter went through his copy of the game program and found the contact information for Bob Geoghan, the cofounder and organizer of the event. Geoghan and Showalter had met but did not know each other well. Showalter wrote a letter to Geoghan stating his interest in serving as a coach for the game. Geoghan checked references and wrote Showalter back asking if he wanted to coach the team.

On Wednesday, March 24, 1999, Showalter sat courtside in Hilton Coliseum in Ames, Iowa, coaching the West team in the McDonald's All-American Game. Chris Kern and Don Logan joined Showalter on the bench, and behind them sat an entourage of Mid-Prairie people, including members of the Mid-Prairie Mafia, the same crew that attended Final Fours together, and a few members of the school's administration. "When he was selected as the coach for the McDonald's All-American Game, he not only invited us along, but he made time for us to go into the locker room and meet the players," recalled Gerry Beeler. "We were part of his team, so to speak."

The West team won 141–128 behind Jonathan Bender's 31 points, a mark that eclipsed Michael Jordan's 30-point performance in the 1981 McDonald's All-American Game. At the end of the game, after the coaches returned to the bench, a person working the game as an usher handed Kern a rolled-up game program.

"What's this?" Kern asked.

"That gentleman over there said he would like you and Coach Showalter to sign it for him," said the usher as he pointed toward an elderly man sitting five or six rows up from courtside, across from the team benches. Kern looked in the direction of the usher's pointed index finger until he caught the eye of Coach Wooden. The coach with 10 national championships just smiled. Coach Wooden attended every McDonald's All-American Game until 2004.

Showalter had pursued the opportunity to coach the McDonald's All-American Game and then backed it up by doing a good job. "People noticed how well he communicated with the kids," said Don Logan. On the court, the game featured the top-level basketball prospects in the United States. But the stands featured a who's who of people involved in the business of basketball: athletic administrators, agents, basketball organizers such as Bob Geoghan, handlers, and representatives from giant shoe companies such as Nike. Not to mention notable coaches like those who signed Showalter's ball a couple years earlier and collegiate recruiters in attendance to see the top players.

A few days after the game, Showalter reached back out to Bob Geoghan and thanked him for the opportunity. He also asked if they needed any help on the game selection committee. Because he asked, Geoghan assigned him to the selection committee. In a one-year span, Showalter coached the top high school players in the United States, both in the USA Basketball Festival and the McDonald's All-American Game, and also coached elite high school players against international talent in the Hoop Summit game. All three experiences challenged him as a coach and seasoned him for future experiences working with elite-level talent. Back home in Wellman-Kalona, he faced a new challenge, a test many coaches face: coaching your own son or daughter.

BRENT SHOWALTER PLAYED WITH the confidence of a coach's son; he knew the game. He had grown up in the gym within earshot of the on-court teachings of his father—wisdom of how the pieces of a team fit together and insight into how to get the most out of your athletic ability. "Brent was a good basketball player, but his best sport was track. Wherever he got that speed, he did not get it from Don," laughed Tony Evans, who coached Brent in junior high. "He was tall and really thin, same build as his dad—skinny as a rail."

If his physical stature aligned with his father's build, his personality aligned more with his mom's type A personality: he liked things organized and perfect. At times he struggled to let things go, such as a loss or when the ball did not bounce his way. "Brent was very strong-willed and could be a handful as a youngster," recalled Vicky. "But he was also very mature for his age compared to how other kids were doing and how they were acting."

It was a maturity based on the experiences he received through basketball, traveling to California each summer and overseas trips, and learning how his father operated a high school basketball program. He witnessed his father working with players individually on different skills, watching film to prepare for the next game, and meticulously planning the next practice session. He observed, like a fly on the wall, his dad communicate with parents and members of the community. Brent traveled with him to basketball camps, participating in the camp while Don coached, including at the famous Five-Star Basketball Camp in Honesdale, Pennsylvania.

There were advantages to being a coach's son: "The best part about playing for [my dad] is that I had open access to the gym," recalled Brent. "Usually on Sundays, he would go up to his office and do some of his AD or coach's work, and I would just shoot in the gym by myself. Then when he was done, he would come down and rebound for me—that was one of the coolest things."

But there were drawbacks: "We were a small enough school," said Brent. "You could not get away from each other, even if you wanted to." Not that Brent wanted to get away from his father, but sometimes his teammates did not want his dad, their coach, to know what they were doing, and they would neglect to include Brent, an experience he shared with Melissa because both their parents worked at the school. "Our kids struggled just a little bit because they knew what they wanted for themselves and they knew what we wanted for them; sometimes that was socially conflicting with the majority of what everyone else was doing," recalled Vicky. "I remember Melissa coming home from college at one point and telling Brent, 'Just hang in there, Brent. Once you get to college, you will find more friends like you.'"

On the court, regardless of how good Brent played, he was always the coach's son. A slight drop-off in his performance and parents started chirping about favoritism regarding his playing time. Fortunately for son and father, Brent's performance stayed consistent; he was Mid-Prairie's top player his junior and senior seasons and became one of the more accomplished Golden Hawks players in history, netting 1,047 points, placing him third on the all-time Mid-Prairie scoring list at the time he graduated. "He had a high basketball IQ and he was not afraid to take the big shot," remembered Tony Evans.

Brent could score in a lot of ways. He derailed opponents when he could spot up beyond the arc and be the recipient of a drive and kick-out pass or a ball-reversal pass for an open jumper. If contested, he put the ball on the floor and maneuvered his way to the hoop, never overpowering or outquickening anyone but using a crafty approach honed from playing his father's bigger, faster, and stronger players over the years. His father pushed him. "Donnie was hard on Brent," remembered assistant coach Bud Bender. Kern agreed, saying, "He was really tough on Brent. But if you are going to treat your son differently, then it is better to be harder on him and let other players know you are not playing favorites."

Prior to Brent's freshman year in high school, his father knew the challenges he could face coaching his son, and he addressed them at the dinner table. "Brent, just so you know, you are not going to play varsity your freshman season, but you can play sophomore ball," said his father between bites of steak. "If you feel better about me not coaching you in high school, let me know. Coach Kern can take over as head coach and I can just kind of come to the games."

Brent said, "Nah, Dad. I'm okay with it."

They never discussed it again, but Vicky laid down a few ground rules at home to avoid disrupting the family. "I said to both Don and Brent, 'Once you walk into this house, we are not going to get on each other about basketball. At home is a safe place for each of you. If you need to have it out, that needs to happen at the gym,'" shared Vicky. Father and son never had it out at the gym or at home. "They ended up further bonding over those years," recalled Vicky. "I remember Don asking Brent, 'What do you think about this and that?' It was really a good time for us as a family."

As a junior in the 1998–99 season, Brent led Mid-Prairie in scoring with 19 points per game. His teammate sophomore Seth Fisher complemented him as a combo guard, switching between point and wing. The younger brother of Jake Fisher, Seth excelled in football and in the classroom, taking his talents in both to the University of Pennsylvania. Mid-Prairie finished the regular season with a 55–48 win over Mount Vernon for their 11th win. In postseason play they reached the district final against the Pella Christian Eagles. The Golden Hawks trailed 12–8 in the first period, and they never got any closer. Showalter's young squad took a beating, losing 74–30 to finish the season at 13–9.

IN THE 1999–2000 SEASON, the Washington Demons led throughout the first half and were up 23–21 at halftime. Fisher kept Mid-Prairie in the game early, connecting on back-to-back threes, and Brent found his rhythm in the second quarter, ending the half with 12 points. The Demons continued to control the scoreboard in the second half, leading 75–68 with 1:32 left in the game. Then Brent scored two key buckets: he canned a three to cut the Demons lead to four, and then, off a missed free throw, he secured an offensive rebound and scored the put-back to put the Golden Hawks within one point at 75–74.

The teams traded free throws. The Demons made one. Seth Fisher made two to tie the game at 76. In the stands, Vicky was tense watching her son play while her husband coached the game. "I was used to the role of the coach's wife," said Vicky. "But the coach's wife and being a mother all wrapped up in one for a few years—all the emotions were heightened."

With 35 seconds on the game clock, the official called the Demons for a five-second violation in the backcourt. With no timeouts and only a few seconds to work with, Showalter called a play his team had practiced all season. The Demons knew the final shot would go to either Brent or Fisher. Fisher had scored 16 in the contest, but Brent was hot, scoring 26 of his game-high 38 points in the second half. (The 38 points topped his previous season high of 37 against the Solon Spartans in an early-December contest.)

Fisher pushed the ball into the frontcourt along the left sideline as the clock ticked below five seconds. Brent, in motion, used two staggered screens to get himself open in the left corner, beyond the arc. Fisher fired the pass. Brent caught the ball in rhythm. He was having one of those nights when everything clicked. With just enough space to elevate and release over the scrambling defender's outstretched hand, Brent let the ball fly toward the basket.

Swish.

The Demons made a desperation play, scoring a two-point bucket as time expired, but Mid-Prairie held the county bragging rights for one more year with a 79–78 win.

After the previous year's loss in the district final, Mid-Prairie won the district championship 49–45 over the Wapello Indians, on Seth Fisher's clutch free-throw shooting. The win set up a rematch with Pella Christian, and the winner would earn a trip to Des Moines. In the rematch, the Golden Hawks employed a first-half

1-2-2 zone defense, but after trailing 37–21 at halftime, Showalter adjusted the defensive style to a switching man-to-man defense. The strategy worked, and Mid-Prairie crept back to within six early in the fourth period.

Pella Christian responded with two quick buckets to pull back ahead by 10 points on their way to a 60–49 victory, ending Mid-Prairie's season at 16–7. The Golden Hawks missed making a state tournament all three years Brent played, one goal both coach and son had hoped to achieve together. Brent earned first-team all-state Class 2A from the Iowa Newspaper Association and second-team all-state Class 2A from the *Des Moines Register*. He followed his sister to Wartburg to compete in basketball and track. He played one season of basketball for the Knights before deciding to focus his efforts on track, where he went on to garner All-American honors in both indoor and outdoor track for three years; he and his 4x400 meter relay teammates still hold the school record for the event.

Showalter would get another shot at Pella Christian with the savvy play of another coach's son, Travis Kern. In each of his 14 seasons as an assistant coach, Chris Kern's role in the basketball program continued to expand. Over the next few years, Showalter would entrust his assistant with more responsibilities as he started traveling more, sharing and teaching the game of basketball.

CHAPTER 16

Nike

Coach Wooden greeted the Showalter family, welcoming them into his condominium in Encino, California. He led them to his den, a room adjacent to the main living space, which was a living monument to a living legend. Wooden's den featured memorabilia from a life in leadership: framed letters of recognition, a Presidential Medal of Freedom given by President George W. Bush, and mementos from championship success. This was not the first time the Showalter family had visited Wooden's den, but this time was different: Melissa and Brent were fully grown. Brent had recently finished his freshman year in college, and Melissa would start medical school in the coming fall.

Coach Wooden no longer operated his summer basketball camp; that had ended in 1992. But his summer camp coaches from over the years converged on August 4, 2001, in Van Nuys, California, for a John Wooden Basketball Fundamentals Camp reunion, which is why the Showalters were there. The Showalters engaged in small talk with the 90-year-old Hall of Fame coach. Wooden deflected any questions about himself and spent most of the time asking questions of Melissa and Brent. Wooden had a quiet charisma about him; he oozed greatness beyond the significance he had achieved and displayed it in how he interacted with others. Through his basketball camp, Wooden became a mentor to the next generation of coaches, including Don Showalter.

Wooden and Showalter's love for teaching the game of basketball and those they taught fueled their relationship. "You know if you talk to people that played for John Wooden, they will tell you that Coach Wooden loved them," shared Steve Middleton, a Snow Valley Basketball School coach and administrator for more than 30 years. "Coach Wooden tapped into the fact that love is the greatest motivator of all. It beats fear; it beats punishment and all the others. If you get someone to understand that you really care about them, they will run through a wall for you, and I think that Don understands that and taps into that."

Wooden showed Don he could stay true to himself as a person and as a coach and find success. "[Don] took that [understanding of love] and, along with the knowledge of teaching fundamentals, he married that with a personality that a lot of people like and trust," explained Middleton. "The combination of those things meant that Don was given opportunities, and he certainty took them, and that is how he got to be where he is."

In the late spring of 2001, new opportunities kept coming for Showalter. He agreed to coach the US All-Star team in the Capital Classic All-Star Game, a secondary All-Star game to accompany the McDonald's All-American Game. Showalter coached in other high school All-Star games featuring top high school talent, including the Jordan Brand Classic. The Jordan Brand Classic experience came about from an old Snow Valley California friend, Tony Dorado. Dorado met Showalter at Snow Valley in the late 1980s, and they formed a friendship cut under the camaraderie of working long hours at Snow Valley. "You bonded because you worked so hard," recalled Dorado. "We all had a passion for teaching." Dorado coached high school basketball before joining Nike and becoming the head of high school basketball, where he oversees Nike's sponsorships of high school teams and Nike-sponsored basketball events involving prep athletes.

A coaching friendship became a business relationship. Through Dorado, Mid-Prairie High School became a Nike-sponsored school, and the boys' basketball program benefited. "We had slicks with outfits. We had sweatshirts. We had book bags. We had gym bags," recalled Aric Kos, who played in the program during the mid-2000s.

Nike's involvement in basketball and basketball coaching extended into coaching clinics. An avid attendee, Showalter had file folders labeled with the name of each Nike clinic and coaching topic in file cabinets, dating back to his days coaching at Lone Tree High School. Showalter expressed his interest in speaking at the Nike clinics to Ed Janka, their longtime organizer, prior to Nike's sponsorship of Mid-Prairie High School. The sponsorship sealed the deal. "I always tried to use those coaches that were affiliated with Nike to speak at the clinics," said Ed Janka.

Janka spent 45 years running basketball clinics, first on his own as a high school and college basketball coach, and then under the umbrella of Nike starting in 1981. During Janka's tenure in securing speakers, every big name in coaching—from Bobby Knight and John Thompson to Jay Wright and Roy Williams—spoke at a Nike clinic. "If you name a coach, they probably spoke for me at some point," said Janka.

Gaining respect on the Nike speaking circuit as a small-town high school basketball coach from Iowa did not come for Showalter because his name appeared on the program. "It's tough for a high school coach to come to these clinics because of the expectations of the coaches that come," said Janka. "A high school coach has to be even better to make a difference."

Showalter made a difference. His passion and knowledge of the game prepared him to deliver a message that resonated with the attendees. "What happens to some people is they only have this topic, and the next time they speak, it's the same topic. Don could come and do different things," recalled Janka. "We had six or eight of those coaches like Don, that I was able to use on the same level as a college coach or pro coach." When he spoke, Showalter's authenticity made attendees feel like he was one of them. "He exudes friendliness, and that makes him very listenable in a clinic," shared Dorado. "That makes him approachable—somebody people can feel comfortable going up to and asking a question."

Always a student at coaching clinics, learning from others, Showalter now found himself speaking more, teaching others. The Nike clinics led to the video production of his clinic presentations through Championship Productions, which produced coaching instructional videos of the Nike clinic speakers. Showalter continued to work with Championship Productions, creating a series of videos on offensive and defensive systems, practice drills, and building a team culture.

The relationship with Nike as a clinician expanded Coach Show's voice to a wider audience and increased his credibility among the coaching fraternity at higher levels of competition. "Having the Nike connection in those days was awfully good," said Ed Janka. "He was well-liked and well-known. Once you get a strong positive reputation like Don had, it was easy for him to talk to and mingle with the so-called upper-level college coaches."

"THAT'S ANOTHER TWO-POINT BUCKET from Kern, with an assist from his backcourt mate, Gardiner!" The voice of Chris Hotchkiss narrated the action on the court. He barely caught his breath as the Golden Hawks' press forced a quick turnover and Travis Kern drained a 20-foot three in the corner. "Threeeeee...pointer. Travis Kern, off the steal and assist from Gardiner," Hotchkiss said.

When spectators visited the Mid-Prairie gymnasium, they did not expect to get a play-by-play of the game from the public address announcer, but that is what Chris Hotchkiss gave them. "I announce everything but rebounds," explained Hotchkiss. "I give compliments to the visiting team as well as the home team. To make excitement in the gym. To make the kids feel good hearing their name."

Hotchkiss started announcing games for Mid-Prairie in 2000. A devoted Iowa Hawkeyes fan, his license plate reads: HAWKS 247. "It's Hawks 24 hours [a day], 7 days a week," laughed Hotchkiss. "That goes for both the Golden Hawks and the Iowa Hawkeyes." The passionate announcer became a part of the Mid-Prairie basketball experience for coaches, players, and spectators, and his signature speech acceleration on the three-pointer became anticipated when Travis Kern got the ball anywhere past half-court.

Before Steph Curry changed the perception of the deep three in leading the Golden State Warriors to four NBA championships, Travis Kern had the green light to let it fly for the Golden Hawks. Kern finished his career as Mid-Prairie's all-time leading scorer, with 1,503 points—a mark he achieved partly because he played varsity as a freshman and because he made a lot of shots.

Basketball was a family affair for the Kerns. Chris Kern opened the gym for free play, he coached his son's AAU teams in weekend tournaments, and they traveled outside Iowa in search of more competition throughout the late spring and summer. "We breathed it from morning to afternoon," remembered Ruby Kern, Chris's wife. "Vacations in the summer were going to AAU tournaments and Snow Valley camps. It truly was our life, but I would not trade it for anything in the world."

With basketball at the forefront of the family, father and son often butted heads. Both were super competitive. When Travis made the varsity team as a freshman, it presented a new challenge to the relationship—and it was not easy. "I felt a lot of pressure about that," recalled Chris Kern. "If it is your son playing, they are probably being watched more than most players. I felt that he had to perform to a certain level. I was very hard on him."

A self-made shooter, Travis grew up going to the gym every day with his dad, where he developed all aspects of his game: ball handling, passing, and the ability to score against taller and stronger players. The skills he developed as a youth gave the 6'1" Kern confidence, and his natural competitive instinct drove him to outshine his opponent, a personality trait that at times was smug, leading to a flamboyant, show-off style of play. His on-the-court mannerisms perturbed his father and needed curtailing by Showalter. But Kern's occasional zest for flair paled to the style of play his backcourt mate James Gardiner exhibited.

James Gardiner passed the ball from his right to left hand continuously, the ball bouncing between his legs as he scissor-kicked them—40 feet from the basket. He paused the sequence and dribbled toward the basket, drawing the Durant defender. With forward momentum, Gardiner moved right to left, using a crossover move, again taking the ball from his right to left, between his legs. Driving hard down the center of the court toward the free-throw line, he spun backward, the ball moved to his right hand for one dribble and then in a split second he picked it up with his right hand and fired a behind-the-back pass in the direction of Tyler Griffith, a hard-nosed, multi-position player who contributed to scoring, rebounds, and assists. Griffith had been open but, in seeing Gardiner penetrate, started to position himself for a rebound and missed the pass. Gardiner's teammates had yet to learn to play with the junior transfer from England.

"HEY, JAMES, YOU HEADING to Foster Woods tonight?" asked his classmate.

"Why?" James replied. "What's going on?"

"It's where we go to—." Without finishing, and in what looked like a game of charades, his classmate put both hands into a fist and rocked them back and forth in front of his chest in a punching motion.

"Sure, I'll check it out," James responded, curious as to what type of boxing his new classmates were doing in the cornfields of Iowa.

Foster Woods is a public wooded park a couple miles southwest of Wellman—a place for hiking, picnicking, and fishing, and a place for adolescents to escape the eye of adults. A perfect place to duke it out in amateur bouts. James Gardiner had arrived from England in the summer of 2002, prior to his junior year in high school. "I showed up [in Kalona], new school. I was on edge," remembered Gardiner. "I was scared because it was all foreign to me."

His classmates knew little about him, other than that he could play basketball. They had no idea Gardiner started boxing at eight years old. "You can tell right away if a guy is going to be good at basketball. You give him a ball and he shoots. You know right then," said Gardiner. "It's the same in boxing. So I just leveled three of the kids that night. I thought no one would mess with me if I beat up the big kids."

A city kid, Gardiner grew up a troublemaker with little interest in school and authority. He took to sports—first boxing, which he did competitively throughout his youth in England and into young adulthood, and then basketball. He matured early, growing to 6'1" as an eighth grader, and he demonstrated a knack for handling the ball. He was a true playmaker, which earned him playing time with men's professional teams in England at just 14 years old. "I got to travel all over the world in front of big crowds," remembered Gardiner. "I had a crowbar and bricks thrown at me."

Gardiner's physical maturity and talents on the court masked his immaturity off it. He needed a fresh start away from England. "I was fighting, getting into trouble at school. I had kind of given up," said Gardiner. His parents didn't give up and found James an opportunity in Iowa through Tom Sherlock, also an international transfer from England and the only Mid-Prairie player in Showalter's 28 seasons to play professional basketball. The 6'10" Sherlock came over from

England through Showalter's good friend Mike Vear, and he only played half a season due to IHSAA transfer rules. "My coach got ahold of Sherlock's parents and they got ahold of my parents," said Gardiner, and in the summer of 2002, James's father dropped him off at the Kerns' house in Kalona. For the next two years, Gardiner lived with the Kerns and teamed with Travis to form one of the best backcourt duos in southeastern Iowa.

For the 2002–03 season, the backcourt tandem often finished No. 1 and No. 2 in scoring, with Gardiner averaging 17.4 points per game and Kern 15.9. Showalter garnered his 400th career win in an early-season victory over Wilton High, and the Golden Hawks finished their season at 17–6, losing in district semifinals. The 2003–04 balanced Golden Hawks roster gave them a legitimate shot at the state tournament. Gardiner, a senior, and Kern, a junior, returned to the backcourt. Other key players included 6'2" senior Brent Yotty, who anchored the inside; 6'0" junior center Aric Kos; 5'10" junior Jordan Montgomery; and the team's best all-around athlete, 6'0" sophomore Josh Berry, a 1600 medley relay state champ and a second-team all-state running back.

The team and the school embraced their classmate from across the pond. The Grady Crazies, a student section in the Mid-Prairie gym, brought a British flag to home games, Gardiner had a girlfriend, and he no longer missed the city life. Both Gardiner and Kern matured from the previous season, and the duo was a formidable scoring machine.

In an early-season matchup with the Washington Demons, Mid-Prairie needed them both. Kern faked a shot from about 30 feet from the left hash mark. The Demons defender put his hand up and inched closer in response; he knew Kern might shoot it. Kern push-passed the ball to a breaking Gardiner at the top of the key. Gardiner caught the pass and squared to the basket. Immediately chants of "USA! USA! USA!" bellowed from the Demons section.

Unfazed, Gardiner shook off his defender and hit a pull-up jumper. Mid-Prairie took the lead in a seesaw affair late in the fourth period. The game went into two overtimes. Then the longtime rivalry ended in a bizarre fashion.

With two seconds remaining, Mid-Prairie was up 55–54. Washington had the ball underneath their own basket. Coming out of the timeout, the Demons inbounder took a couple steps back, wound up like a quarterback, a threw a Hail Mary pass. The ball sailed through the upper rafters, the length of the gym, skimmed through the narrow opening in the beams, and landed in Demon Nick Spencer's hands.

Spencer spun and tossed a point-blank shot in the direction of the basket. Seeing the play develop, Gardiner anticipated Spencer catching the ball and burst across the lane, jumping to block a potential shot, but he arrived late. Spencer's shot made the rim at the same time Gardiner's hand brushed the net. When the shot rimmed out, Mid-Prairie started to celebrate. But the official blew his whistle and called Gardiner for interfering with the ball in the rim by hitting the net, and the Golden Hawks fell 56–55.

The Golden Hawks went 12–2 the rest of the way to win the EIHC championship. They won the first two games at the district tournament to enter the district final at 20–3. But something was missing; they never discovered the right team chemistry. "[Coach Show] wanted the team to have chemistry, to be close-knit, a kind of a family-oriented type of togetherness," said Chad Showalter, Don's nephew and Doug's son, who graduated in 2002. The chemistry Chad described happened with most of Showalter's teams but for some reason never came to be with the 2003–04 squad. In the district championship game, against Central Lee, the lack of chemistry overshadowed their talent.

Trailing by as many as 16 in the fourth quarter after missing 18 of their first 19 shots to start the game, Central Lee point guard

Garrett Reising hit a 10-foot shot as time expired to give Central Lee a 62–61 win. When Central Lee made the comeback, Mid-Prairie did not seem to be able to come together and stop the slide—they lacked togetherness.

Travis would get another shot to lead Mid-Prairie back to state for the first time since the 1996–97 season. Gardiner's run was over. He stayed in the area and enrolled at Kirkwood Community College to play for the Eagles. But he never made it to the first game. One day he told his coaches he quit and walked out of the Kirkwood gym. But before he reached his apartment, his phone rang.

"James, this is Coach Show. What's going on down there at Kirkwood? I heard you quit the team."

"Yes, Coach. It's not for me."

"James, if you quit now, you will always be quitting," said Showalter.

James let his high school coach finish and hung up the phone. Then he muttered to himself, "I'll show him." Gardiner reflected, "I was pretty low at that point. To go out of his way to call me even when he had nothing to do with me anymore, that was pretty cool—even though I did not think it was cool at the time. I spent a lot of time trying to prove him wrong."

Gardiner quit the Kirkwood team, but he did not quit on himself. He proved Showalter wrong—which is what Showalter had hoped for. Gardiner went back to England and reignited his boxing career for a few years until love brought him back to Iowa. He married a local girl, started a family, and learned the plumbing trade, eventually opening his own business in Wellman-Kalona. "Basketball was the reason I came [to Iowa], but I don't think that was the goal for everyone else," reflected James. "What [the Kerns and Showalters] did for me outside of basketball far outweighs that stuff on the court. I was kind of a punk, and they stood by me and helped me graduate."

Although Gardiner made an impact and became a member of the community, Showalter did not dabble in any more international transfers at Mid-Prairie. Instead the Mid-Prairie Golden Hawks went into the 2004–05 season with homegrown kids, youth who grew up in the system ready for their turn to play for the hometown team. Showalter's summertime focused on building the Snow Valley Iowa Basketball School while he became more involved in USA Basketball. And over the next two years, USA Basketball would need a reboot, changes that would affect Showalter in ways he never imagined.

Donnie helped lead the Mid-Prairie football team to an undefeated season (9–0) in 1969. The state of Iowa did not implement a state playoff system until 1972.

An 80 percent free-throw shooter his senior year, here Donnie gets set to make one against Paulina at the 1970 state tournament.

Steve Mast (left) and Donnie pose with the second-place trophy at the 1970 state tournament.

Donnie heads to the bench in Mid-Prairie's 91–73 1970 state semifinal victory over La Porte City.

Seated first row, center, with the 1970 Mid-Prairie state runners-up.

Vicky Bauer and Don Showalter at their senior prom in 1970.

Vicky Bauer and Don Showalter, senior year, 1970.

Vicky Bauer and Don Showalter, Mid-Prairie graduation day, 1970.

Vicky Bauer and Don Showalter marry on August 26, 1972, at the West Chester United Methodist Church.

Don Showalter (middle) watches his Lone Tree Lions warm up during the 1974–75 season with former Mid-Prairie teammate and Indianapolis Colts player Dan Dickel (right).

The 1974–75 Lone Tree Lions, the first team for which Don Showalter was head coach.

Don (far right) was a member of the Show-No-No's, a lip-sync band at Wartburg College in the mid-1970s.

The 1981–82 Central Elkader Warriors. The team finished the season at 22–3 and qualified for the state tournament for the first time since 1976.

The 1985-86 Mid-Prairie boys' basketball team went 19–3 overall, finished undefeated in conference play, and captured both a conference and district championship.

Don instructs the 1998 USA Basketball Hoop Summit Team.

Coach Showalter addressing Junior National Team hopefuls at a USA Basketball minicamp held during the NCAA Final Four.

Don's last City High team was conference champ and beat No. 1–ranked Iowa City West.

2010 gold medal
U17 Junior
National Team.

2012 gold medal U17
team.

2014 gold medal team.

2018 gold medal U17 Junior
National Team.

Coach Showalter in a timeout with the 2016 U17 Junior National Team.

Capturing the gold medal is always an honor and a thrill.

Mr. Perfect. Celebrating 62 straight wins leading the U16–U17 Junior National Team.

Don and Vicky with the championship trophy after winning the Gold Medal U17 Tournament in 2018.

Cal Hickman in 1970.

And Don (right) with Hickman in 1985.

Coach Showalter with Jalen Suggs.

Coach Show with Scottie Barnes.   Don and Coach K.

Don worked many camps, including Hall of Fame member Pete Newell's Big Man Camp.

With basketball greats. (Standing, left to right) Howard Garfinkel, Don, unidentified McDonald's Game staff, Joe Wootten; (seated, left to right) Morgan Wootten, Dean Smith, John Wooden, and Bill Guthridge.

The Showalter family visit Coach Wooden in 2001, one of many visits with Coach Wooden over the years.

The Showalter legacy beyond the court. Celebrating Don's Hall of Fame induction into the Iowa High School Athletic Association are (to Don's right) Brent, April, Cade, Kasen, and Cam Showalter and (to Don's left), Vicky alongside Melissa, Scott, Landon, and Owen Kahler.

The Showalter family in Hawaii, a family favorite.

CHAPTER 17

Coach K

The 2004–05 Golden Hawks took the court for warm-ups. One side of the gym was stuffed with Mid-Prairie fans decked out in black and gold; the other side was filled with Pella Christian fans, many wearing T-shirts that read: WE'RE GOING TO STATE! A bold statement by their fans, but the arrogance of the Eagles players to wear the same T-shirt during warm-ups backfired as a motivational tactic. "They just had that walk about them. Very confident in themselves," said Mid-Prairie junior Josh Berry, an undersized, athletic forward. "Then they were wearing state tournament T-shirts. It does not take much for me to get my juices going."

The Eagles were 20–4 and featured six players who were 6'5" or taller. Mid-Prairie was 17–7; the cochamps in the EIHC entered the contest with no player over 6'3". Kern led Mid-Prairie in the 2004–05 season with 21 points per game. Now a senior, the point guard with 30-foot range added an ability to slash more to the basket, beating opposing guards off the dribble, scoring in different ways, and setting up his teammates for baskets. He tallied more assists but still had big games making buckets, scoring 39 points in a win over Durant.

Jordan Montgomery joined Kern in the backcourt. A role player his junior year, Montgomery started as a senior and became a frequent recipient of a drive and kick-out pass from Kern for a three. He earned his minutes as a hustler, defender, and leader. The 6'1"

Josh Berry returned to the starting lineup. The Golden Hawks' tallest starter, he continued to complement his natural athletic skills with the development of his basketball skills, increasing his scoring output while still guarding bigger and taller opponents. He led the team in rebounds and finished second behind Kern in scoring.

Aric Kos, a 6'0" senior—the fourth of five brothers—provided a presence in the post. A physical enforcer type, Kos always guarded a taller opponent, using his experience playing against his older brothers to outwork and outthink his taller foes in the pursuit of rebounds and put-back baskets. Kyle Graber, a 5'10" sophomore guard, rounded out the starting five. His willingness to compete and play defense, coupled with his approach to conditioning, kept him on the court; he could run all day.

The 2004–05 Golden Hawks were fundamentally sound basketball players, using skills honed during Showalter's youth programs, but they were also blue-collar. Many of Showalter's teams embodied a blue-collar approach, a mentality that aligned with the Wellman-Kalona economy that comprised the fabric of the communities. This is what his players knew. Many did not come from money, or they had to work hard for it. The Mid-Prairie program provided stability, with strong role models. "As a kid I did not have that much consistency with a lot of things," remembered Berry. "Basketball was a very positive thing in my life. My father was there, but he was not always around. He did not go to any of my games. I just felt like [the coaches] were there to keep me on the right path—trying to help me become a better person and a man."

The program provided structure, guidelines appreciated by parents. "I liked the rules he made them follow, as a parent," recalled Allen Kos, Aric's dad. "You knew where you stood with Don. If you broke [his rules], you paid the price." The rules were simple, such as dressing up for game days, away or home: dress shoes, slacks, a buttoned shirt, a tie, and a recent, neatly trimmed haircut. On the court jerseys were to be tucked in. Everyone wore the team shoes, and all the shoes were the same color. Each player had to present himself in a certain manner as a member of the team. It was about pride in the school, pride in themselves. The 2004–05 team had pride and confidence, and they played with an edge. The Eagles' success and physical size did not intimidate them. "They were all string beans, and we had some pretty solid kids that had been in the weight room," recalled Graber.

Jim Buitendorp, assigned to officiate the substate game, did not need to remind Chris Kern to keep Showalter on the bench this time. Kern nearly ripped Showalter's suit coat pulling him down in the first quarter. The game would ultimately feature 17 lead changes. Late in the second half, the Golden Hawks found themselves down by four with fewer than two minutes to play. During a timeout, Showalter felt a surge of confidence from his team. "You could see it in their eyes," said Showalter after the game. "We were not going to lose this game."

With 1:39 on the clock, Kern drove hard to the hoop. Buitendorp called a block on the Eagles defender, who then slapped the floor in frustration, resulting in a technical foul. Kern had two free throws from the foul, and Showalter had him shoot the two technical foul shots. The best player on the court was at the line with a chance to tie it. Kern missed the first but made the next three to put the Golden Hawks within one at 48–47.

After a Graber steal and Kern layup, giving him 26 points on the night, Mid-Prairie held a one-point lead. Pella Christian still had a chance. The Golden Hawks helped them by missing three consecutive free throws. But neither team scored again, and Mid-Prairie advanced to Des Moines.

"This is a dream come true for me," said Kern following the game. "Ever since I was a little kid, all I've ever dreamed of is playing in the Barn." Nicknamed the Barn, Veterans Auditorium was a staple of the Des Moines community from 1955 to 2004, serving as a community hub of sport and musical entertainment. The Barn hosted Elvis Presley in 1956 and 1977 and hosted numerous state high school basketball tournaments.

The excitement of a return trip to the state tournament, the first time since 1997, shut down Wellman and Kalona. "Each time you go to state, the community just closes down and everyone goes to Des Moines," said Vicky. "They have the send-off with the fire truck, and all the downtown windows are painted, posters are made, buttons are made, everybody is just so rallied around the team." The caravan of cars from the Wellman-Kalona area to Des Moines included more than Mid-Prairie fans. IMS beat WACO High School 55–48 in a 1A substate game, sending the 26–0 Mennonite school to the state tournament for the second year in a row.

But today the Golden Hawks had more important things to think about as they waited for the school bus to take them to Des Moines.

"Quiet," said Showalter, raising his voice above the din of the talking kids. He waved his phone in the air. "Quiet down. I have someone on the phone who wants to speak to you."

The bus went silent.

"Hey, Mid-Prairie Golden Hawks! Congratulations on making it to the Barn!"

The ever-so-familiar voice of Dick Vitale filled the team bus through Showalter's cell phone.

Mid-Prairie would face Bondurant-Farrar in their first game at state. The Blue Jays starred high-scoring guard Kerwin Dunham, who averaged 27 points per game. Dunham, who later played Division I ball at Northern Iowa, scored 28 and the Blue Jays held Kern to 13 points to advance to the state semifinals with a 61–41 win. Kern finished his Mid-Prairie career as the all-time leading scorer, surpassing Randy Jirsa. His accolades filled a plaque, which hangs on a wall outside the Mid-Prairie gym: McDonald's All-American nominee; all-state honors from the Iowa Newspaper Association, the *Des Moines Register*, and the *Iowa City Press-Citizen*; Team MVP for three seasons; and numerous school records in assists, steals, and points scored. He signed to play at NCAA D-2 Truman State.

The 2004–05 team had a star in Kern and they had team chemistry, but they overachieved to reach the state tournament. Many of Showalter's earlier teams featured more talent across the roster and failed to make it to Des Moines. Getting to a state tournament is an achievement; winning state is a significant accomplishment. Showalter would get another shot with an unlikely group soon. But before he could begin thinking about the next season, he had an off-season full of basketball activities planned, including one with USA Basketball.

A SIXTH-PLACE FINISH AT the 14th FIBA World Basketball Championships, held in Indianapolis, followed by a bronze medal performance at the 2004 Olympic Games in Greece softened the swagger of USA Basketball (USAB) as the best in the world. Jerry Colangelo, a well-respected sports executive, agreed to serve as managing director of the USAB Men's Senior National Team program and rebuild USAB's dominance in the world. USAB needed to change their culture, what it meant to play for Team USA.

To implement change, Colangelo needed a buy-in. First, players selected for the 2006 World Championships in Japan had to commit to the 2008 Olympic Games in Beijing: a three-year commitment. Second, Colangelo needed a coach to lead Team USA for three years. Two options emerged: Mike "Coach K" Krzyzewski and Gregg Popovich. A highly successful college coach, Coach K understood the pride of representing your country as a graduate and former coach of his alma mater, West Point. The other candidate, Gregg Popovich, a professional coach with three NBA championships leading the San

Antonio Spurs, also understood representing the US as a United States Air Force Academy graduate. Colangelo wanted Krzyzewski.

USAB found the perfect advocate and leader in Jerry Colangelo and the right coach at the right time in Mike Krzyzewski. Changes to the culture of USAB were underway, including additional changes with their developmental program, and Showalter was right in the middle of it.

Three NCAA Division I national championship banners were draped from the rafters. The navy blue bounced off the maple floor, illuminated by the lights hanging above the court, leaving the upper-level seats under a shadow. The wood-paneled walls circling the court below the upper level gave the sense of nostalgia. Cameron Indoor Stadium—small by NCAA D-1 basketball standards, especially for a team as storied as the Duke Blue Devils—presented a collegiate feel. Even when empty of spectators, a visitor could picture the Cameron Crazies, Coach K storming the sideline, and future NBA players gracing the court.

Showalter found his seat among the other coaches; practice started in 15 minutes. Each October, at the beginning of the NCAA men's basketball season, Coach K held a coaching academy in conjunction with his team's early season practices. Coach K was heading into his 27th season as the head coach at Duke University. He spent the 2006 summer with USA Basketball, winning gold at the 15th World Championship in Saitama, Japan. The Blue Devils ran through a practice session, and then Coach K met with the coaches in attendance. He shared his thoughts about the practice session they observed, added more information on the techniques used, and answered questions from the attendees. Afterward, coaches had a chance to mingle with the Hall of Fame coach and introduce themselves.

Showalter had met Krzyzewski at the USA Basketball Festival in 1998, and their paths crossed because of Showalter's role on the

Developmental National Team Committee; Coach K and Showalter were familiar with one another. Showalter mentioned a few things about USA Basketball, the commonality they shared, and asked a few questions about the Duke team and the practice he had observed. The conversations between Showalter and Coach K continued as both became more involved in USA Basketball.

To learn, Showalter enjoyed being in live settings with coaches and talking with them; he went where coaches shared knowledge and where other coaches were going. He no longer worked camps each week throughout the summer, but occasionally he did one such as Pete Newell's Big Man Camp. Although Pete Newell was 90 years old, he still operated one of the most respected teaching camps for post players in the United States. In the summer of 2005, after Mid-Prairie's run to the state tournament, USA Basketball conducted their first-ever youth camp at the Knicks' practice facility in West Chester, New York. They invited Pete Newell to lead much of the instruction, with Showalter and other coaches ready to assist the legendary coach.

HEADING INTO THE 2005–06 season, Mid-Prairie boys' basketball players knew Coach Show spent time among notable players and coaches in the sport of basketball. The McDonald's All-American Game in 1999 exposed the Wellman-Kalona community to the fact that their hometown son had national recognition as a coach and connections with people they saw on television. His work coaching at the Nike basketball camps and growing role with USA Basketball hinted that his teaching skills carried a national audience as well. "When we were young, we were well aware of everything he was doing," shared Josh Berry. "That kind of made you want to play harder for him."

Kyle Graber remembered riding back with his coach from the Snow Valley camp: "He took a phone call, and I heard him say 'Riley' at one point, and after he got off the phone and we were talking—he was talking to Pat Riley." Jordan Montgomery realized this was not normal for a coach from a 300- to 400-person high school in rural Iowa and had trouble convincing his friends that he played for Coach Show. "One year, he was on a USA Basketball commercial that aired routinely during the Final Four," said Montgomery. "Coach Calipari, Coach K, and Coach Show. It was just the three of them in USA Basketball polos. I remember telling my friends, 'That's my high school coach,' and they didn't believe me. They were like, 'You grew up in Kalona, Iowa.'"

On the surface, it might appear Showalter lived two lives. But his basketball interests away from his Mid-Prairie program helped to better his athletes back home and provide them more opportunities and exposure. Travis Kern participated in an NBA Top 100 Camp at Virginia Commonwealth University before his senior year. He helped players get to Snow Valley Iowa each summer, such as giving Graber a ride or reducing the participation fee. "We were pretty poor, my family. So we did not have money to do all [the summer stuff]," recalled Berry. "But he would help. He would help me pay for Snow Valley or he would just pay for it—give you the camp for free."

The information Showalter learned teaching basketball around the country and overseas, and observing other coaches, funneled back into the basketball program at Mid-Prairie—how he taught the game, new drills, and ways to build a team culture. "He was constantly doing things with the team outside of basketball. Like taking them to an Iowa game, taking them bowling, that kind of thing," shared Pete Cavanagh, the longtime Mid-Prairie football coach who also coached the freshman basketball team under Showalter from 2000 to 2002. "But he was very demanding of them. I think the kids accepted it because of the family atmosphere that was already there."

The 2005–06 Golden Hawks bonded and found team chemistry en route to a 17–9 season, winning the district championship before falling short of a return trip to state; again, it ended at the hands of Kerwin Dunham and the Bondurant-Farrar Blue Jays, this time 70–49. Senior Josh Berry led the way in scoring at 16.2 points per game and all-around play for the Golden Hawks, earning team MVP honors. The next season the 2006–07 team benefited from the family culture as they faced challenges individually and together unlike any team Showalter had coached in his 28 seasons at Mid-Prairie.

ON DECEMBER 5, 2006, 76-year-old Donald Showalter passed away from renal failure after a long battle with diabetes. Don knew his father's death was imminent. Donald's health had deteriorated over the past few years, and he had attended fewer Mid-Prairie games. Still, his passing hit Don hard. "That was really hard on my dad, because they were pretty close," remembered Melissa.

Donald's physical presence in the stands offered steadfast support for Don—a psychological reminder always to do his best work, to do it until it was done, and to remain humble about what he accomplished. Donald's passing occurred right as Mid-Prairie opened the 2006–07 season. Don needed time to grieve, and he found solace on the basketball court.

The Golden Hawks started the season short-handed, with senior point guard Jason Kern and senior center Josh Showalter on the bench, both nursing broken legs. Josh, Don's second nephew from Doug's family, was a rugged role player. He used his steady, consistent play to earn minutes for three varsity seasons. Chad and Josh were the last of the Showalter family to prep under Coach Show. Uncle Don's presence in both Chad and Josh's lives took on a greater meaning than being their coach: "I think both sons really looked up to Donnie as a father figure after all that happened with Doug's accident," shared Judy Showalter.

With the graduation of Travis Kern, the attention of the Kern family turned to Jason. A student of the game, lefty Jason earned his opportunity for court time through his heady decision-making skills. He thought like a coach on the floor: waiting for the right shot, getting the Golden Hawks in the right offensive set, and being the ideal team player. With Jason and Josh on the bench, the Golden Hawks started the season at 5–4. They had experience in senior Kyle Graber. In his third varsity season, the defensive specialist turned into one of the top scorers, averaging 13.6 points a game. The lefty scored mostly on spot-up three-point shots and crafty moves around the basket, posting up smaller guards. Another Kos, senior Braden, provided a physical presence in the low block similar to his cousin Aric, often guarding taller players. Braden often led the team in points when Graber or Darian Patterson had an off night.

Patterson played varsity minutes as a sophomore but became a go-to player his junior season, averaging 14.7 points per game. Like Randy Jirsa, the 6'3" Patterson could score in a lot of different ways. He had size, length, and the skills to play on the perimeter or be physical in the post. Patterson joined the 1,000-point club at Mid-Prairie, finishing with 1,022 career points. He earned a scholarship and played collegiately at Wartburg College.

In early January, the Golden Hawks received a jolt of energy with the return of Jason Kern and Josh Showalter. They both worked their way back into the rotation coming off the bench. At full strength, Mid-Prairie proceeded to win three straight games to up their record to 8–4. Then nothing seemed to work. The Golden Hawks lost six of the next nine games to finish the regular season 11–10. "At one point in time we were just trying to determine how we were going to finish out the season over .500," recalled Kelby Bender, who had returned in the 2003–04 season to coach in the program he starred in. "Show was working hard to get the kids to buy in. We knew we had a good team. We had a group of kids that would not give up and a group of coaches that kept fighting."

This had been a trying season. Prior to the passing of his father, Don coped with the news of his old coach and mentor Cal Hickman's untimely death at the age of 68, while chopping wood on the family farm in Missouri. In addition, the community felt the sorrow of a popular Mid-Prairie teacher's wife's death, and the aunt of two players on the team passed in a tragic car accident just a couple weeks before the district tournament.

To add to the trauma, on Saturday, February 20, 2007, an ice storm engulfed many parts of Iowa, leaving thousands without power, including Wellman and parts of Kalona. The power outage forced cancellation of school and local extracurricular activities for a week. However, state-sponsored activities continued, as other communities had power. Unable to practice in their home gym, and with many athletes dealing with no power at home, the Golden Hawks practiced at the middle school gym in Kalona while participating in the district tournament.

In a difficult year, the team stayed together, a result of the program's culture. The players never stopped listening to their coach. "Everybody looked up to him," said Josh Showalter. "When he spoke, we listened." And Showalter kept them believing: "He just kept preaching to us: 'You have to persevere, overcome adversity,'" recalled Jason Kern.

The Golden Hawks rolled through the district tournament, surprising everyone. In the district final they blew out Louisa-Muscatine 65–45 behind Patterson's 29 points. "This hasn't been an easy year for us, as you notice from our record," said Showalter following the game. "But we've had a lot of things happen within our team that I think our kids have overcome."

Even with a district title, the Golden Hawks played the role of underdog going into the substate game against Montezuma. They stunned the 21–3 Braves for a 12-point win, 64–52, earning a trip to the state tournament, Showalter's fourth trip with the Golden

Hawks and his second in the past three seasons. The eighth-seeded team from Wellman-Kalona continued to embrace their underdog role, and the team that struggled to find themselves late in the season pulled it all together at the right time.

When Showalter walked into the locker room before the semifinal game against the Tri-Center Trojans, the Golden Hawks team grew silent. During their postseason run, players developed greater confidence in themselves and in each other, and they knew what to expect from their coach. Showalter stayed consistent in his pregame speech: offering a few key points about the Trojans and how they were going to defend their strengths. He finished by reminding his team to play their game and play together. As he finished his final thoughts, he noticed team manager Erik Schneider fidgeting, like he had something to say.

Erik, who was autistic, had served as team manager for the past three seasons. He was the son of school superintendent Mark Schneider, and he participated in every activity the athletes on the team did, except practice and game play. "Not only as a father but as a superintendent, I appreciated the way [Don] treated everyone on the team, including my son, as a unique role and person on the team," shared Schneider. "[Erik] was just as much a part of that team as anyone else. Don made sure he was treated like an equal."

"Erik," Coach Show said, looking at his junior manager. "Is there something you want to say?"

Without hesitation, Erik looked at the team and stated, "When we have the ball, I am going to be like this." With both hands, Erik crossed his index and middle fingers and closed his eyes, demonstrating to the team he would be wishing they would score.

Smiles crossed the faces of the Mid-Prairie players. They knew Erik and his personality; he was their biggest supporter and an important part of the team. And they knew he had more to say. Erik continued, "When they have the ball, I am going to be like this."

Erik uncrossed his fingers and looked straight ahead. They all knew what he meant: he would not be wishing for the other team to score. The team burst out laughing. Erik successfully lessened the tension in the room and calmed the nerves of the players. Realizing the moment, Showalter sent the team out to the floor on a high note.

In the crowd, Erik's parents watched the game, but like parents watching their child play, all their focus was on Erik. Erik performed just like he said he would in his pregame speech: he crossed his fingers when Mid-Prairie had the ball and he left them open when they were on defense. The Golden Hawks snuck out another victory, 59–58. For the first time since he wore the black and gold back in 1970, 37 years prior, Showalter and the Golden Hawks were playing in the championship game—his first state title game as a coach.

In the championship game, Graber led the Golden Hawks with 25 points, but Erik Schneider's magic wore out, the Western Christian Wolfpack took the 2A state championship 67–62. Showalter would get another shot at a state title with the Golden Hawks, but not before going for an international title with USA Basketball.

CHAPTER 18

USA Basketball

In April 2009 USA Basketball (USAB) selected Don Showalter, a coach from a 2A rural high school in Iowa, to lead the inaugural U16 team, the best 15- to 16-year-olds in the United States. "I thought he was the perfect person for us. I say that because he understood us. He understood the process," recalled Sean Ford, who was chair of the committee that selected Showalter. "But also from a coaching standpoint. He might not have been the most well-known name, but he was very organized, very committed to his craft."

Ford and Showalter worked together to select the top youth players in the US for the Youth Development Festivals and the Hoop Summit team. Ford started as the manager of basketball operations for USAB in 1995 and worked his way up to his current role as men's national team director. His familiarity with Showalter gave Ford and those in and around USAB a comfortability with who he was. Just to be sure, Ford consulted a few coaches about the idea, running Don's name by George Raveling, not knowing that Showalter knew Coach Raveling from his days as the Iowa Hawkeyes' head men's basketball coach. "Raveling said Don would be a great choice. Maybe not the most well-known because he was coaching in Iowa, but Don would be a great person to lead that," said Ford.

Showalter was not expecting an invitation to coach the U16–U17 teams. "Our minds are kind of blown away that this coach from Iowa gets chosen for this opportunity," said Vicky. "But in my estimation, that speaks to how giving Don is, always being there to do whatever needs to be done. USAB acknowledged that and felt that he was someone they wanted to coach their team."

Showalter's reputation as a coach diminished any hesitancy about his ability to lead the elite players. "What separates him is his vast experiences throughout the game and his knowledge of the game—but above all else, it is the spirit and the way he coaches and the way he is able to connect with people," said BJ Johnson, former assistant national team director. "Everyone felt he would be the ideal person."

Each action Showalter had taken over the years set him up for the opportunity to coach this group. Along the way, and throughout his entire career, he continued to work on his craft, and to work with players of all skill levels. He was ready for this moment, and he timed it perfectly with the changes going on in international competition and with USAB.

The International Basketball Federation (FIBA) governs international basketball competition. FIBA originated in 1932 and since 1950 has operated World Cup competitions every four years, alternating with the Olympics. A significant moment in FIBA history occurred in 1989 when they voted that professional athletes could play in the Olympics, leading to the 1992 USA Basketball Dream Team. In 2007 FIBA made structural changes to international competition. They dropped their U20–U21 tournaments and added a U16 qualification tournament beginning in 2009 and a U17 World Cup in 2010. Countries qualified for the U17 World Cup through one of four zones in the U16 tournament: Asia, Europe, Africa, and the Americas. FIBA offered the same structure for the U18–U19 junior national teams, whereas the U18 teams qualified through the four zones for the U19 World Cup the following year.

With the changes occurring at the international level, USA Basketball adapted. Instead of operating the USA Basketball Men's

Youth Development Festivals, they created the Developmental National Team, later renamed to the U16–U17 Junior National Team, to coincide with the already established U18–U19 Junior National Team. The World Championships for U17 and U19 were held in alternate summers, as were the qualifying tournaments for U16 and U18. This system allowed for many of the elite players to participate and represent the United States across multiple summers, although selection to one team did not guarantee selection the following summer. The FIBA changes coincided with USA Basketball's decision to build a National Team program, where all the components aligned, from the Senior Men's National Team under managing director Jerry Colangelo and Coach K to the new U16–U17 team.

"It was not just about selecting Don; it was our approach to it. You were not just a coach; you were going to help us run a program," said Ford. "We did it by having a National Team approach. We had a pool of players. Even if you were not selected for this team, you were still on the National Team, and you could compete for a spot next year and come to a training camp."

Showalter agreed to a two-year commitment. If the U16 team succeeded in the 2009 FIBA U16 Championship as one of the three teams to quality from the Americas zone, then he would lead them in the 2010 FIBA U17 World Championships. For Showalter, his selection to coach the U16–U17 team served as another step along his coaching journey, a challenge he had yet to experience: coaching the best of the best.

BRAD BEAL PASSED UP a wide-open jump shot. On the next dead ball, a teammate replaced him.

"Why did I get taken out of the game?" asked Beal to assistant coach Kevin Sutton.

"Well, you passed up an open jump shot."

"You mean to tell me that I got taken out of the game because I passed up an open jump shot?"

"Yeah," replied Sutton.

Beal responded, "I'll never do that again."

Beal did not turn down an open jump shot the rest of the tournament. The U16 squad beat Brazil 110–82 in the first game at the 2009 FIBA Americas U16 Tournament in Argentina.

Kevin Sutton, the head boys' coach at Montverde Academy in Florida, along with Herman Harried, the head boys' coach at Lake Clifton High School in Maryland, accompanied Showalter to Argentina, and like Showalter, both agreed to a two-year commitment. The same committee that selected Showalter appointed the assistant coaches. Sutton and Harried sported impressive résumés. By 2009, as a high school coach, Sutton had amassed a 489–102 record at five nationally ranked programs, winning two national championships. Harried, a former Syracuse player in the mid to late 1980s, became the head boys' coach at Lake Clifton in 1997, and by 2009 he had led them to three state titles.

Like Showalter, Sutton and Harried were teachers of the game. While all three had worked with high-level athletes at the high school level, none had worked with 12 elite athletes on one team at one time. Showalter reverted to what he knew best—teaching the fundamentals of basketball—and Sutton and Harried offered their seasoned assistance. In addition to teaching the game, Showalter knew they needed to build a culture, a climate that aligned with the Senior National Team and the gold standards established by Coach Krzyzewski. Following Coach K's lead, Showalter started every practice with a short meeting in the team meeting room adjacent to the practice court at the United States Olympic and Paralympic Training Center in Colorado Springs. In this classroom environment, he focused on developing a sense of pride in playing for your country. Like Coach K, Showalter showed videos of past

USA Basketball Men's National teams, including highlights from the 2008 Olympic gold medal game in Beijing.

During practices, in team meetings, and when the team traveled, Showalter established expectations to align with USA Basketball's vision. "He set the tone our first day in training camp. It was no-nonsense. He held us accountable," recalled Quinn Cook, a guard from the famed DeMatha Catholic High School who later starred at Duke before embarking on an NBA career. "My training camps were very tough. We used to do two-a-days."

The small-town coach from Iowa earned the players' respect with his approach. "He treated us like pros—high, major college athletes," said Cook. "He pushed us every day in practice and film and in the games. But he made it fun and he kept it balanced."

With Showalter's focus on coaching the team and getting them to bond, USA Basketball's staff took care of the details, ensuring this was a special experience. "Everyone involved in the [National Team program] wanted [the players] to know that this was different," said Ford. The staff created an atmosphere that playing for USA Basketball was first-class, from the accommodations at the training center to the Nike team apparel. On the court, the players received instruction focused on helping them improve as top-level athletes. Off the court, the coaches and staff provided care and consideration for their personal growth through life lessons and cultural experiences. "When players landed in Colorado, the guys knew instantly that this was much bigger and much different than they had ever been a part of before," recalled Sutton.

The atmosphere USA Basketball created around the team, and the accountability provided by the coaching staff, helped them bond in a short period of time. "We all came from different backgrounds and cities, and we all came together and bonded," said Cook, one of the team captains. "We had 12 of the best players at our age, at that time, and we were the youngest USA Team ever to play."

A connected group, the USA U16 team prevailed in two more preliminary-round games, disposing of Venezuela 102–76 behind Cook's 22 points. Then they beat Puerto Rico 126–73, getting 18 points from Beal, who was now shooting open jump shots. With a 3–0 record, Showalter and the first-ever USA men's U16 team entered the medal round. The top three teams, the medal winners, would receive a berth in the 2010 FIBA U17 World Championship the following year in Hamburg, Germany. The U16 players received little resistance from their neighbor to the north in the semifinals, running away from Canada 126–78 to qualify for the U17 World Championship.

With only the gold medal to play for, Team USA, undefeated at 4–0, wanted nothing less. So did the host team, Argentina, also undefeated at 4–0. Cook contributed 22 points and Beal hit for a team-high 26 in a 101–87 victory. James McAdoo added 20 points and snagged 12 rebounds. Statistically McAdoo led the U16 inaugural team with averages of 16.8 points, 8.6 rebounds, and 2 blocks. For his accomplishments, USA Basketball named McAdoo the 2009 Male Athlete of the Year. McAdoo went on to star at the University of North Carolina.

As Showalter, Sutton, and Harried, along with the 12 U16 players, took their place for the medal ceremony; they appreciated the moment. "We all grew up watching Team USA and the Olympics and our favorite players," recalled Cook. "Now, for us to represent our country and finish the job with the gold medal—it meant a lot to us." For Showalter, the significance of the moment hit him when the American flag went up and the national anthem started to play. He thought about how representing the United States on the playing field is bigger than any one person, any one player, and any one coach. "When they play the national anthem, it gives you goose bumps," remembered Sutton. "You set out to do this, and then you actually end up doing it. Then in the moment, you end up taking it all in."

After receiving his Male Athlete of the Year Award in December, McAdoo reflected on the experience with his U16 teammates the previous summer: "It is a very humbling experience to travel and see different cultures, to get away from home and do what I love to do most, which is play ball and kick it with some of my best friends. The people you play with can definitely make you better, and playing in Argentina, I think that was probably the best ball I have ever played in my whole life. Getting to practice with pretty much the best 16-year-olds in the world with great coaches really helped us all hone our skills. The competition was top of the line every day."

Although USA Basketball did not really know what to expect with the inaugural U16 team, McAdoo's experience summed up what they hoped to achieve: an experience young, elite basketball talent in the United States wanted to be a part of. In the process, USA Basketball also found their coach. Any doubt about Showalter being the right person for the role ended in Argentina.

"The USA Men's Developmental National Team could not have had a more impressive inaugural year, and Don deserves credit for much of the program's success," said Jim Tooley, USA Basketball executive director/CEO, when asked about Showalter's contributions after Don received the 2009 Development Coach of the Year Award for USA Basketball. "With a gold medal performance in the U16 championship and two training camps this year, Don has prepared USA Basketball for success at the 2010 U17 World Championship."

Showalter returned to Wellman, Iowa, with a gold medal, an undefeated record in FIBA competition, and confidence in his ability to lead elite-level talent. And his 2009–10 Mid-Prairie team featured a high-level athlete—one capable of leading the Golden Hawks to their first state title in school history.

TANNER MILLER CAUGHT THE ball and squared to the basket, 19 feet from the hoop. His defender, outmatched, dropped back, giving Miller enough room to launch a shot. Miller studied his defender. He could hit the three, but he liked to use his quickness to penetrate and use his leaping ability to bounce off the floor for a midrange pull-up jumper, a fade-away shot, or a leaping leaner, maneuvering his way around taller defenders while in the air to get off a short shot or a layup.

With the Golden Hawks leading their substate matchup against the Albia Blue Demons 35–31 in the fourth period, Miller went at his defender, getting into the lane for a fade-away. On the next possession, Miller received the ball again and penetrated. This time, he bounded upward a few feet from the basket. The taller defender rose with him to contest his shot. Except Miller hung in the air longer, floating as the defender started his descent, giving Miller an open look for a two-point bucket. The Golden Hawks led 39–31. The Golden Hawks won the low-scoring contest 46–34, sending them to the state tournament for the third time in five seasons and Showalter's fifth state appearance leading the Golden Hawks.

Tanner Miller was a star. A three-year varsity starter, Miller's athleticism backed his competitive mindset. The 6'2" guard was victorious on the basketball court, winning 54 varsity games over three seasons; on the track, winning state in the 400 meter hurdles his junior and senior seasons; and on the football field, leading the Golden Hawks to the playoffs, where he rushed for 1,846 yards, scored 23 touchdowns, and made 68 tackles at free safety his senior year. "He was an amazing athlete," said Michael Aldeman, his teammate on the football team. "I had friends call us the Mid-Prairie Golden Tanners. We'd hand the ball to Tanner and he would score a touchdown. Then 10 plays later we would give him the ball and he would score another touchdown." His athleticism and stat line earned him interest from collegiate recruiters as a running back and defensive back, including from the University of Iowa.

In his 35 seasons as a head coach, Showalter had coached athletic and talented multisport athletes before, but none possessed the combination of athleticism, competitiveness, and savviness of Miller. "He's got a mindset of how to win games whether it's on the football field, basketball, track—whatever it is," said Showalter after their substate win. "You let him dictate what's going to happen in a game because he's got a great feel for what's going to work."

The 2009–10 team was a tight-knit group. Earlier in the season, on February 1, 2010, after a road win over Fairfield High School, the team bus was headed back to Mid-Prairie. A victory made for a jolly ride home, and the athletes often broke out into song. A medley of different songs filled the back of the bus. Midway through a tune, Tanner Miller received a phone call.

He gestured to his teammates to quiet down as he answered the phone. The jubilant moment on the bus paused as Miller held a short conversation on the phone. When he hung up, his teammates waited for Tanner to explain. Something felt important. "That was Coach [Kirk] Ferentz from the Hawkeyes. He just offered me a full-ride scholarship to play football at Iowa," Miller said calmly. His teammates erupted. The Golden Hawks caroled the rest of the way home.

Miller's teammates on the bus included the two Aldeman brothers, Mark and Michael. They formed a three-guard tandem, with Michael coming off the bench. Mark, a senior, starred as the quarterback on the football team and led the basketball team from the point guard position. Michael, a 5'10" junior scoring point guard, played with confidence and aggression. He attacked the rim and competed all the time in everything.

Other players saw significant court time also: Kaleb Duwa, a 6'0" heady power forward, made big plays at the right time, often while guarding the other team's bigger and taller players; 6'2" Quinn Hollan, the son of Steve Hollan, the Mid-Prairie track-and-field coach, contributed in multiple ways at the forward position; Aaron Smit, a lanky 6'5" post, altered shots and scored down low; and 6'7" junior Dylan Hochstetler provided size for scoring and defense to complement Smit.

Similar to other Mid-Prairie teams, the 2009–10 team took a blue-collar approach to match their competitiveness, with their success dependent on their ability to rebound and run. "I remember at the end-of-the-season banquet, Coach Show said this team never had one bad practice," recalled Michael Aldeman. "I never was on a team that did not have a bad practice, and that team never had one."

The Solon Spartans presented Mid-Prairie's first-round matchup at the state tournament. Solon had more talent player for player, but Mid-Prairie had confidence they could win. The Golden Hawks had beaten their rival 55–52 at Solon earlier in the season, ending Solon's 35-game winning streak, which included a 2009 Class 2A state championship. The two teams no longer competed in the same conference, but they still played one nonconference game each year. Brad Randall continued to lead the Spartans, and he continued to throw candy to the spectators before home games. The Spartans were making their fourth state tournament trip in five seasons.

In their first matchup with Solon back in December, Mid-Prairie had jumped out to an early lead and hung on to win. In the state quarterfinals, the Spartans took the early advantage to go up 4 at the half and 14 by the end of the third quarter. After Mid-Prairie went without a field goal for the entire third period, the game felt out of reach, but Showalter knew his team had more. With Michael Aldeman hitting the long ball and Miller working his midrange game, the Golden Hawks rallied, cutting the lead to three with 3:17 remaining in the contest on a Michael Aldeman triple, his sixth of the game.

When Miller hit a fade-away jumper with 1:25 left, it appeared Mid-Prairie had rallied at the right time; they were within two points. The state tournament–savvy Spartans responded, making their free throws and controlling the ball down the stretch to win 50–46, ending Mid-Prairie's season at 19–6.

Showalter's sixth state tournament appearance as a head coach ended without a state title. "He kept it in perspective. He had chances to go other places," said Chris Kern. "He could have gone to some big schools and probably had that state championship." His coaching colleagues understood the challenge of winning a state championship, how difficult it was. "There are a lot of great coaches that have never won a championship," said Randall. "When we won [in 2009], we got a few breaks here and there."

The 2010 team was Showalter's last Mid-Prairie team to make the state tournament. Wellman and Kalona would have to wait 12 years before the Mid-Prairie boys' basketball team returned to state. Between 1960 and 2010 Mid-Prairie made seven state tournament appearances; hometown kid Don Showalter contributed to six of them. As Miller prepared to attend the University of Iowa in the fall of 2010, Showalter headed to San Antonio to prepare for the 2010 FIBA U17 World Championships.

CHAPTER 19

Gold

The 60,000 people in the crowd cheered and waved the German flag as the Germans scored their second goal to go up 2–0 on Australia in the 2010 International Federation of Association Football (FIFA) World Cup in South Africa. They packed into downtown Hamburg, Germany, to watch the match on a giant screen as part of the Fan Festival. Walking among the crowd were overly tall teenagers, members of the USA Basketball U17 Team, in town for the 2010 FIBA U17 World Championships.

In their opening game, Michael Gilchrist got hot midway through the third quarter. The 6'7" 16-year-old came off the bench in the third period and scored 8 of his team's 13 points in a 13–0 run to give the USA a 61–50 advantage and later an 82–70 win over Argentina. In the second game, they dismantled Lithuania 102–66 in the early afternoon and then partook in the activities of the Fan Festival for dinner and early evening entertainment.

In 2006 FIFA started Fan Festivals as part of the World Cup soccer experience—a place to watch the games on large screens, eat, and enjoy musical artists. Hamburg hosted a FIFA Fan Festival as part of the inaugural Fan Festival program in 2006, but the Fan Festival the U17 team attended in Hamburg was not one of the official FIFA Fan Festival locations in 2010. Still, the city of Hamburg put on the event. When the Germans won the game 4–0, the American basketball players joined in the revelry, celebrating with the fans—caught up in the moment.

The 2010 U17 team featured nine players from the 2009 gold medal–winning U16 team in Argentina and three new players, including Michael Gilchrist, who later changed his last name to Kidd-Gilchrist before starring for the University of Kentucky, helping them win a national championship in 2012. The 12-member team demonstrated maturity beyond their years. When a heatwave engulfed Hamburg, the best 17-year-old players in the world, future major college and NBA players, accepted it for what it was. "The hotel had fans, with no air-conditioning," recalled assistant coach Kevin Sutton. "They never complained…a group of guys that really came together, sacrificed, and understood the magnitude of what we were trying to accomplish."

As the team enjoyed their time together, Vicky captured the moments on and off the court in photos and shared them in a blog for family and friends of the players, coaches, and staff back home. She had traveled to Argentina in 2009 and again with the team in 2010. "It became a big part of our culture, the reporting from Vicky on a daily basis when they were out of the country," said Sean Ford. "When she traveled with the team, that was the moment I realized what a team [Don] and Vicky were. You don't get Don without Vicky. The support she gives him and the joy that she had traveling with him, being the 'den mother,' if you will, because not a lot of parents went the first couple years."

Vicky captured photos from each game, including their final preliminary-round win—125–75 over Serbia to remain undefeated at 5–0. In the opening game of the medal round, Brad Beal scored 25 points and James McAdoo added 17, making all eight of his attempts, to lead the U17 squad to a 105–70 quarterfinal win over Australia.

Up in the stands, Showalter's good friend from England Mike Vear watched him coach. After Vear and Showalter met at a basketball camp in England back in the mid-1980s, they continued to stay in touch. When Vear was in the States, he would contact Showalter to see if their travels would cross in the same city on the same date. Showalter did the same when traveling overseas. In this case, Vear ventured to Germany to watch the USA team compete and practice, impressed with his friend's ability to lead the elite athletes. "They listened and respected him in what he was putting across to them," said Vear. "His presence on the sidelines...he is the coach. Nothing seems to faze him."

In his second summer leading the U17 team, Showalter felt confident his approach worked, and Vear could see it from the stands. "He's very good at getting across the fundamentals, the basics of how to play the game," stated Vear. "His read on the game is excellent; he can assess a situation very well." Showalter's ability to adapt in the games resulted from his preparation. "He knew everything about each team. He knew them from front to back," recalled Cook. "He did not assume we could just throw the ball out and win. Coach Show pushed us every damn practice. If we weren't competing or if we were not going as hard, he would let us know."

Showalter pushed them early in training camp; he wanted them to be uncomfortable. The time frame to get the players ready for competition was short—a quick turnaround from the first day of training camp to when the team began competition. "His real coaching starts once he gets them out of their comfort zone," said Ford. "Don did it in a way that was always within teaching, in a way that made the team better and the individual better and never made anyone feel less of themselves."

In Germany the team played with confidence, and they trusted each other going into their semifinal game against Canada. They prevailed 103–83, getting 30 points and 15 rebounds from Gilchrist.

The U17 team expected to win gold, but the pressure to win came from the pride they felt as the first U17 team in USAB History; their finish would set the standard for future teams.

In the championship, an undefeated Poland made it tough early, trailing by only five points, 46–41, with 2:54 left in the first half. USA went on a 12-point run to close out the half and extended the lead in the second half for a 111–80 gold medal win. The first U17 team went undefeated at 8–0. Showalter completed his two-year term leading the U16–U17 team unscathed, with two gold medals.

To work as a coach for USA Basketball fulfilled one of Showalter's aspirations as a younger coach. At one time he aspired to work with high-level basketball talent at the collegiate level, thinking he would work his way up and become an NCAA Division I coach. He never chased that dream, unwilling to risk the potential pitfalls that came with the life of a college basketball coach when marriage, family, and job stability take second place to the pursuit of winning. Now, as he entered his 27th season at Mid-Prairie—his 37th as a head coach—Showalter had the best of both worlds. With his two-year commitment ending as the U16–U17 team coach, he wondered how he could keep it going.

BY 2011 CONVERSATIONS ABOUT basketball between Coach K and Showalter occurred with more frequency. Coach K continued to lead the men's Senior National Team and Showalter the Developmental National Team. A phone call from Duke to Mid-Prairie High happened on more than one occasion.

To maintain consistency in the USAB developmental teams, Nike suggested the coaches continue beyond two years. "USA Basketball kept switching coaches. Each year they had a different coach," said Tony Dorado, head of high school basketball for Nike. "Nike made the suggestion to them: Why not…have coaches stick around a longer period of time to create consistency in the teaching?"

Whether USAB and the Developmental National Team Committee heeded Nike's advice is unconfirmed, but Nike played an important role in basketball across the United States, through sponsorships of high school teams, youth programs, and coaching clinics. On January 11, 2011, USAB announced Showalter would return as the head U16–U17 coach for another two-year cycle. "Keeping [Showalter] provided a consistent continuity," recalled BJ Johnson. "It bred trust with everyone—[players, coaches, and staff]."

Billy Donovan, head men's basketball coach at the University of Florida, continued on as the U18–U19 coach for three summers from 2012 through 2014. He relinquished the role when he left for a coaching job with the NBA's Oklahoma City Thunder. The U18–U19 coach must come from the collegiate level, whereas the U16–U17 coach must come from the high school ranks. In the winter of 2011, Showalter had no plans to leave high school coaching. On the same day of the announcement that he would return to lead the U16–U17 team, his Mid-Prairie team hit 11 three-pointers, including six from senior Christian Swartzentruber and four from senior Michael Aldeman to upend Wilton High 82–52, improving their season record to 9–3.

The 2010–11 Golden Hawks looked to shoot the three-ball. A couple weeks after the Wilton win, Aldeman broke Travis Kern's record for three-pointers in a season, only to have his teammate Swartzentruber break it a few weeks later. Although Mid-Prairie fell short in the district tournament, the Golden Hawks finished another strong season under Showalter, with a 17–7 record. Aldeman led the team with a 20.8 scoring average, becoming Showalter's ninth all-state player at Mid-Prairie.

"WHERE'S DON?" ASKED GERRY Beeler, peering into Showalter's office.

"He was there a few minutes ago," replied Carmela Ulin, whose office neighbored Showalter's. Ulin did not work for Showalter; she worked in the district office. But they worked together, and due to the proximity of their office space, they shared daily conversations; she knew his habits. "He would make his rounds daily just to say hi to the kids," remembered Ulin. "There were quite a few kids on his teams that did not have a father figure. It might be as simple as giving them rides, giving them shoes, or shooting baskets with them."

Following his 27th season back in his hometown, nothing had changed: Don Showalter was still the person who grew up on his parents' farm just a few miles northeast of Mid-Prairie High. "He was just a farm boy," said Bud Juilfs, a custodian at the school toward the end of Showalter's career. "He helped me line the football fields." Michael Aldeman noticed his coach helping out the custodian staff. "He was always in the gym sweeping the floor or in the bleachers taking out the trash, putting water bottles away," said Aldeman. "He did everything."

The recognition and notoriety received beyond the cornfields of Iowa did not change Don or his approach to how he interacted with others in Wellman-Kalona. "One day he will be eating a steak with Coach K in New York City and the next day he's driving the school bus to West Chester—and it's the same Donnie," said Marc Pennington, who served as girls' basketball coach at Mid-Prairie for nine seasons.

Don wanted to be visible in the community and support local businesses. On most days, he grabbed lunch at Casey's convenience store (for their tenderloins) or at the local diner. His interaction with others often occurred over food. He liked to eat, leaving others to wonder how he did not gain weight. "He must have a high metabolism," said Chris Kern. "Whether it was Mexican or Italian, I don't know if there was anything he didn't like."

Jaynie Bontrager, who worked as Showalter's administrative assistant for five years, often made big meals at home and would bring in a plate of food for him to eat at work. "He would eat the whole thing," remembered Bontrager. "It became a game to me to see how much I could put on that plate and see how much he would eat. He always made you feel good; whether he liked it or not, he finished it." Showalter rarely turned down food or a can of Pepsi. "Whenever you'd see him walking around, it was not uncommon to see a Pepsi in his hand or a Pepsi nearby," remembered track-and-field coach Steve Hollan. "You would walk into his office and see piles of stacked Pepsi cans."

Showalter showed his appreciation for others through food, such as Chris Hotchkiss, the Mid-Prairie public address announcer. "He treated me really good. He always asked me to do these things: go to Iowa games, go out to eat, and whatnot," said Hotchkiss. "He was the only coach that did that." Mid-Prairie superintendent Mark Schneider felt that Showalter understood how to get to know people on a personal level. He called it "making emotional deposits into a person's bank account." Said Schneider, "It was a genuine interest; it was not fake. He made sure he made those connections first before he asked anything of you." Showalter would need those emotional deposits as his commitments with USA Basketball increased, often taking him away from Wellman-Kalona.

"HEY, COACH," SAID ALLEN Kos as he knocked on Showalter's open office door.

"Hi, Allen, come on in," said Showalter. "You got a letter?"

"Yeah, I thought you should see this," Allen stated as he handed Showalter an envelope. "I can't believe some of the things they said about the program and our family."

Showalter pulled the folded piece of paper out of the envelope and asked, "Is it signed?"

"No, anonymous," replied Allen.

Showalter unfolded the letter and read it. Then he looked at Allen. "Do you know what I do with these if they are not signed?"

he asked. Before Allen could respond, Showalter tossed the letter in the trash.

The seasoned coach and athletic director dealt with disgruntled parents from time to time. If they were not willing to put their name behind a note, he did not chase down the writer. The community expected success from their boys' basketball team, and along the way they may have forgotten to enjoy it or appreciate what they had. "There were a few parents over the years that just thought their kids were a little better than they were, and there was some friction there," said Tony Evans.

Showalter handled any resistance he received from parents. "Show always told the players, 'Your parents can't be fair about you because they love you,'" recalled Kern. "It's hard to make everyone happy all the time." Showalter focused his efforts on each player, not the parents. He felt that if a player was happy with what was going on, then the parents would have a better understanding as well. During the season, Showalter often mentioned the contributions of bench players or players receiving less attention when speaking with the media. He understood that the coach and parents come at a child's experience from different perspectives and with different expectations. The parents focus on their child, and the coach sees a player and his role on the team.

Showalter strived to build a relationship with parents, a mutual agreement to work together in the best interest of their kids. He communicated with parents and talked with them, giving them an opportunity to express their concerns. Allen Kos observed Showalter coach all five of his sons. Kos, a farmer, may not have agreed with every decision Showalter made as a coach, but he respected his approach and communication. "Donnie was always coaching them. He'd pull a kid out and have an arm around them—coaching them," said Kos. "Donnie called me when my son Anthony was a sophomore. He wanted to know if it would be okay with me if he brought him up to the varsity level. I respected that he called me and wanted to know my opinion."

With the success of the U16–U17 team, requests for Showalter to speak at coaching clinics increased. He rarely turned down a request; he just found a way to do it. "He just does more and sleeps less," said Vicky. "Sometimes I have to remind him, 'You can't be everything for everybody.'" The demands on his time started to stretch him thin. He managed, but there were whispers in the community that maybe it was too much. "He was always on the go, always on the phone. I chuckle because I would see him in the morning driving and shaving to save some time," shared Pennington. "Toward the end some people might have thought he was spread too thin. I could sense a little bit of change in the community."

Showalter's speaking opportunities and commitments with USA Basketball didn't change the amount of time he spent involved in basketball. Earlier in Showalter's tenure at Mid-Prairie, principal Gerry Beeler asked Showalter about his weekend plans and learned he was flying down to San Antonio to work on player development with the Spurs. "I was like, 'What, are you kidding me?' There was no off-season with him when it came to basketball," stated Beeler. "One summer he mentioned to me that he was only going to spend one or two nights at home because of his commitments to basketball."

Nothing changed in terms of travel and his passion for basketball. "A lot of his summers were away from Iowa," said Tony Evans, the longtime middle school coach. "At first, when Show got more involved in the USA Basketball stuff, the community did not really know what he was doing with his time. It was not really public knowledge."

As Showalter neared the end of his career, the veteran coach shared his love of basketball and teaching the game with the same enthusiasm as before, but now people recognized him, which may have created some resentment among coaches at the high school when their athletic director was out of the office in the summer. "It did create some animosity, and I did take some heat for that," said Superintendent Schneider. "There were only a few times where we had personnel issues in the summer and it could not be taken care of because Don was overseas. Very few and far between."

Schneider knew Showalter wanted to do a good job and was always responsible. So they worked out an arrangement that he could be gone, but he had to be reachable. "No matter where he was at, if there was an issue, he would take care of it," said Schneider. "He earned the right to do that. If I felt like Don was taking advantage of it, I would have said something. Obviously we wanted Don to be a part of Mid-Prairie as long as he wanted to be a part of it."

After the 2011 season, Showalter did want to be a part of it, but only as a head coach. On June 1, 2011, Vicky and Don retired from the Mid-Prairie School District. "Don and I were fully vested at that time in our state's retirement system, and our school was also offering an early retirement package," said Vicky. "We kind of put those things together with our increasing travel and schedules, and it just seemed like retirement would help us evolve into the next season of our life." Mid-Prairie wanted him back for his 28th season, but Showalter had to go through the hiring process due to state retirement regulations on rehiring retirees. Eventually he was rehired and would be the returning Mid-Prairie basketball coach for the 2011–12 season.

JABARI PARKER FOLLOWED THE tour guide through the Mayan ruins of Chichen Itza, an archaeological site selected as one of the New Seven Wonders of the World. The tour guide rarely had to look upward when giving a tour of the historical location, but Parker and his 11 teammates all towered above him, each listed at 6'0" or taller. The teenagers, like students on a class field trip to a museum, rolled their eyes initially at the idea, but once the team made the 117-mile trip from Cancun to Chichen Itza to spend time learning history, taking photos, and picking up a few souvenirs, none of them complained about the experience. "There is so much out there in the world that is different from our country. I was always pretty adamant of at least allowing the kids out to see something cultural or historical from the country that we are in," said Vicky, who became a travel guide for off-court activities when the U16–U17 team traveled for competitions. "If we are just going to be in the gym and the hotel, we just might as well be in Chicago or L.A."

Jabari Parker was one of 12 players on the 2011 USA Men's FIBA Americas U16 Team roster. He was also a player in the USAB National Development Team program—a pool of players selected by the USAB Men's Developmental National Team Committee. The six-member committee includes five voting members: two appointed by the Amateur Athletic Union (AAU), two appointed by the National Federation of State High School Associations (NFHS), one athlete representative, and Sean Ford, who as men's national team director for USAB, chairs the committee in a nonvoting position.

The national team committee, in consultation with coaches involved in USAB's developmental program and the national assistant team director, identifies and evaluates the top youth players in the United States throughout the year. They observe players in live settings and utilize the assistance of well-established scouting services and youth player-ranking systems to develop a list of players with potential to compete for Team USA in international competition.

On October 9–10, 2010, Parker took part in a two-day, four-practice minicamp. He was one of 31 14- and 15-year-olds selected from the pool of athletes developed over the preceding year. During the minicamp, the coaches evaluated the abilities of each player and learned how coachable they were. The minicamp serves as an early tryout for the U16 training camp roster taking place the following summer; youth players from other age groups (U17–U19) in the national team development program also participate in the minicamps.

Not every player at the minicamp made the training camp roster. The 2014 Texas Basketball Coaches Association Player of the Year, Justise Winslow, did not make the U16 team, but he did receive feedback on how he could improve his game, motivating him to work hard, improve, and earn a spot on the 12-member 2012 U17 team. He later joined two of his U17 teammates, Tyus Jones and Jahlil Okafor, at Duke University, helping the Blue Devils to an NCAA national title in 2015.

"WHAT DOES PLAYING FOR USA Basketball mean to you?" asked Showalter, sitting a few feet from Jabari Parker after an early practice session at the 2011 training camp to select 12 players to represent the USA in the 2011 FIBA U16 Americas Qualifying Tournament in Cancun, Mexico.

As Parker responded, Showalter jotted down a couple notes on a piece of paper. Then he continued, "What do you think separates talented players?"

Parker responded. His answer was short, but the interviews were short by design. Each response packed a lot of meaning and provided the coaches insight into the player's mindset about what it means to be a part of a team. Showalter finished the questions in a few minutes, ending with a question about playing time: "If you are chosen to travel but as the 11th or 12th player that might not get many game minutes, how will you react to this?"

The interview was nonconversational. Showalter and his two assistant coaches asked the question, listened, wrote down the response, then moved to the next question. Each coach took a third of the training camp roster. Once they completed the interviews, they met and compared notes. The evaluations helped to determine the first cut. Showalter and his staff evaluated each player's individual basketball talent and his ability to play with his teammates on the court, but they needed to know if a player would sacrifice the team in pursuit of individual, selfish goals. The final 12 players selected for competition needed to be able to come together as a team.

The 27 players practiced twice a day over three days. The focus of the practice sessions involved fundamental skill work, game-based drills such as Cutthroat, and scrimmage situations. Showalter designed every part of practice to be competitive, so the coaches could observe how each player competed; they watched for body language, how they conducted themselves, and whether other players liked to play with them. After the last practice, USA Basketball announced the final 12-member roster.

The final 12 players selected would not represent the best under-16-year-olds in the United States but the most balanced group of the 27 invited players—multitalented players who could play different positions, a mix of good shooters and rebounders. The coaching staff met individually with each player cut to offer suggestions on what they needed to work on. The nonselected players were still a part of the USAB National Team program and had the opportunity to improve and make the team the next year.

The 12-member U16 team stymied Brazil 105–70 in the first game in Cancun, with Parker scoring 27 points and grabbing 10 rebounds. The future Duke All-American and second overall pick by the Milwaukee Bucks in the 2014 NBA Draft led them in the second game against Argentina, tossing in 21 points in a 102–81 USA victory. Parker's teammates starred in the third contest. Aaron Gordon, the future All-American at the University of Arizona, toyed with a quadruple-double, garnering 18 points, 18 rebounds, 8 blocked shots, and 9 assists in a 118–46 win over Costa Rica.

Showalter let them play as long as they played together. These 12 of the best individual players in the US needed to set aside their egos to pursue a gold medal and qualifying for the FIBA U17 World Championship in Lithuania the following summer. Playing for USA Basketball meant something. "The mindset is different. It's not all about me, me, me, I got to prove this or I got to score this," said assistant coach Mike Jones. "We're playing for USA Basketball, and that means we have to win a gold medal."

In the medal round, Gordon led Team USA in both games, recording 22 points in a semifinal win before pacing the U16 squad with 24 points and 15 rebounds in the gold medal game victory over Argentina, 104–64. Showalter, for the third time, joined his team on the medal stand to receive their gold medals. For the athletes, this was their first experience. FIBA only allowed the 12 players and the head coach on the medal stand during the ceremony; the assistant coaches would receive their medals later. That didn't lessen the experience for Jones. "It's hard to articulate unless you have gone through it," recalled Jones, who played and later coached at the famed DeMatha Catholic High School. "To stand and hear the national anthem played is really an experience I will never take for granted."

Showalter remained unblemished, a perfect 18–0 as the head coach of the U16–U17 team. He shared his passion for basketball with the elite players just like he did with his high school players. When Jabari Parker appeared on the cover of *Sports Illustrated* on May 21, 2012, Showalter kept a copy and brought it with him to the 2012 training camp for Jabari to sign. Parker left him more than a signature: "I'm so grateful to have had you as a coach to remind me and also tell me the most important things. Because of you and your desire, you fed it off on me and now I have a better passion." Showalter's USA team and high school team differed in basketball and athletic talent, but his passion rubbed off the same way: the teenagers he led learned to enjoy the game. But for the

Wellman-Kalona community, Showalter's days of sharing his passion as the Mid-Prairie basketball coach would soon end.

In the Mid-Prairie School District office, postcards covered the side of a file cabinet. Pictures from across the United States, of places such as the Empire State Building in New York City, the Golden Gate Bridge in San Francisco, and Wrigley Field in Chicago. And photos from around the world: a double-decker bus in London, a pyramid in Egypt, and a sunset over the city of Seoul, South Korea. "Wherever he was at, he would always send us, in the office, a card from where he was," shared Mark Schneider. "He understood the value of the relationships he had with other people and maintaining those relationships."

The photo-littered file cabinet signified Showalter's ability to stay connected with the office staff at the school and document many of the places he had been over the years. Going into the 2011–12 basketball season, home for Don and Vicky remained in Wellman. But after retiring from their full-time positions, their lives seemed to be moving in a different direction. They both wanted to travel more, and they had more opportunities to do so, as Don's success with USAB garnered him requests to speak at coaching clinics overseas.

He faced a rebuilding year with the 2011–12 Golden Hawks, a young team of sophomores and freshmen. They took their lumps, managing five wins all season—the first losing season for Showalter in 19 years. In March, following the season, Showalter intended to return for his 29th season, but he heard about an opening for a head boys' basketball coach at City High School in Iowa City. The position captured his interest: a new challenge, an opportunity to make a difference at a larger school.

CHAPTER 20

Elite

Tucked among the vernacular architectural style of residences scattered about east Iowa City, the City High School campus has the look of a small private college. City High opened its doors in 1939 with 700 students and today averages an annual enrollment of around 1,500, placing the school in the IHSAA's highest classification level, 4A. The City High boys' basketball program never experienced sustained excellence, but they have had memorable moments. After a subpar regular season in 1989, City High stumbled into the state tournament. They caught fire during the postseason and made a memorable run, winning the state 4A championship.

In 1992 City High returned to the state tournament but lost an early-round game. They endured a considerable drought of talent from 1993 to 2007 before returning to basketball glory in 2008 when Matt Gatens led the Little Hawks to the state 4A championship, garnering Iowa Mr. Basketball honors and becoming City High's all-time leading scorer with 1,928 points. The 2007–08 season is one of the greatest in City High boys' basketball history, but the program took a nosedive in the next three seasons, winning 17, 10, and then only 2 games by the 2010–11 season.

After finishing the 2011–12 season with nine wins, City High principal John Bacon—a former City High basketball player who had returned to his alma mater as the principal in 2010—went in search of a new head coach. The personable Bacon gives off the energy and approachability of a popular athlete—someone others want to be around and interact with. He engages with others as he moves about a crowd, a trait that allows him to interact with students, staff, and colleagues in unison.

Not overly pleased with the pool of applicants, Bacon consulted with the Gatens family. Matt Gatens's father, Mike, at 6'9", was a formidable prep player at West High in Iowa City and in college at the University of Iowa under Coach Lute Olson in the early 1980s. Bacon and both Gatenses were sitting in Mike's office, the wall littered with sport photos. In one photo, taken at the Kobe Bryant Basketball Camp, Matt, Kobe, and Coach Showalter are standing together. Bacon recalled looking up at the picture and asking both Gatenses what they thought of Coach Showalter. Both father and son agreed that Bacon should reach out and talk with the longtime Mid-Prairie coach.

"HI, DON, THIS IS John Bacon at City High," said Bacon when Showalter answered the phone. "I noticed you are listed as a reference for a few of the applicants for our open boys' basketball position."

"Hi, John," responded Showalter. "Yes, a few coaches I know shared with me they had applied for the position and asked if I could be a reference."

"I would like to get your thoughts on some of the candidates, if you are willing." Bacon paused briefly, then said, "If *you* are interested in the position at all, we would love to talk to you about it."

Without making a commitment, Don replied, "I will come up and look over the candidates with you."

A couple days later Coach Showalter appeared at City High dressed like he was getting ready to conduct a basketball practice—adorned in a T-shirt and basketball shorts. Showalter met John Bacon in the main office. Bacon skipped over the discussion of the other candidates; he wanted Showalter. "He had the experience

220   CORNFIELDS TO GOLD MEDALS

to deal with a diverse student body and…players at all levels of competition," said Bacon. "He would have instant trust as head coach." Now, after 28 years in the Mid-Prairie School District, the Showalters had a decision to make. In the past Vicky and Don always chose to stay when new opportunities presented themselves. But with their children out of the house and building their own lives, they felt comfortable moving on. It was a new adventure and a new opportunity to see what they could do at a larger school.

On April 12, 2012, Don Showalter accepted the position of head boys' basketball coach at City High. The farm kid who, out of college, stated he would never return and work for the high school he had played for, who was convinced he could never earn respect in his hometown, who then returned and gave his alma mater 28 years of everything he had. He earned respect with 446 victories, 8 conference titles, 11 district championships, and 5 state tournament appearances. More important, Showalter left a legacy of sharing his love of basketball with youth in the community, instilling a love of the game in them, while teaching them life lessons along the way. Now Showalter would trade sharing his joy of the game with the Golden Hawks of Mid-Prairie for the Little Hawks of City High. But first the FIBA U17 World Championship awaited him and his U17 players in the summer of 2012.

JUSTISE WINSLOW TOOK ANOTHER rep, catching a pass from Showalter on the move and pivoting into a 15-foot jump shot. Winslow, a lefty, needed reps going to his right, coming off his left pivot foot. Showalter built his coaching career on working with teenagers, high school athletes like Justise Winslow. The U16–U17 players were the same age as the youth he worked with in Iowa. Yet as basketball players they were different, and he expected that they would be different his first summer with the U16 team in 2009. But he misjudged their ability on the court, making the assumption that he could not teach the elite teenagers anything they did not already know. His perception of their basketball skills, knowledge of game situations, and ability to make good decisions on the court was skewed by their physical size. "Sometimes they are 15 years old and they look like grown men," said Mike Jones, a U16–U17 assistant coach. "Sometimes because they are so big and strong, you forget they are 15 years old."

Initially Showalter had hesitations about his ability to coach a high-level athlete even though he had experience at Nike Elite Camps, the USA Basketball Hoop Summit, and numerous All-Star games, including the McDonald's All-American Game. He questioned himself, wondering if anything he said to the U16–U17 team athletes would matter to them. He discovered that the top 14- to 15-year-olds on the court didn't know as much as he had assumed. They needed to be coached like high school athletes, not like college or professional athletes; mentally they were still teenagers. Once he adapted his approach, his confidence grew and he believed the U16 players would listen and have respect for what he said.

Still, the players were different. He needed to teach them while giving them some space; they did not need him yelling at them for every little detail or each time they made a mistake on the court. "With the top players, you can't sweat the small stuff because they won't let you coach them," said Tony Dorado who, in his role as head of high school basketball for Nike, has observed hundreds of coaches over the years. "If you harp on every little thing, they won't respond."

Off the court the elite players were different in regard to their experiences in basketball, what they were playing for, and the people with whom they were involved. They participated on the best AAU teams and traveled among the upper echelon of basketball players. People knew who they were; followed them on Instagram; and some even wanted to be involved with the kids, to be in their inner circle when they signed professional contracts.

The influence of others based on their own self-interests tainted the message the elite athletes received about their abilities as basketball players because people could not be honest with them, hesitant to offer any criticism that might destroy a relationship or potential connection with the elite players. Showalter didn't have to worry about this; USAB's only goal was to put together the best team to represent the United States in international competition. "It's pure basketball. There is no agenda outside of winning a gold medal and representing your country," said BJ Johnson.

Iowa Hawkeyes men's basketball coach Fran McCaffery said Showalter checks all the boxes for USAB because he does not want anything from the elite athletes other than to coach them and help them get better, which is exactly the type of person USAB needs to develop young talent in the US. "He has no agenda. It's a pretty simple game plan, but it's not always easy to execute," said McCaffery. "You need the right person to execute that, and the United States has found the right guy for that position."

Thus, Showalter could be honest with players and tell them what they needed to hear to get better on the court while offering support and information from a neutral position about how to handle things off the court, such as working with coaches at a higher level, what to expect in the professional game, and how to recognize people only interested in associating with them for their own self-interests.

Emotionally, the elite 14- to 16-year-olds were like any other teenagers: they struggled to communicate, respond to criticism, and handle praise. They also experienced stress, like at the training camp, where they compared themselves to other players. Off the court they liked to goof around and have fun. "They are teenage guys," shared Vicky. "They can be gross at times—with burping contests and stuff like that." Showalter's approach to working with teenagers stayed consistent. He pressed players to get out of their comfort zone, pushing them to learn how to challenge themselves to get better.

Simple things on the basketball court, such as swishing five straight free throws before leaving practice or making three three-point shots in a row before going to a different spot.

Tyus Jones wanted to develop as an elite point guard, but he needed to improve his verbal communication. Showalter created opportunities in practice when Jones needed to verbalize. Once Showalter got Jones out of what he was accustomed to doing, he could teach him. "He is good at getting them out of their comfort zone," said Debbie Jones, who had two sons, Tyus and Tre, play under Showalter on the U16–U17 team. "Tyus was not very vocal, and that was a big thing to Coach Showalter—telling Tyus he needed to be more vocal."

Getting out of your comfort zone was one of the four C's (choice, comfort zone, communication, and compete) Showalter taught the elite athletes—his advice on how to separate themselves from other talented players. He taught them to make good choices on and off the court, to push themselves out of their comfort zone, to communicate as leaders through verbal and nonverbal communication, and to strive to develop a competitive mindset. The 4 C's served as one method Showalter used to help bring the team together in a short period of time while aligning his approach with the 15 Gold Standards and the culture of USAB.

What are these Gold Standards? Coach K developed the Gold Standards with the 2008 Senior National Team, and they filtered down through USA Basketball's National Team program. They comprise expectations for all the developmental teams and act as a framework to guide consistency in the program. The Senior National Team earned gold in the 2008 Beijing Olympics and then again in the 2010 World Cup; and with the 2012 London Games less than a month away, the change in culture at USAB was working. Jerry Colangelo, Coach Krzyzewski, and the Senior National Team received the media attention; they were the face of USA Basketball, but responsibility for implementing the daily culture change happened behind the scenes through the efforts of the full-time USAB staff. "We have a philosophy that the players play, the coaches coach, and [USAB] takes care of everything else," explained Sean Ford, the National Team director. "For me, I give structure to all of it, from a planning standpoint, a budget standpoint, as chair of the committee, and oversight, but I have never personally been to a U16–U17 competition."

While Ford did not travel with the U16–U17 team, Caroline Williams, the former assistant director for media and public relations, did, and she observed Showalter coaching the team and also how he interacted with the elite players. "He holds them accountable for the things that they do, and he has a way to really get them to buy into the system," said Williams.

The system was Showalter's coaching style mixed with the culture established by USAB. "I have seen some really selfish players [in other environments] turn around and be the most unselfish players [here] because they have USA across their chest," shared assistant coach Mike Jones. "You cannot attribute that to anything except for the culture of USA Basketball and Coach Showalter's leadership."

Showalter embraced the USA Basketball culture and helped contribute to it by creating a climate focused on developing players' fundamental basketball skills and helping athletes discover their love of the game. Showalter has always been a teacher of the game first, and he used his platform as a teacher to mold the elite athletes into a team in a short period of time, using both the USAB Gold Standards and his Mind Candy, a short phrase or saying used to inspire, reinforce, or stimulate action.

Showalter emphasized the Gold Standards and Mind Candy in the pre-practice classroom settings and reinforced them on the practice court. For example, if a player showed up late for practice, he could remind them that they failed to meet their responsibilities as a member of the team by violating the Gold Standard of respect. He also stopped practice to ask them what a specific Gold Standard meant to them, how they could meet the expectation, and how it would make them a better player.

Showalter took the same approach with his Mind Candy. The concept was simple, but the implementation needed to be purposeful, an approach that demonstrated to the athletes what the phrase or saying meant to them. An approach Debbie Jones noticed had an impact with Tyus and Tre, who both later starred at Duke University. "It's a great example of how he put emphasis on the mental part of the game being just as critical as the physical part of the game," said Debbie Jones. "He pushed them both mentally and physically."

Showalter meshed his ability to push them individually while remaining approachable; he took an interest in them as people and got to know them. "Any kid that has ever played for him is going to feel the care he had for them," said Mike Jones. "But he has not done it to an intensity level so much that the kids are not unable to relate to him off the court."

His relatable approach earned him respect among the elite players. "He's got that really, really good feel at that high level of talent, which [allowed] him to coach those guys and [allowed] those kids to believe in his coaching," said Dorado. "This [made] him very unique coming from the high school ranks." They trusted the small-town coach from Iowa. "This older guy from Iowa [was] able to relate to and communicate effectively with kids from Chicago, New York City, Los Angeles, and…DC," said Mike Jones. "You would say they [had] nothing else in common but the game of basketball. Coach Show is Coach Show; he's able to reach anybody."

If there was any question about the comfort level of the elite athletes with their coach, all anyone had to do was observe the communication circle, an activity designed to generate interaction and open up channels of communication between the athletes and coaches. Showalter used the communication circle to end a practice session. "He [had] them holding hands—looking each other straight in the eye," said Caroline Williams. "Fourteen- to seventeen-year-old boys don't hold each other's hands."

The development of each individual basketball player provided the first step in helping the United States put their best team together to compete for a gold medal, but the goal of the team in competition was to *win*, to bring home the gold. With Showalter leading the effort, the U17 team was poised to represent the United States and strive for gold in the 2012 FIBA U17 World Cup.

With his future Duke teammate Jabari Parker nursing a sore foot, Jahlil Okafor stepped up in the preliminary round, scoring 10 points to go along with 14 rebounds in a 95–57 win over the Czech Republic, and he followed that with another double-double two games later, grabbing 13 rebounds to go with 21 points in an 86–50 win over France. For his performance over eight games, Okafor earned tournament MVP honors.

Team USA finished 5–0 in the preliminary round and faced Canada in the quarterfinals. Throughout the U17 World Championships, different players stepped up and contributed. Against the Canadians, Tyus Jones tossed in 22 points and added 6 assists in a 113–59 victory. Justise Winslow made his presence felt with 17 points and 13 rebounds. In the U17 team's 95–66 semifinal victory over Spain, Winslow again scored 17 points to go with 13 rebounds to lead the team in both categories; he led the team in steals for the tournament with 21 over the eight games, earning him all-tournament honors. Winslow's work ethic since not making the U16 team in 2011 started to pay off, and he emerged as a leader among his peers at the World Cup. "The coaches really motivated me.... Last year I didn't make [the U16 team], and they just told me to keep working," said Winslow following the World

Championships. "That's what I did. I just tried to play my role, get rebounds, and get some hustle points, and everything worked out."

In the gold medal game, USA faced Australia again. Showalter's U17 squad combined a strong defensive effort, holding Australia to 32.3 percent shooting from the field, with a stellar offensive performance, shooting 60.3 percent from the field and 44.4 percent from three-point range to capture the gold medal, 95–62.

Showalter's ability to teach the game and connect with the elite players started early in his career at Lone Tree and Central Elkader, and only improved over his 28 seasons at Mid-Prairie. He developed new methods during summers working basketball camps, and he refined and tested his skills working elite camps and clinics. Showalter fit right in, embracing the culture of USA Basketball while contributing to it. Now, in his new position at City High, he had to establish a new culture.

CHAPTER 21

City High

Showalter had an idea. He approached John Bacon, the principal at City High, about visiting the homes of each returning varsity player. At Mid-Prairie, Showalter had an established presence; City High parents and athletes were less familiar with him. Bacon liked the idea and teamed Showalter up with Emily Dvorak, the welcome center coordinator at City High, a position designed to help new and existing families acclimate to the school. She started what she termed "touching base" with students; she visited families at their homes to check on students' truancy, help align them with resources, or work through myriad other scenarios they might be dealing with.

Because Dvorak had made connections with a few of the basketball players and their families, she helped Showalter line up the home visits and often accompanied him. One visit led Coach Showalter to the home of Luke Posivio. Standing at 6'8" and weighing 265 pounds, Posivio played on the block and had never developed basic basketball skills. He attributed this to a combination of poor coaching in youth basketball and his rebellion toward authority as an adolescent. "I was kind of a frustrating case," stated Posivio. "I had a chip on my shoulder and a little bit of an attitude."

The visits lasted up to 45 minutes. Showalter shared a handbook outlining his vision for the basketball program. He highlighted key points in the handbook, including information on how parents could be involved. Luke's parents, Brent and Tami Posivio, remembered

Showalter's visit, because no other high school coach had done this before. It left them with a positive impression, a sense of comfort that their son was in good hands. "You could tell that Coach Showalter is all about the basketball," said Tami, "but that he also cares deeply about the kids. He wants them to have good character and good values. I don't think we could have asked for a better coach for Luke to finish his high school career with."

At first, not all families welcomed Showalter in their homes, a bit leery of the outsider. "A few families changed their mind once word got around what his intentions were," said Dvorak. "I think it was just refreshing for them to actually have somebody take that individualized time to talk to them about what he wanted for the program. Making those home visits would not be the easiest approach for any coach. But he did not do what was easiest for him—he did what was best for those families and those kids."

The experience helped Showalter connect with each player; he knew how they lived and who the key people were in their lives. The connection with Posivio changed the player's basketball experience. "The coaches never gave up on me as a basketball player and a person," recalled Posivio. "Coach Show taught me how to accept constructive criticism, and he instilled in me many life lessons," which Posivio termed Showisms. Posivio's positive experience with coaches and athletics at City High pushed him toward a career in education. He later became an elementary school teacher and coach—passing along Showisms to his students.

To assist him in building the City High program, Showalter hired Tyler Griffith. Griffith had stayed in touch with his former Mid-Prairie basketball coach through the Snow Valley Iowa basketball camps and was living in Iowa City at the time. Griffith had familiarity with Showalter's coaching style and knew many of Iowa City's youth through his work in the numerous junior high programs. "A lot of the challenges we faced in growing the program

were with developing standards," recalled Griffith. "We were
working with a diverse group of individuals from many different
backgrounds, and we had to pull everyone together and get them
playing for each other."

Showalter kept Ryan Lee on staff from the previous head coach,
and both Lee and Griffith became an important part of Showalter's
long-term vision for the program. With Showalter's commitment to
USAB in the summer and occasional weekends throughout the year,
both Lee and Griffith took on a variety of responsibilities, including
the coordination of summer camps, youth tournaments, and off-
season weekend basketball tournaments with the City High players.
In addition, they supervised open gyms and organized strength
and conditioning sessions. "He trusted Tyler and I quite a bit with
the program in the off-season—[with] the behind-the-scenes stuff
and also the growth of the players," said Lee. "Even though he was
juggling all these different things at once, like USA Basketball, if he
committed to something, he was all in, and the players recognized
that. It inspired us [coaches] to push ourselves to be better, because
he was willing to work hard."

Progress in the win column would take some time, as City High
finished the 2012–13 season 8–14. In previous coaching stops early
in his tenure, Showalter had a rival high school and another coach
who provided a competitive challenge, a more talented team to test
his team's improvement. At Central Elkader, the Postville Pirates and
Paul Jungblut provided the test. At Mid-Prairie, Washington High
and Dave Tremmel offered the challenge. At City High it would be
crosstown rival the West High School Trojans.

A basketball juggernaut, the Trojans dominated 4A basketball
in the state of Iowa from 2012 to 2018. They accumulated 165
victories and captured 4 state titles and 2 runner-up finishes, a
run that included three straight 4A titles (2013, 2014, and 2015).
During the same era, the Trojans controlled City High's Little

Hawks, winning 11 straight contests, with two of those wins coming in Showalter's first season. During both contests with West High, Showalter recognized his players seemed beaten before they even took the court; they lacked confidence in their ability to win. Showalter needed to instill in them a belief that they could compete. Thus, he began setting small goals they could achieve, such as outscoring the other team by four points over the following four minutes or a goal to win the next quarter. Over time, each of the smaller goals lay the groundwork in helping the players believe they could win basketball games, but it would take some time against West High.

West High won three meetings against the Little Hawks in Showalter's second season, by scores of 70–34, 73–41, and 74–50. While West High continued their reign over City High, the Little Hawks made progress and fared well against some formidable opponents, growing their confidence as their skills improved. City High athletic director Terry Coleman recognized the challenge Coach Showalter faced in building the program. "He desperately wanted to bring winning basketball to City High, and that was not something that came quickly," stated Coleman. "Even though you would never see it on the outside, I am sure that was difficult for him." While progress in the win column was slow to develop, Showalter utilized his experience with USA Basketball to build a culture at City High that went beyond winning.

SHOWALTER BARRELED DOWN THE two-lane highway. Eric Flannery shifted in the passenger seat. His body tensed each time Showalter rounded a corner faster than the recommended speed. Flannery and Showalter were returning from Cripple Creek, a historic gold-mining community outside Colorado Springs. Flannery, an assistant coach with the U16–U17 team, was accustomed to Showalter's driving. "Don's driving is terrible. He goes too fast," said Flannery. "But for some reason he is always behind the wheel. One time we drove up to

Pikes Peak; I was literally laying down in the back of the car because I thought he was going to drive over the cliff." Pikes Peak, with an elevation of 14,115 feet, is accessible by a 19-mile paved road that climbs at an average grade of 6.7 percent and includes 156 turns.

Flannery's stomach didn't care much for moving vehicles at high speeds, especially on curves. Yet here he was again, a passenger, leaving his fate in Showalter's hands. Showalter continued to zip down the mountain highway, ignoring the speed limit.

"Oh, crap," said Showalter suddenly as he pushed on the brake, slowing the car down. Flannery looked in his mirror and saw the flashing blue and red lights. Showalter eased the vehicle over to the shoulder of the road, and the two USA Basketball coaches waited for the highway patrol officer.

"Hey, where are you guys going?" asked the officer as he looked in the car. "You are going pretty fast here."

"We are USA Basketball coaches heading back to Colorado Springs," replied Showalter.

"Oh, really?" asked the officer as he eased back. He could see Showalter and Flannery were wearing USAB logoed apparel.

"Throughout the rest of the conversation, the officer seemed in awe, like he thought we were Mike Krzyzewski or whatever," recalled Flannery. "The officer ended up shaking our hands at the end of the conversation and gave Don his business card and said, 'Let me know if you ever need anything.'"

In the summer of 2014, Flannery, along with L. J. Goolsby, an AAU coach and owner of KC Run GMC out of Kansas City, served as assistant coaches helping Showalter select and prepare the U17 Team for the FIBA U17 World Championships in Dubai, United Arab Emirates. Flannery got involved in USAB in 2001 when the National Federation of State High Schools appointed him to the National Team Committee. As head coach at St. Edward High School in Cleveland, Flannery has now won more than 500 games and led the Eagles to nine state tournament appearances, including a state championship in 1998.

The U17 team returned nine players from the U16 team's gold medal performance in the 2013 FIBA U16 Americas Tournament in Uruguay the previous summer, where they went 5–0, setting a record for point margin of victory, besting the field by an average of 53.4 points per game. En route to the 2014 U17 World Cup in Dubai, the U16–U17 team stopped in Doha, Qatar, to spend three days training. In Doha the U17 team visited the Al Udeid Air Base, home to the United States Central Command (USCC) and the United State Air Force Central Command (USAFCC). Team USA put on a coaching clinic for the troops stationed at the base. The team practiced each day and played a game against any member of the troops willing to lace up their sneakers.

The air force base provided a place to practice and prepare for competition and an opportunity to learn about how our military personnel live and what it is really like to serve your nation. The young USA Basketball players learned that there are a lot of more important things than the game of basketball and that they are playing for something bigger than themselves. While playing basketball for your country is incomparable to serving your country in a military uniform, when the U17 team members put on the USA Basketball jersey, they know they are representing the United States of America. "It really hits them when we get over in another country and they put on their uniforms with USA across their chest," said Vicky. "How impactful that is that they are representing our country."

In their opening game of the U17 FIBA World Cup, the U17 team battled a tough, experienced Greece squad throughout the first half, leading by only one, 32–31. They settled down and controlled the game for an 83–73 opening win. They got their World Cup jitters out of the way and recognized they were going to get everyone's best game. "It let us know that we can't just walk on the court and beat someone by 40 just because we're the USA. We have to play hard to get the win," stated Malik Newman after the game. He later played one season for the Kansas Jayhawks, earning Big 12 Newcomer of the Year honors in 2018.

The USAB team stomped Angola 99–63 in the second contest of the preliminary round. After the first two games, the U17 team had a day off; they had time to sightsee and take in all the things Dubai has to offer. "These kids need to experience things beyond the basketball court," said Caroline Williams. "They are wide-eyed; most of them have never traveled out of the country, and many have not traveled out of their geographical regions."

The USAB travel party piled into the Land Rovers parked outside their hotel for a desert safari. Once the parade of SUVs carrying the next generation of great basketball players in the US arrived at the Big Red Sand Dune, the drivers asked them to get out of the vehicle while they let air out of the tires. Coach Flannery should have sat this one out, but since Showalter was not driving, what did he have to worry about? Flannery and his wife, who accompanied the team on the trip to Dubai, settled in the back seat of one of the Land Rovers.

The SUVs raced over the sand dune—sliding, skidding, and spinning. Not everyone handled the roller-coaster ride through the desert the same. "Some fared better than others," said Vicky. "Had we known, we probably would have taken Dramamine." Flannery only held his stomach on the Pikes Peak drive with Showalter, but this was too much; he threw up all over the back seat. Flannery and the rest of the team would get to power and steer their own vehicles later in the day when they rented some dune buggies to go along at their own speed.

The team returned to the court for the final game in the preliminary round to best the Philippines 124–64. Seeded into the round of 16, Team USA disposed of Japan 122–38 behind Jayson Tatum's 19 points. Tatum, a future NBA All-Star for the Boston Celtics, came off the bench for the U17 team in four of the World Cup games. Showalter was able to get players to accept their roles for the betterment of the team and not lose the respect of the players in the process. "He's really smart about how to put it all together but has the gift of being able to deal with one-on-one as well," shared Fran McCaffery, the head men's basketball coach at the University of Iowa. "I think a lot of people are able to be good at one of those two things, but he is good at both of them."

Tatum and his teammates bested China 113–71 to earn a spot against undefeated Serbia in the semifinals. Serbia utilized a switching defensive scheme, along with increased physical play, to fluster their opponents from the US. The strategy worked early, as Serbia trailed by only three at the half, 39–36. But Team USA adjusted at halftime and rolled to an 89–68 victory.

Showalter entered the championship still undefeated as the U16–U17 coach. Australia was ready to end the streak, finding success from behind the arc early and throughout the game. When Dejan Vasiljevic of Australia hit his second three of the first quarter, Showalter's squad faced their largest deficit of the tournament, trailing 17–7. As they had throughout the U17 World Cup, the U17 team used a big spurt to pull ahead, and by the end of the first period, they had taken the lead 28–27. Australia kept the game close; every time they fell behind by double digits, they rallied back, using their three-point marksmanship to bring the game within single digits, trailing by only six with 2:25 left to play, and then by five with only 30 seconds left. They finished the game making 11 three-pointers, shooting 44 percent. Still, the U.S. prevailed 99–92. Showalter maintained his perfect record and notched his sixth gold medal.

Coaching with USA Basketball in international competition challenged Showalter to be a better coach. He became more intentional in building team culture, making connections with athletes, and in his preparation; each was a strength he had developed as a high school coach, but coaching for USA Basketball sharpened and expedited these abilities.

The 12-member U16–U17 team convened for two weeks of practice and competition in the summer. Showalter had to believe it could be done—that he could connect with them. "There's a perception that elite athletes need to be treated differently. I don't think that's true, and Don has proven that," said Fran McCaffery, who observed Showalter coach elite athletes and who coached elite talent throughout his more-than-40-year coaching career. "He connects with them. He recognizes that each person is different, and he will connect with that individual."

Tre Jones was the last person invited to the U16 camp in 2015. "I went out there and just played hard. He noticed how hard I was playing, and he noticed what I was doing and what I wasn't doing," said Jones. "He would tell me to focus on my strengths and do what I can to add to the team and winning; he was interested and just trying to help me get better."

Showalter thought more about what he was going to do on the court and what he would do off the court. He stepped back and considered what the players he was coaching needed to develop at that particular point. Over time, Showalter improved his ability to put players in a position to be successful; he spent less time talking and telling players what to do, instead helping them learn how to make decisions on their own. Coaching the international game didn't change who he was, but his coaching success with the U16–U17 team gave him confidence in his ability to lead elite talent and coach at that level. It was a confidence he carried through to his high school teams and into the 2014–15 season at City High.

THE GOLDEN STATE WARRIORS entered their game against the Milwaukee Bucks on Saturday, December 12, 2015, with a 24-game winning streak, the most consecutive wins to start a season in NBA history. The Bradley Center, home of the Bucks, was filled with fans, with one section sporting green 24–1 T-shirts. The crowd also included members of the City High basketball team. Showalter made arrangements for the team to attend the game, which featured three players from his U16–U17 teams: Johnny O'Bryant III and Jabari Parker for the Bucks and James McAdoo for the Warriors. The Little Hawks left Iowa City in a pair of vans on a Friday after school and made the drive North to Milwaukee. Friday evening, they practiced in the Bradley Center and conducted a second practice Saturday morning.

The game turned out to be historic, as the Bucks defeated the Warriors 108–95 to end their record-setting winning streak. Parker had 19 points. The Warriors finished the season with 73 wins, adding another NBA record for the most wins in a season. After the game, the Little Hawks players met O'Bryant and Parker. Naeem Smith, a City High point guard with slick handles and an aptitude for finding the open man, had never been to an NBA game before. "I really did not know what to expect," said Smith. Neither did Henry Mulligan, a senior that season: "The trip we took to Milwaukee for the NBA game and practicing on their court my senior year was one of my best memories of City High," recalled Mulligan.

For City High principal John Bacon, the NBA game was just one example of the impact Showalter had on the City High basketball program. "We got kids from backgrounds of poverty that had never experienced anything like that in their entire life," said Bacon. "He really gave the kids a first-class program to be a part of. The kids just knew they were part of something so special."

For the first time in his coaching career, Coach Showalter didn't have any teaching or administrative duties to attend to during the day; he used the extra time to get to know each of his athletes better. Showalter ate lunch in the cafeteria at school or made appearances in their study hall or free period. For Smith, Showalter made an impact. "I can't really describe all the things he has done for me. He was really almost like a father figure," stated Smith. "He really cares about everyone and wants everyone to succeed. From everyone that started to everyone on the bench." Smith was the floor general who made Coach Showalter's offense run. He spent two years on the varsity as a sophomore and junior before electing to focus on football his senior season.

Henry Mulligan was one of the few players during Showalter's tenure at City High who would go on to play college basketball. A tough defender, Mulligan was a savvy player who could get a hot hand. Mulligan remembered Showalter's individual player meetings. "I was kind of intimidated because he would just stare at you. But he was really just listening to what you were saying," said Mulligan. "The individual meetings were just one of the things he had us do that continue to help me today."

Team bonding activities off the court were frequent. Beyond the NBA game, the team attended Iowa Hawkeyes basketball games and organized team bowling nights, and often the team ended up at the Showalter home, a place where players could relax and just be kids. The Showalters' commitment to be all in aligned with who they were. Yet City High challenged them to give more, fulfill a greater purpose to develop boys into young men through basketball. Vicky remembered one incident when Don heard from a teacher that a player had been disrespectful toward her in class. "I don't remember exactly what the punishment was," said Vicky. "But the players quickly realized that you had to be a good person of character in all areas of your life—not just what you brought to the gym and the game."

Showalter carried over methods he used at Mid-Prairie to help players develop pride in themselves. He required City High basketball players to dress up on game days with dress trousers, shirts, and matching ties. If a player did not have dress clothes and could not afford them, Vicky and Don would find something for them to wear, even if it meant purchasing the clothes themselves. Terry Coleman noticed a culture change and Showalter's ability to create an atmosphere where students just wanted to be a part of the team. "The kids looked good, felt good, and they had pride. Kids just wanted to be there—even if they never saw the playing court," recalled Coleman. "One year he kept 24 guys on his roster—they wanted to be a part of it. What makes that impressive is we were not winning basketball games at that time."

At City High, Showalter used his recent experiences with USA Basketball and emphasized that the legacy you leave as a player is not about you as a ball player but what you do for other people. He linked the Little Hawks to local organizations and had the players give back to the community. The team volunteered at the Ronald McDonald House in Iowa City. The Ronald McDonald House Charities provide families of seriously injured or sick children a place to stay while the kids receive care at a local medical facility. No family is turned away for inability to pay. "He would give us various jobs. Some of us would clean around the house and some of us would make meals for the families," recalled Smith. "That was something that really brought us together, as we got to help out those families—many of them that were really going through a hard time."

The team also assisted with food drives, cleaned up Kinnick Stadium after Iowa Hawkeyes Football games, and would read to elementary school students. Each experience exposed City High basketball players to a greater purpose beyond themselves. While the efforts off the court were turning boys into men, the results in the win column were slow to develop. In Showalter's third season (2014–15), the team slipped to a 7–16 record, finishing the season with nine straight losses.

The losing was tough, but Showalter continued to remain positive. "Coach Show was really good at communicating to each player that we were not going to give up on each of them," recalled Lee. "We would not cast anyone aside when they were going through a rough patch." This was a mindset the Little Hawks needed in their second matchup with West High after losing 64–40 in the first contest. In the second game, something changed. The Little Hawks kept the game close but fell a few points short as West High squeaked by with a 66–63 win. It was a significant moment for the City High program under Showalter's watch. His team believed they could not only play with West High but that they could beat the Trojans.

THE LITTLE HAWKS OPENED the 2015–16 season winning six of their first nine games. West High won six of their first eight. Once again, the Little Hawks appeared to be no match for the Trojans, whose roster featured five starters with Division I scholarship offers. In their first matchup at West High, the Trojans proved they were better, jumping to a 16–5 lead and then adding to it, prevailing 45–31, notching their 11th straight victory over City High.

In mid-February, West High visited City High. The Little Hawks had gone 4–4 since their last encounter. The Trojans carried an eight-game winning streak and a No. 2 ranking in Class 4A. On paper, the Little Hawks looked defeated; West High was too good. But from the tip, everything was clicking for City High. "We all seemed to be playing at a different level that night," remembered Smith. "In the first half, I shoveled a pass to Micah Martin and he slammed home a thunderous dunk."

At 6'9" Martin was a presence in the post, but displays of rim-rattling flair were a bit out of character for him. It set the stage for the rest of the game; Smith slid by defenders, getting to the paint and dishing to sharpshooter Henry Mulligan. One time Mulligan hit a three off a dish from Smith in front of the student section. A few fans spilled onto the court in excitement as City High retreated on defense. "When Henry hit that shot in front of the student section, I remember people jumping around, and the floor was shaking," said Smith. "A couple times I could not really feel my legs, I was so lost in the moment."

The Little Hawks never trailed in the game, winning every quarter, for a final score of 63–53. For Bacon, this was a special night. "If you would have put the two teams next to each other, it would not even have looked like a fair fight," said Bacon. "To win that game was a great achievement. I still have that newspaper article on my office wall."

Beating West High was a defining moment in Coach Showalter's four-year run at City High, and definitely a highlight for the basketball program. The Little Hawks finished the season at 13–10 and captured the Mississippi Valley Conference title. Showalter earned conference Coach of the Year honors in his only winning season at City High. Although he never intended to leave high school coaching, after 42 years he decided to pursue a full-time opportunity with USAB in the spring of 2016. Vicky, like Don, felt proud of what they had accomplished. "City High was a perfect fit for Don," said Vicky. "He was able to turn around the program in four years, and we were able to serve the community and try to make a difference in the players' lives along the way."

For Showalter, his time at City High might be his best work as a coach. Drawing on the experience of a storied high school career, coupled with international experience coaching elite athletes through USAB, he was able to adapt his approach to best meet the needs of the student-athletes at City High. While his focus on developing those under his guidance was nothing new, the position at City High had refreshed him; Showalter became more deliberate in his approach and reflected more on his life in coaching.

On February 16, 2016, Showalter had achieved a career milestone. He notched his 600th career win in a 62–44 victory over Dubuque Senior High School. The 600 wins placed him in rare company on the all-time career wins list for Iowa boys' basketball coaches. At the time, he was the 12th coach to accomplish the feat. He finished his career with an overall record of 601–346. The 10-time Iowa Coach of the Year was inducted into the Iowa High School Hall of Fame in 2017 for his accomplishments on the court and contributions to Iowa basketball, but Showalter's true impact along his path to 601 wins is the number of people he helped to fall in love with the game of basketball, and those he supported over the years.

"He has given people access [to the game]," said Dwight Gingerich, the IMS coach who coached just a few miles from Showalter for most of Don's career. Showalter stayed in touch with former players—such as Jason Dumont, a two-year starter at Mid-Prairie in 1987 and 1988—long after he left the Golden Hawks. "I went through a health scare, a cancer scare, at one point, and he was one of the first guys to pick up the phone and call me," said Dumont.

And Showalter built lasting relationships with coaches he worked with. "We were such good friends beyond coaching. I miss the day-to-day interaction, talking basketball, Iowa sport, and life in general," said Chris Kern. "I got a lot of opportunities because of him; meeting coaches like John Wooden, Red Auerbach, and Bobby Knight—people I would never have had the opportunity to meet without Show's connections."

Later in his career, Don took a special interest in mentoring the next generation of coaches. "He helped me balance coaching while being a good husband and father," said Ryan Lee. "I picked that up from him. All the lessons we have learned from him are the 'bigger than basketball' kind of thing."

Showalter kept winning in perspective throughout his career. He always had a goal to develop youth on and off the basketball court. Now, more than ever, who he was coaching and who he could help his athletes become became more important than winning. Showalter's legacy as a high school coach is set. Yet his legacy as a basketball coach continues to grow as his influence expands around the world and he mentors the next generation of coaches.

CHAPTER 22

Mentor

In 2018 Snow Valley Iowa celebrated their 25th year as Showalter watched over the activity below him, each court alive with the sound of players engaged in competitive drills. From this particular vantage point, Showalter's view was in the moment but offered a reflection of his past and a glimpse into his future. From his days hoisting two-handed set shots at a basket fastened to the side of his parents' barn to this moment, basketball continued to evolve, from how it was played to how it was taught. The athletes below him felt the expectations of society, the year-round commitment and the pressure to train for one sport. Coaches at all levels felt an expectation to win and pressure to develop collegiate-level skills in their athletes. But as Showalter looked out over the coaches working the camp, he could see the future, the next generation of coaches—young coaches, passionate, and ready to make an impact.

Jason Kern was one of those coaches. Kern commanded the court; the youth before him were attentive to his instruction as he led them through a defensive drill called the Perfect Defense Drill, where a team must stop the other team from scoring for a total of 24 seconds. Showalter watched Kern teach an instructional clinic, just like Herb Livsey had observed him teaching an instructional clinic at the Snow Valley Basketball School in 1984. A coach's son, Kern spent hours in the gym around Showalter and his father, Chris Kern. He was set up to coach. He taught with an energy and enthusiasm—he shared his passion, just like his former coach. Now, as a young coach, Kern found a mentor in Showalter. "When I got my first coaching job, I called him and asked him things. I struggled my first year, and I talked to him that summer," said Kern. "The next year we built the program, won the conference, and got 20 wins."

The Snow Valley Basketball School is inextricably linked to Showalter's coaching career; there he made connections that would advance his coaching career, and built his reputation as a teacher of the game. Now he mentors the next generation. He hires the coaching staff with a focus on giving young coaches an opportunity. But like Livsey, Showalter keeps a balance of veteran and novice coaches, a dynamic that keeps the experienced coaches sharp as they respond to all the questions from younger coaches trying to learn as much as they can.

Showalter struggled saying no to a coach wanting to work the camp. "He always overstaffs it," said Dave Schlabaugh, a longtime camp director of the Iowa camp. "So if you are a young coach and you want to work it, somehow, some way, he finds a way for you to work it." Yet to become a member of the Snow Valley Basketball Camp fraternity of coaches, new coaches must prove they belong and make it through a week of camp. Similar to a probationary period for a new employee or an initiation to join a club, Snow Valley tests a coach's commitment to teaching the game of basketball. Not every coach survives a day that begins at 6:30 AM and often does not conclude until past 10:00 PM.

Thus, Snow Valley creates a fraternity-like atmosphere where coaches benefit from their association with the camp, so much so that a coach working the camp might get labeled as one of "Show's guys." Ken Spielbauer, a Snow Valley camp coach turned camp director, benefited in being one of "Show's guys." One summer Spielbauer celebrated his 30th year running his annual basketball camp at Wapello High. He invited Showalter to be a special speaker.

"At the time, Showalter was at City High and had been working with USA Basketball," recalled Spielbauer. "I always paid the coaches, and at the end of his session, I gave him a $100 check. He took the check, tore it up, and said, 'I ain't taking your money.'"

Spielbauer may have benefited from his association with Showalter, but Showalter's approach toward other coaches is the same wherever he goes, whether you are labeled a "Show guy" or not. "He never turns anybody down; he makes time for everybody," said Mike Vear. "He'll do anything. I have seen him at the end of a [coaching clinic] session in London, and 20 people want to talk with him, and he stays and talks to all 20 and he hands out his email address."

At Snow Valley, codirector Jerry Slykhuis shared in the responsibility with Showalter to build an environment for coaches in Iowa similar to what Livsey had created in California. Slykhuis also mentored coaches. "He really got me on track that [coaching] is what I was going to do," said Rob Brost, a successful high school coach in Illinois, who considers Slykhuis the most influential male in his life other than his dad. "I knew from a young age that I wanted to coach, and playing for him cemented that fact. I wanted to be like him," said Brost, who played for Slykhuis at Cedar Falls High School, then coached with him.

Under Showalter and Slykhuis's leadership, the camaraderie, built on a shared experience among coaches, became a support group. Camp coach John Walz was a direct recipient of that support. A high school coach in northwestern Iowa and a father of three, Walz lost his wife to cancer in 2015. "Some of the first people that reached out to me were Snow Valley coaches," said Walz. "When we had my wife's funeral, we had a great showing of coaches from Snow Valley, some driving as many as five hours to get there."

Two years later the same camp coaches gathered to mourn and support each other when news of a car accident reverberated throughout the group. Jerry Slykhuis and his wife, Jane, were traveling a rural highway, Route 56, in western Kansas. A semitrailer truck ran a stop sign, killing them both instantly. The emotional toll of the Slykhuises' passing was difficult. Jerry was a true teacher who got the best out of kids. His presence left an impression on others. "Jerry had this really dry sense of humor. He was able to make people laugh, make people grin," said Don Logan, executive director of the IBCA. "He was always kind of smiling." Slykhuis made a difference, and coaches—including Showalter—carry on his memory, each of them who interacted with him a better person and a better coach for it. The Snow Valley Iowa Basketball Camp recognizes his contributions; the registration website still lists him as camp director, in memoriam.

IN 2003 PRESIDENT GEORGE W. Bush honored Coach John Wooden with the Presidential Medal of Freedom. The coach, who taught his players the game of basketball, taught everyone else about life in the 35 years after his retirement. He became a mentor to many, including Showalter. Mike Dunlap, who met Showalter at Snow Valley California in the 1980s, noticed the impact Coach Wooden had on Showalter's approach as a coach. "He knows John Wooden inside and out. Wooden was his model, his No. 1. He's emulated those behaviors," said Dunlap, who won two NCAA D-2 national championships as a head coach at Metropolitan State University in Denver and later an NBA title as an assistant coach with the Milwaukee Bucks.

Now, in the twilight of his career, coaching for USA Basketball, Showalter's role as mentor to others followed many of Wooden's characteristics: love for teaching, being a role model for a way of life, and putting family first. "[Showalter's] passion for teaching goes to coaching the coaches just as much as coaching players," said Tony Dorado. "That passion has allowed him to teach all over the world."

Showalter models a way of living off the court. "He was such a role model for me, just his character and in how he carried himself," said Todd Bontrager, who played on Showalter's first Mid-Prairie team before becoming a coach. "Just his professionalism. How he presented himself, and his love for basketball." Showalter could also be direct in his mentorship, like Wooden, asking coaches questions to challenge them to figure it out on their own. "He always threw out an idea that you could bounce around in your head and come to your own conclusions," said Bontrager. "He put you in a position where you were deciding; he was not just giving you an answer."

Over time, with age, Showalter took on a fatherly role. "I see a father figure, not just from the players but from the high school coaches that come, many from really good programs," said Stan Waterman, who assisted Showalter with the U16–U17 teams. A fatherly role built on his commitment to family first. He models putting family first. "Probably his greatest strength is that he is an unbelievable family man," said Dave Schlabaugh. "He finds a way to make it all work. He is in Hong Kong giving a clinic, and then he is back at his grandson's birthday the next day."

With no high school team to coach in the spring of 2016, Showalter felt a greater purpose to give back to basketball. For years, he had given his energy to the players he coached, to youth in the communities he lived in through his youth programs, and to other coaches as a mentor. Now he was in a position to become an ambassador of the game. He had the credibility and influence to help grow the game on an international level and help coaches on the national stage. "I think he feels a responsibility to share what he knows and to mentor young coaches to better the game," shared ESPN basketball analyst Jay Bilas, who also runs a coach-development program as part of his annual Jay Bilas Skills Camp, where Showalter is a frequent guest speaker. "Don feels an important responsibility to leave the game better than he found it, and he has done that. He has grown the game. Don's done it, for most of the time, out of the spotlight." So when USA Basketball needed someone full-time to work in their new Youth Division, to grow the game and impact coaches, Showalter jumped at the opportunity.

SHOWALTER PUSHED A CART loaded with bags. The elevator near baggage claim was malfunctioning, so he headed toward the escalator, following the rest of the USAB travel party. The U17 team arrived in Spain for the 2016 FIBA U17 World Cup with 40 large bags. Showalter, the assistant coaches, and a few of the USAB staff often handled the luggage carts.

Showalter caught up to the group as they stepped onto the escalator. The group of players and the team manager, Samson Kayode, paid him no attention, joking around with each other as Showalter maneuvered the luggage cart onto the moving stairway. One of the front wheels caught the first step, leaving the second front wheel hanging off the same step. Showalter recognized the awkward tilt of the cart, unbalanced and at an angle. He tried to adjust it, lifting the rear end of the luggage carrier as the moving walkway climbed. The ruckus caught the attention of Kayode and the players. "Literally every piece of luggage was falling on top of him as he was struggling to lift the cart on the escalator," recalled Kayode. "Everyone was dying laughing."

Showalter saved the luggage and avoided taking a fall. He never thought twice about pushing a luggage cart as the head coach of the best U16–U17 players in the world—he was always willing to help. "Don will come into an event, and there will be 30 boxes that got delivered, and there will be two or three of us, and Don is one of those two or three, and he is cutting boxes open and pumping up the balls—moving this or that," said Andrea Travelstead, associate director of youth sport and development and Showalter's coworker at USAB.

Prior to the 2016 FIBA U17 World Cup in Spain, Showalter accepted a full-time position with USAB as coach development director. Travelstead noticed how Showalter brought a level of energy to the office. "He brings a youthful vibe to us. He makes us feel excited and appreciate where we are and what we are doing," said Travelstead. "He also brings a level of credibility to what we do. He is the most passionate person I have met about the sport of basketball."

Showalter's credibility is what attracted youth and sport development division director Jay Demings to hire Showalter in 2016. Demings leads USAB's youth development initiatives, including player development and coach education and safety. The Youth Division began in 2013. In 2015 Demings launched Coaches Academies, coaching clinics sprinkled around the US. "I was sort of the face of the Coaches Academies. We knew fairly quickly that that was going to have to change; we needed someone credible, qualified, who could stand up and be the voice," said Demings, who knew his limitations in terms of coaching experience and connections among coaches. "While they might call me back because my business card says 'USA Basketball,' they call [Showalter] back because he has built relationships for 40-plus years."

Showalter found a perfect fit in his new role with USAB, a chance to give back to the game with the backing of a well-respected organization in the basketball community. "He's come full circle from helping build the National Team program, coaching the junior national team to now coaching coaches," said National Team director Sean Ford. "In a way he is giving structure to the game for others. He's gone from a master coach to a master teacher of coaches."

When Showalter went full-time with USAB, the organization needed to create an exit plan from his role as head coach of the U16–U17 Junior National Team; all coaches for USAB have to be volunteers. Showalter would coach one more two-year cycle after the U17 World Cup in Spain. USAB didn't make the decision public.

THE 2016 U17 TEAM made it look easy. The roster, loaded with future college and NBA talent, was led by tournament MVP Collin Sexton. Sexton, who like Justise Winslow didn't make the U16 Team. Now he was a dominant player, leading the U17 team in points per game (17) and assists (4.2). USA ran through the preliminary round, scoring more than 100 points in two of the three games. They netted 109 against Argentina in the round of 16 and 133 against South Korea in the quarterfinals. They beat Lithuania 98–70 in the semifinals and Turkey 96–56 for the gold. For the tournament, the U.S. finished with a scoring average of 106.1 points per game.

Showalter shared his eighth gold medal with BJ Johnson. "We had a saying between us that it never gets old," said Johnson. The assistant national team director had been with him every summer. Sean Ford, the National Team director, never shared in the gold medal experience with Showalter at the event, but he called once or twice during competitions and always before the team traveled back. "The joy in his voice never changed, and it never got old—the winning," shared Ford. "Winning never became a relief for him."

USAB expected to win gold, and as Showalter kept winning with the U16–U17 team, that belief increased and the desire to keep the streak going became a conversation piece among the coaching staff. "You're afraid to fail. You don't want to be the first one to lose, screw this up," said Flannery. "[The pressure] is always there. We don't avoid it; we talk about it. As long as we're prepared, if we make them as good as they possibly could be, and strive to be perfect, we are going to be pretty hard to beat."

As the national team director, Sean Ford observed the pressure a coach faced across all the National Team programs. "There is an incredible amount of pressure that builds on a head coach as he is going into the gold medal games," said Ford. "They own it—their legacy." Even with an expectation to bring back a gold medal, Ford and USAB did not actually expect Showalter to win every game.

Ford even told Showalter at one point that he might lose a game, trying to relieve the pressure. Still, the expectation was there from those in the basketball community, and to maintain the high level of success was not easy. "It is a challenge to find ways to get better when you've been winning and you're considered good enough already," said Ford. "You are raising the bar every time you win, because people are figuring out ways to get closer to you and ways to get better."

At times Showalter's U16–U17 teams made it look easy, almost too easy, winning by 40, 50, 60, and even 70 points. The large margins of victory can create a perception that anyone can coach an elite group and win, but Mike Jones, who was an assistant under Showalter three different summers, had an insider perspective. "I know people look at the margin of victory," said Jones. "But if people knew the work that goes into it…. Each time has been incredibly difficult to prepare. The pressure of having that standard before you and you making sure that you take this group of kids that are very unpredictable and getting them to meet that standard each and every time is just amazing."

Not every game was a blowout, and one particular game—the gold medal game against Canada in the 2015 FIBA U16 Americas Tournament—put everyone on edge. The U16 team featured a balanced scoring attack with four players averaging double figures: future NBA talent in Gary Trent Jr. (16.8), Markus Howard (15.0), Wendell Carter Jr. (13.6), and Kevin Knox II (10.6). The team also featured Tre Jones, the brother of Tyus Jones, marking the first and only time Showalter coached two brothers with the U16–U17 teams.

In his seventh summer leading the U16–U17 team, Showalter held a high level of respect just when he walked in the room. The elite youth knew who he was; they respected his six gold medals and undefeated record. "They have such a high level of respect for him. It's almost like they are speaking to their father," said Sharman

White, a highly successful high school coach in Georgia, who assisted Showalter with the 2015 U16 team.

The rapport Showalter developed with the elite players before his current team, many of them now in the professional ranks, gave him street cred—they listened to what he had to say. The players knew he would help them get better. "He spoke to you how you would want to be coached," said Tre Jones. "Everyone knows how he coaches is how he is as a person. He keeps it real. He doesn't care what your ranking is in high school. He knows his basketball and he knows how to win, and he will do anything possible to win."

Showalter's confidence and the confidence he instilled in his players was tested against the Canadian squad, who they took too lightly after beating them in a friendly pretournament game. "We kind of put it to them," said White about the friendly game. "We won by more than 30 points. At the end of the day, I felt like our guys came out with their guard down a little bit."

When Canada led 23–3 early in the second quarter, Vicky thought, "This could be it. Maybe we are not going to win this game." White had the same feeling, except this was his first time working with the U16 team; he did not want it to end this way. "I was nervous because it was my scout," said White. "But [Show's] message was, 'Let's get it down to 10 to 12 points by halftime, and then we can go out and get it in the second half,' and he did it in such a calm manner." Ahead or down, Showalter stayed on an even keel. "His confidence in knowing whatever the situation is—whether we are up by 20 or down by 20," said Flannery. "We're going to keep the same body language and we are going to keep the same focus as far as what we need to accomplish."

The team listened and picked up their defensive intensity to cut the lead at the half to 37–27. But Canada continued to lead in the second half, up five early in the fourth quarter. In the low-scoring contest, Team USA turned to their defense to win the contest. They held Canada to four points in the last 8:25 of the game, while Gary Trent Jr., who scored all his 19 points in the second half, and the rest of his teammates netted 22 points for a 77–60 win. The streak remained intact—for now. Trent earned tournament MVP honors and Jones recorded a USAB U16 record of 19 steals in five games.

Even after USA pulled away late in the game, when the game ended, Don and BJ looked at Vicky. "I just burst into tears," recalled Vicky. With the win over Canada, the U16 team won the 2015 FIBA U16 Americas Tournament with a 5–0 record and left with a gold medal. If Showalter felt any pressure going for gold against Canada or the following year at the U17 World Cup in Spain, the pressure only increased as he began his final two-year run coaching the Junior National Team.

CHAPTER 23

Legacy

Jalen Suggs received the inbounds pass with 3.3 seconds left in overtime. He pushed the ball. On the third dribble, with one second left, he passed half-court, gathered himself, and released a running jump shot. The ball banked in. Suggs jumped on a courtside table and pumped his fist in celebration as his Gonzaga teammates mobbed him. The undefeated Bulldogs advanced to the national title game with a 93–90 victory over UCLA on April 3, 2021. It was an iconic shot, making Suggs an instant hero.

"[Suggs] is a kid that plays as hard as I have ever seen a kid play anything," said Scott Fitch, an assistant coach with the U16–U17 team in 2017–18. "There were times we had to just have a trainer watch him because we were afraid of him playing himself to exhaustion." Fitch recalled a four-minute stretch during a scrimmage at the 2018 U17 training camp when Suggs controlled the court. "He blocked a shot, made an incredible layup, got a steal and a dunk, then hit a half-court shot," said Fitch. "After four minutes, we were like, 'We can't not have him on the team; he's too valuable of a competitor.'"

Suggs joined a U17 roster loaded with talent, with nine of the players returning from the U16 gold medal–winning team at the 2017 FIBA U16 Americas Tournament in Formosa, Argentina, in which Suggs and his teammates stormed through the preliminary round games, beating Puerto Rico 110–69, the Dominican Republic

94–45, and Mexico 127–53. In the semifinals, USA topped the century mark again with 121 points in a victory over Argentina. Future 2022 NBA Rookie of the Year Scottie Barnes recorded a team-high 20 points and 6 steals. In the gold medal game, USA crossed the century mark one more time, netting 111 points in a 51-point win over Canada. Vernon Carey, the future Duke star, scored 19 points and added five rebounds and four assists to lead the effort.

After the gold medal ceremony, pictures with the media, and some time celebrating with fans, the players returned to the locker room. They went nuts; for many, this was their first gold medal. Showalter and the coaching staff joined the youth to share in the moment of jubilation and a little bit of relief. They had kept the streak going. Showalter gave them time to celebrate, but there was still a teachable moment with this team. Showalter gained their attention and offered a few closing words about their experience together, and then he asked each player to state something they had learned from their experience on the U16 team. "It's a powerful moment. Guys get emotional," said Fitch. The players expressed themselves; they were honored to have this opportunity. "To be picked as one of the top 12 players in the country, and to go play against the rest of the world, is a great honor," said Suggs. "It makes you feel real special. I never really lost that feeling."

With the postgame reflections over, it was time to celebrate, and for the USAB coaches and staff, that meant enjoying one last meal together in Argentina, which they all knew would include steak. In 2012, at the FIBA U17 World Cup in Mendoza, Argentina, Showalter learned just how good Argentinean steak could be. "We found a steak house and we ate there every night," recalled Kevin Sutton, who served as an assistant that summer. "The food was good. We got to the point where the owner walked up and sat us down and knew exactly how to cook Don's steak."

Anyone who shared a couple steak dinners with Showalter could place his order: a ribeye, medium, with mushrooms and a wedge salad. He did not care too much for vegetables; the wedge salad was to appease Vicky, as she wanted him to get more greens in his diet. "If the vegetables are touching the steak, he almost has to throw the steak away," laughed Demings. Because of Don's love of food, it became a running joke among the USA Basketball staff at the tournament and back home. "Our CEO, [Jim Tooley], might text me after a win and write, 'Well-done—tell Don he can have two desserts tonight,'" said Caroline Williams.

Coaches and friends wondered why Showalter did not gain more weight based on the number of calories he consumed. "He should weigh 450 pounds. He gets a dessert every time, and the meal takes about three hours," said Fitch. "But those are special moments where you are bonding and you don't even know it." Fitch, along with people in and outside of basketball over the years, realized time spent with Don is best spent in conversation over a meal. He enjoys the conversation. He wants to get to know you. Plus, his personality makes him easy to talk to. "He's an aw-shucks human being," said Mike Dunlap. "He just loves to have a good meal and a good yak, and he asks great questions."

Showalter's notoriety for his steak habit rivals the recognition he receives as a basketball coach. "I think he may love steak more than he loves basketball, but I could be wrong," laughed Kayode, who searched for the best steak houses when the team traveled. In 2017 Showalter had new steak houses to find in Formosa, Argentina, and another steak lover in assistant coach Stan Waterman to share in the fun. "We were out each night trying to top the night before. [We'd say,] 'There has got to be a better one than this or a better one than that,'" laughed Waterman.

Coaches and others revere Showalter's passion for basketball, his commitment to the game; people tease him good-naturedly for his love of steaks. But what amazes his friends is his energy. Tony Dorado travels extensively as head of high school basketball for Nike, evaluating players and meeting with sponsored high school programs. Dorado's travel is mostly domestic. Because Nike sponsors USA Basketball events, Showalter and Dorado often end up at the same coaching clinic or camp. Dorado's trip might be from Oregon and Showalter's from overseas. "He's addressing the coaches and coaching the coaches with the energy as if he had just slept 12 hours in Iowa," said Dorado. "I think his secret is sleep and steaks. Don will be the first to admit that he's asleep before the plane even takes off."

Wherever Showalter rests his head each night, either in Iowa or on an airplane, he still gets up the next morning ready to share his love of the game with youth or impart wisdom to coaches. On the day before Father's Day 2018, he slept in Colorado Springs, and the next morning, he ended the U17 training camp practice with a message for the young players.

THE COACHES AND PLAYERS grabbed each other's hands while forming the communication circle to end practice. The routine was the same, but this day was different—today was Father's Day. By now the players and coaches were comfortable enough with each other, so Showalter started with a personal question.

"Who is the father figure in your life, and why?"

"A lot of these kids don't have a father [in their lives], and it was great to hear who the figure was," said Fitch. "Then we talked about being a good father."

At one point during the communication circle, Showalter paused to share a story about his late father. He choked up. His father had passed away before Don coached one game for USA Basketball. He knew his father would be there watching, doing his best to travel and be in the stands; when in good health, he rarely missed a game Don played in or coached.

Don and Vicky and a few others knew: this was Don's last run, his final time coaching the U16–U17 team and probably the last time he coached in competition. Don and Vicky adjusted to Don's full-time job with USAB, moving to Colorado Springs but keeping a house in Iowa City. They planned to do more international travel, with many of the trips connected to basketball. Showalter retired from teaching and administration, he hung up his whistle as a high school coach, and soon he would finish his 10-year run leading the top U16–U17 players in the country. Yet no one expected him to retire from basketball, he still had too much to give.

THE U17 TEAM JOGGED off the floor in jubilation after winning the pretournament in Argentina. Showalter carried the first-place trophy toward Fitch, Waterman, and Kayode. As the team celebrated, the staff gathered outside the locker room, something they always did before entering, to converse and ensure they were on the same page with their postgame message. Showalter looked at the trophy in his hand.

"Do you think USA Basketball will care if I smash this?" Showalter asked his staff as he lifted the trophy in their direction. "I don't want these guys thinking we've made it; we have a long ways to go." Waterman, Fitch, and Kayode all looked at Showalter. No one knew the answer to this question or how best to respond. They affirmed his idea with passive agreement, a shrug of "I don't know" and "Go for it."

Showalter walked into the locker room. He grabbed the trophy with both hands and threw it to the floor. The trophy shattered and everyone went quiet, mouths agape. The moment was out of character for Showalter. The celebration turned sour.

"This trophy means nothing!" shouted Showalter. "We have not done anything yet!"

Then his voice softened. "This is nothing, but great job closing out the tournament. Let's go on to the real tournament." A smile crossed his face on the last sentence, and the players read the vibe and started laughing. He had made his point: time to move forward.

In a teachable moment, coming off the emotion of the game and realizing his team needed a boost, Showalter still paused. He checked with the assistant coaches. He confirmed with Samson. Although none of them had any idea if the top brass at USAB would care if Showalter smashed a trophy, Showalter took the time to consider the consequences. USA Basketball had meant so much to him, and he to them. He did not want to fracture the relationship.

"USA Basketball was great for Don, but I think Don was great for USA Basketball as well," said Fitch. "USA Basketball needed a guy that could get the buy-in and culture piece. They could have gotten a lot of great coaches that did not have that focus on culture, and it may not have gone as well." The confirmation from his staff gave him the momentum he needed to follow through, step out of his comfort zone, away from his usual postgame decorum. He wanted one more gold. So did the players, and so did USA Basketball.

THE USA TEAM DOMINATED each opponent in the preliminary round of the 2018 FIBA U17 World Cup in Argentina behind the play of Jalen Green and Scottie Barnes. Team USA entered the quarterfinals against Croatia poised to make a run for gold. They scorched the nets for a 126–52 win over Croatia, followed by a 120–71 victory over Canada. Green led them against Croatia with 27 points. In the semifinal win over Canada, Green scored 25 points and Scottie Barnes added 25 points and 4 assists.

Undefeated France awaited Showalter and his squad in the gold medal game. If they felt any pressure, they met it head-on. "I embraced the target on our back because I know we are going to come out and get everyone's best game," said Suggs. "For me being a competitor, that's the way I like it—I would not have it any other way."

Knowledge of this being Showalter's last game as the U16–U17 coach was limited to a select few. "He never mentioned it until the last night we were out and celebrating the gold medal and championship," said Waterman. Undefeated, with 61 straight wins and 9 gold medals, Vicky knew he needed to get this one. "As Don's wife, I wanted nothing more than for him to go undefeated—to finish up with 10 gold medals," said Vicky.

Within the first 10 minutes of the game, she could relax, as the U17 squad raced to a 23–14 advantage at the end of the first quarter. Jalen Green contributed five points in the early run. Showalter needed three more quarters to cement his legacy unscratched. Yet his legacy was already complete. Jay Bilas, who played for Coach K and observes and interacts with coaches in his role as a college basketball analyst for ESPN, considers Don one of the great coaches in the game. "He is one of the examples I use that great coaches aren't subject to levels," said Bilas. "It's not that the NBA has the best coaches or college has the best coaches. Don's been one of the iconic high school coaches in the game for years and has such a command of the game."

Showalter's knowledge of the game was unquestioned at this stage of his career, and the U17 team had command of the gold medal game, forcing turnovers and outrebounding France to take a 20-point lead into halftime. The fact that he was in this position seemed surreal. The high school coach from Iowa on the verge of 10 gold medals.

Green, Suggs, and their teammates were too much for France, as Team USA extended their lead in the third period and into the fourth. USAB knew they were losing Showalter as the U16–U17 coach, but his transition to a full-time position the past two years was exactly what they hoped for—Showalter is a coach for everybody: youth, elite talent, and the next generation of coaches. His voice resonates with those involved in the game of basketball, whether playing, coaching, or working behind the scenes in administration, management, or media. A gift he will continue to share with others in his role with USAB. "He has a preferable personality and style, and it translates to young people, it translates to his peers, it translates to younger coaches," said Jay Demings. "But it also translates to coaches and celebrity-level basketball coaches and general managers, because when they want to know something about a player and they want the truth—they go to Don and they get the truth."

With the game no longer in doubt, Showalter would win his 10th gold medal and finish his tenure coaching the U16–U17 team with a 62–0 record. As the game reached the final minute, Showalter glanced up and caught Vicky's eye. They shared a smile. This run was over, and another chapter in their lives was complete: Don forever the coach. Don and Vicky forever a team. Both ready for the next chapter.

Afterword

A few months after my last game coaching the U16–U17 team, Vicky and I walked the Ke'e Beach on the island of Kauai. Hawaii is our place. A place we go to vacation. At times Melissa and Brent, with their families, have joined us, but usually this is where we go to relax and rejuvenate—the one place we travel where basketball is not part of the trip. As we walk, we talk and reflect on the last 10 summers with USA Basketball, and we are still amazed by all of the experiences we have had with the players and coaches traveling the world. Our shared love for travel and my passion for basketball have given us many wonderful experiences together and with others over the years, on and off the court.

One of my favorite Mind Candy sayings is: "Success does not happen in a vacuum." I was fortunate to have some success coaching the game because so many people helped me along my journey. I grew up a country boy. I just loved the game of basketball and pursued all angles to stay a part of the game. My path in coaching is different from that of other coaches; we each have our own story. I hope that by reading my story, you found inspiration in pursuing your passions in life and understand the impact you can have on others when you share your passion with them.

Today I continue to share my love of basketball with coaches and athletes all over the world. For USA Basketball, I set up and direct

Coach Academies across the country, work with organizations to educate their coaches, and serve as a Junior National Team advisor, where I help scout the next generation of players and coaches for the U16–U19 teams.

Now in the latter part of my career, I enjoy being a mentor to the next generation of coaches. When I speak at coaching clinics or appear on a coaching podcast, I try to leave tips for young coaches. In closing, I leave you with five pieces of advice I often share with young coaches. I often preface each tip with the phrase, "I always tell young coaches…"

I always tell young coaches to be careful of destination addiction. Have the mindset that you are where you are supposed to be at the moment. Do a good job where you are. Nobody is going to ask you to pursue a job that is more difficult than the one you have. Work hard to improve your craft and validate yourself in the eyes of the people you are working for, and more opportunities will come your way.

I always tell young coaches to be available to take advantage of opportunities. Be willing to volunteer your services as a coach. Get involved with local, regional, and national organizations in coaching to grow your professional network. Take the initiative to pursue opportunities. Had it not been for that letter I wrote Coach Wooden, I don't think I would have had the opportunities I did later on with USA Basketball.

I always tell young coaches you are a much different person when you are coaching than when you are not coaching. Work on how you present yourself while coaching, but be who you are. Players trust you when who you are matches how you present yourself. Away from the court, wherever you go, the community views you as a leader. People will lose trust in you if you come off as someone you are not. Realize your role in the community while being the person people recognize as someone they can trust.

I always tell young coaches to know what they want to accomplish in their practice session. Plan your practice session to accomplish a specific goal, such as increasing competitive intensity or improving ball movement. Coaches need to be cognizant of setting a pace in practice that requires the players to move at game speed. Players will try to set the pace to their liking, but coaches need to set the pace, not the players.

I always tell young coaches the most important thing you have to do is bring passion and enthusiasm every day. Players don't have bad practices—coaches do. Your players will feed off what you do. When your players see you have the same enthusiasm and passion on a daily basis, it will rub off on them, which will drive your success.

—Don Showalter

Gold Lessons

Gold Lesson 1: Work Hard, Stay Humble, and Surround Yourself with Good People

"Be comfortable being uncomfortable." —Coach Show

I glance at my phone as the coaching staff and I wait in the dormitory lobby. At 3:00 AM, in unison, we each knock on doors and shout, "Get up! Time to rise!" Within a few seconds, teenagers appear, eyes squinted, brows furrowed, inquisitive expressions on their faces, curious about the early wake-up call. We hand them a piece of paper with no explanation.

We are in the middle of an eight-day training camp in preparation for the 2018 FIBA U17 World Championships in Argentina. The directions on the piece of paper state to be outside in the commons area by 3:10 AM in full workout gear. We meet the athletes in the commons area. A Navy SEAL named Pete Naschak joins us. Over the next four hours, Naschak takes the players through a series of activities to challenge their physical stamina and mental fortitude. He instills lessons about the importance of communication, teamwork, and caring for your teammates. After we break for breakfast, we reconvene for a debrief, where Naschak reiterates the key takeaways from the morning activities with personal stories that focus on hard work, staying humble, and surrounding yourself with good people.

As a coach, I deliberately teach the importance of hard work. For example, during a defensive drill, if an athlete displays increased intensity in rotating positions, taking a charge, or diving on the floor, I will acknowledge the effort immediately with verbal praise. I teach them to recognize when a teammate displays extra effort by clapping, cheering, or giving fist pounds. This purposeful approach instills a team atmosphere where hard work matters and players are rewarded for effort.

I understand the value athletes place on playing time; I may reward less skilled athletes for their work ethic with increased court time in an upcoming game but not at the expense of what is best for the team to achieve competitive success. By doing this, I acknowledge the athlete's work ethic while at the same time teaching another important lesson: although hard work often precedes success, it may not always lead to the outcome you are seeking; a less skilled athlete may work hard to become a starter, but this may not lead to his desired outcome.

Hard work is one part of the equation to achieve success and come together as a team. The other two components are to stay humble and surround yourself with good people. When an athlete has success, such as a career-high scoring night, it is important for him to demonstrate humility and appreciate his teammates' role in their achievement. An individual work ethic can only take athletes so far; they will need their teammates and coaches to achieve long-term success. Thus, it is important to surround yourself with good people. While athletes do not always get to select their teammates or coaches, they can select the people they associate with away from the court. During the Junior National Team selection process, we consider each athlete's personal attributes as much as their skill level—an approach that means the team is not always composed of the most talented 16- or 17-year-olds in the United States, as a few may not make the team.

Hard work can be uncomfortable, challenging, mundane, and time-consuming. But through hard work you become resilient and adaptable, and you learn to persevere. Furthermore, it can be difficult as a leader to be the person you want to be when those around you are either selfish or have goals that stray from the organization's goals. To implement the concepts of working hard, staying humble, and surrounding yourself with good people, consider the following **Gold Strategies**.

Grow others by celebrating and recognizing hard work. Do not assume that everyone knows how to work hard; you will need to demonstrate and teach what hard work looks like in what you do.

Optimize the work environment. Recognize those who contribute to your success or the success of others. When you or your subordinates reach an achievement, reflect on all the individuals involved in the accomplishment and take action to acknowledge their contributions.

Lead by placing good people around you. Use caution when hiring staff and consider what personal attributes they offer beyond their skill set.

Develop humility. Stay humble when your hard work pays off. Remember the role others played in helping you along the way.

Gold Lesson 2: Actions That Require Zero Talent

"These require zero talent: being on time, work ethic, effort, body language, energy, attitude, passion, and being coachable." —Coach Show

Beyond the daily physical practice sessions on the court, each day includes time in the classroom for mental preparation and personal growth.

We were about to begin our seventh practice session in four days. While the overall effort of the team had been good, and they were coming together as a group, I knew that each individual player could take more responsibility for his own development and thought this might be a good time to challenge them, individually, to be better. I entered the classroom and instructed the players to open their notebooks. They were familiar with this routine, as almost all the classroom sessions involved note-taking.

I instructed them to write down the following phrase: "These require zero talent: being on time, work ethic, effort, body language, energy, attitude, passion, and being coachable."

I repeated the phrase as they wrote, then continued, "There is no shortage of basketball talent in this room, but there are things you can do that require no talent, things you can control. For instance, **being on time** is just a matter of respect—respect for your teammates and coaches. Being on time shows you are a team player and not a selfish player. It takes no talent to be on time but shows respect for everyone."

I could tell they were attentive as they scribbled in their notebooks. "It takes no talent to work hard all the time. It only takes focus and concentration. Each of you can be known as a player who has a high **work ethic**. You can separate yourself from others by simply working hard. Work ethic and **effort** go hand in hand. Work ethic is a mindset. First decide that you are going to work hard, then put forth the effort in everything you do. For example, get rebounds out of your area, take charges, and get deflections on defense. Work ethic and effort require no talent, but when put with the elite talent each of you has, you become a special player. It is easy to be average but hard to be elite in all you do."

Then to emphasize the next point, I raised my voice: "There are other things you can control that take no talent. Did you know that people judge you who don't know you or have never talked to you?" This made them straighten up in their chairs; they were curious as to where I was going with this one.

"People judge you by your **body language**. It is not fair, but they do. Do you communicate to others with your body language a sense of entitlement when coached? Think about the message your body language sends when you are on the bench or after you come out of the game. In these moments, others judge you. It takes no talent to have great body language."

I paused to let the information sink in, then continued, "You can combine your work ethic and effort with body language to develop a sense of urgency or **energy** in how you approach your time on the basketball court. Create a vibe that you are here to work and get better. For example, give off a positive vibe on the court by controlling your emotions after a play that does not go your way and by celebrating the play of your teammates. Off the court, smile, engage in conversation, and show genuine interest in others."

The athletes nodded at me and continued writing. This point seemed to resonate with them immediately.

"Displaying and giving positive energy to others is a choice you make; you control this, and it is a reflection of your **attitude**. Like work ethic, your attitude is a mindset. How do you respond when a teammate does not catch your pass? Or when I or one of the other coaches gets on you for making a bad play or even when you make a good play?"

I could tell my questions were getting them thinking about their own actions. I continued, "Right now, think about how you can have an attitude of servitude toward your teammates and USA Basketball. It is not about you and how we at USA Basketball can help you. Yes, we are here to help you become a better player and grow as a person, but you are representing the United States of America. That name on your chest means you have a responsibility to think about how you can best represent our country in international competition. This means on and off the court. This starts with your attitude, and it takes no talent."

I noticed the players had stopped writing and were just listening to my last point.

"Every team before you has done this; each player learned to recognize that the team and representing the USA are bigger than themselves. That is what playing for USA Basketball is all about."

I could have ended the meeting right there but wanted to lead them into the next practice session by finishing the lesson.

"**Passion** is real love for what you are doing. When you love something, there is a natural tendency for you to display this through your actions. Yet at times we hold back. Be genuine, be enthusiastic, and share your love for basketball with us. This relates back to your work ethic, your effort, and bringing a sense of urgency or energy to how you play each day."

By now many of the team members were fidgeting in their seats as their effort to stay focused began to wane. I picked up the cadence of my speech: "All of you have done a great job of listening for the last 20 minutes. Your concentration here in the classroom is a great example of **being coachable**. You make a choice to be coachable. Being coachable is really the sum of everything we have talked about."

I told them, "Look at what you have written down and recognize how each of these actions can give you a competitive edge." As a leader, think about how you can get better by taking actions that require zero talent. While the concepts I teach are related to basketball, many of the same concepts apply to the setting you work in. To help you implement actions that require zero talent in your personal or professional life, consider the following **Gold Strategies**.

Grow personally and professionally by focusing on what you can control. Each of the actions that require zero talent is within your control, choices you can make each day.

Optimize your interactions with others by reflecting on how your attitude and body language impact those you lead.

Lead by example. Make it a habit to be on time for events and meetings. Do not hold back; share your passion for your craft. Be coachable by accepting feedback from those with more experience or knowledge.

Demonstrate effort and energy in the leadership of your organization or team. Combine this enthusiasm with a strong work ethic.

Gold Lesson 3: Culture Supersedes Success

"As a coach you should strive to give your players an
opportunity to love the game." —Coach Show

The ball spins off the rim. Two hands, belonging to a 17-year-old phenom, reach high above the rim to secure the ball. As his feet return to the floor, he reels into a forward pivot. With the ball still above his head, his wrists snap. The ball sails, like it's on a string, right to his teammate, who is already making his way up the floor. The other team retreats on defense. The offensive players start to fill their lanes in anticipation of a fast-break bucket. One defender lags behind. After two forward passes, the offensive team scores a 10-foot bank shot. I immediately blow my whistle and shout in the direction of one of my assistant coaches, "Get him out!"

I turn toward the players on the court, my voice raised so all our players in the gym can hear me. "If you don't sprint back on defense, you are coming out. To stay on the court, you have to give your best effort on every play. We play hard on every possession. Remember our Gold Standards."

We continue the scrimmage for a few more minutes. Then I call everyone together and conclude the morning session. We are in the second day of a two-day minicamp in Colorado Springs to evaluate and develop elite basketball talent for the Junior National Team.

We put the participants through a variety of drills to improve their fundamental basketball skills, exposing the players to the culture of USA Basketball by teaching and reinforcing the USA Basketball Gold Standards. As the players head toward the cafeteria, I walk over to a coach sitting near the sideline. He is a high school teacher and coach in his early 30s. Through an acquaintance he reached out to me and asked if he could attend the minicamp, observe, and take notes.

I take a seat next to him. "Looks like you are taking a lot of notes."

"This is great," responds the coach. "Thanks for letting me come. What are the Gold Standards?"

"Coach Krzyzewski established the 15 Gold Standards with the USA Olympic gold medal team members in 2008. The Gold Standards are simple, such as 'No excuses' and 'Hard work.' But how we describe and use them to hold each other accountable is what is important. We use the Gold Standards to help establish culture."

The coach nods and asks, "How do you establish your own standards and culture as a coach?"

"First, culture is how you do things. Over time how you do things becomes a habit. The habits displayed by everyone involved define your culture. You need to decide what is important to you as a coach. What are your nonnegotiables? Your nonnegotiables become your standards. For me, sprinting back on defense is nonnegotiable. It does not take any talent to sprint back on defense, only effort. If players are lazy getting back, they violate our team standard to work hard on every possession."

I continue, "We talk about the Gold Standards in team meetings and reinforce them on the court. Even though the players buy into the culture, we still have to fight for our culture every day, and this takes communication. Also, you have to hold your best players accountable to the team standards or it won't work."

As I stand up to catch up with our coaching staff for lunch, I leave the coach with one more piece of advice. "In sport, sometimes coaches think of culture and team chemistry as the same thing; they're not. Chemistry is how kids relate to each other. Culture is how they behave together for a common good. You may have a good team, and players on that team have fond memories of their time together; that's chemistry. You know when you have a good culture if players can reflect back on their time with you and remember what the expectations were, the standards you held them too."

As a coach, I create culture by reinforcing what is important to me (my nonnegotiables) through standards that align with the core values (Gold Standards) of the organization I work for (USA Basketball). Thus, the actions taken by our coaching staff in the short term (at the minicamp) will impact the long-term success of the organization (USA Basketball) in international competition.

To help you establish a culture for success using standards to guide you, consider the following **Gold Strategies**.

Gain the trust of those you lead by holding your most talented player or employee to each standard. If you don't, then the standards do not mean anything and they will be ineffective.

Organize situations to teach your standards. Utilize meetings, events, and individual conversations to share and reinforce the importance of striving to meet your expectations. Help those you lead to develop daily habits, based on the standards, for long-term success.

Lead by communicating the team, group, or organizational standards in all settings. Introduce, remind, and reinforce your standards on a consistent basis.

Develop a list of nonnegotiables. What is important to you as a leader? What will you hold others accountable for? What behaviors need to be exhibited by the team, group, or organization to achieve success? Adapt your list of nonnegotiables into shared standards and align them with the core values of the organization or institution you work for.

Gold Lesson 4: End on a Positive

"When you coach your team, your goal is never to win a game;
that is your objective. Your goal is to develop the players you have
into young men who are a real plus to society and become great
dads, spouses, and leaders in the community." —Coach Show

"Let's form our circle," I say to the nation's best young talent as we finish practice.

I step back and present my hands to the two players nearest me. As each player grasps a hand, I shuffle backward. The entire group of athletes and coaches on the court follows my lead to form a large circle, each player linked to another player or coach, facing each other. I turn to a tall, slender 16-year-old and say, "Share one thing that the teammate to your right did in practice today that made the team better."

The young athlete pauses, gathers his thoughts, then states, "I like how my teammate dove on the floor for a loose ball. That really picked up the intensity of our practice." The circle continues as each player and coach recognizes another member of the team by sharing something positive that occurred during practice. I call this the Communication Circle, and we use it each day to end practice. The questions are never the same, and over time they become more personal, such as, "Tell us something about yourself we do not know."

The purpose is to generate interaction and open up communication channels for relationship-building. The Junior National Team features athletes from all over the US. While some members of the team may know each other from travel team competitions, this is the first time they have been together as one group. By finishing practice with the Communication Circle, I provide a positive way to end our time together.

I understand that not every moment is positive, but I still strive to end each interaction with others in a positive manner. As a coach this might mean I control my emotions after a tough loss or provide feedback that focuses on skill improvement when correcting an athlete's technique or behavior. Off the court, I might offer positive words of encouragement at the end of a conversation or conclude a staff meeting by highlighting the good work everyone is doing.

Making an effort to end on a positive does not mean you abandon discipline or avoid exerting your position power to motivate and teach an important lesson. If you keep your focus on ending communication in a positive manner, you will likely diminish the need to exercise your position power and generate more positive feelings about you as a leader, opening the door for effective relationship-building. Consider how you will interact with your staff during meetings, one-on-one conversations, and collaboration projects. Within these small daily interactions, how can you leave everyone feeling more upbeat, confident, and connected to each other?

Use the following **Gold Strategies** to help you end on a positive:

Generate a list of daily activities where you interact with those you lead (meetings, corporate events, individual conversations, etc.), then determine how you can end these interactions on a positive.

Optimize current relationships by reflecting on how well you are relating to those you lead. Be honest with your self-assessment. Then consider how you can end with a positive interaction to build better relationships.

Learn to reflect on your interactions with others. Then adapt to end more interactions in a positive manner.

Develop activities to implement at the end of group interactions. This could be a onetime activity or a repeated activity such as the Communication Circle.

Gold Lesson 5: It's Not What You Teach but How You Teach It

"Players don't care how much you know; they care how you can help them get better." —Coach Show

Early in the training camp in preparation for the 2017 FIBA U17 World Cup, I implemented one of my favorite drills: Cutthroat, a four-on-four live scrimmage situation used to develop both offensive and defensive skills. I discovered that Cutthroat increases the intensity level of practice and helps the elite athletes gel in a short period of time. How I use Cutthroat demonstrates one of the lessons I learned about leadership that I use as a coach: It's not what you teach but how you teach it.

Cutthroat is a structured drill with set rules. In other words, Cutthroat is *what I am going to teach. How I teach* Cutthroat will determine if the players improve their skills and their ability to work as a team. I apply the three basic rules of Cutthroat: catch and square, move after a pass, and thank the passer when you score. I add additional rules to improve ball movement. For instance, I might limit each player to two dribbles after they catch the ball or require the offensive team to pass the ball three times before attempting to score. In this example, I teach Cutthroat (the what) to improve ball movement by modifying the basic structure of the drill (the how). This creates a learning environment that accomplishes our objective to work better as a team.

This same concept applies outside of sport. For example, with the rise in social media marketing over the past decade, organizations have identified the need to hire new talent or train current employees in promotional methods related to social media. In training employees, the social media marketing skills are *what you teach*; the manner in which the training improves the employee's social media marketing skills related to the organization's purpose is *how you teach it.*

To implement this approach as a leader, consider the following **Gold Strategies**.

Guide the training and teaching process for improved performance. Take an active role in how skills are taught to those under your guidance.

Organize what you are going to teach first. Then maximize your time and effort by planning instruction in a manner that meets the needs of your organization or team.

Learn new methods and strategies to teach skills. Make a list of the current skills you are teaching to others and consider how a different approach might be more effective in reaching your objective.

Develop a method to assess the effectiveness of your teaching or training program. Step back and reflect on your approach, then adapt your approach as needed.

Gold Lesson 6: The Four C's That Separate Talent

"Nothing ever grows in your comfort zone." —Coach Show

A selection to the Junior National Team is an honor—the end result of an ongoing talent evaluation through events organized by USA Basketball, such as our minicamps and training camps, in addition to talent evaluation during AAU tournaments and high school games. In the talent-evaluation process, I work closely with our national team director, assistant director, and the rest of USA Basketball's talent evaluators. When observing players, I employ my five pillars of player talent evaluation, or as I like to call it, a player's DNA: smart, tough, skilled, versatile, and resilient.

A **smart** player demonstrates a high basketball IQ. They know the proper spacing and angles on the court, can read what the defense is doing, and understand time and score situations. **Toughness** is a hard quality to describe; a coach knows it when they see it. Often a tough player will make big plays in the game, such as hitting a tough shot, or actions that might go unnoticed by a fan, such as stopping a good offensive player's favorite move. When evaluating a player's **skill** level, I focus on a player's ability to execute the eight basic skills of basketball: shooting, ball handling/dribbling, screening, rebounding, passing, balance/footwork, whole offense, and whole defense. A **versatile** player is one who can play multiple positions. For example, does a player have the ball-handling skills to move from a wing position to a point guard role, or from the low post out to a wing? To evaluate **resilience**, I observe a player's ability to

283

overcome a mistake or a series of miscues. Can he move on to the next play?

Undoubtedly, the United States has the most talented roster, player for player, in the World Championships; we expect to come home with a gold medal. I know this, but I also know my responsibility to USA Basketball goes beyond winning gold; I need to develop young men—elite-level basketball players—to best represent the United States in international competition.

During our time together with the athletes, our entire coaching staff challenges them to be better. The Junior National Team players know they are talented, at the top of their class in the country. Still, we need to make sure they understand how they can separate themselves from others. To do this, we teach them the four C's that separate talent—actions they can take to gain an edge in sport and in life: making good **choices**, **communicating** expectations, developing a **competitive** mindset, and getting out of their **comfort** zone.

Making good **choices**. In practice, we utilize drills that require players to make decisions; I want them to learn how to think on the court. For example, in a four-on-five drill, four offensive players go against five defensive players. The offensive players must make a decision about who is open. Point guard Jeremy Roach, a U17 player in 2018, demonstrated making good choices on the court. He knew when to make the extra pass or who to get the ball to when our team needed a bucket. He also adjusted to the flow of the game, knowing when to push the ball and when to control the tempo. We also teach making good choices off the court. I remind players they will make choices every day; choices that could impact the rest of their lives, such as whom they choose to hang out with or simpler choices that could have an impact on their next performance, such as what type of food to eat.

Communication. I always end practice with the Communication Circle (see Gold Lesson 4). This helps to improve team chemistry and establish an environment where individuals can gain their voice as leaders, confidence to help them communicate with their teammates and coaches. Forward Scottie Barnes, the 2022 NBA Rookie of the Year, found his leadership voice with our U17 team in 2018. Never bashful to lead a drill or be the first one in line, Scottie bought into his leadership role not only by being vocal but also through his ability to lead on the court with his work ethic and being the first in line for drill work. I never had to worry about our team being able to buy into what we were doing, as Scottie made sure this happened; he often started the Communication Circle after practice.

Competitive mindset. I cultivate a competitive mindset by building competition into practice. For example, I might pair certain players together, knowing it will make each player compete harder, or I use highly competitive drills such as Cutthroat (see Gold Lesson 5) and create time and score situations within drills and scrimmages to mimic game-like conditions. We knew as a coaching staff that Jalen Suggs's competitive mindset was already a part of his basketball DNA before he joined the Junior National Team. Suggs, the fifth overall pick in the 2021 draft, combines all five pillars: a high basketball IQ, an ability to hit the big shot, he can execute all eight of the basic skills, play more than one position, and he bounces back from an error or poor play with an intense desire to win. I believe the competitive mindset Suggs displays is part nature—he was born with it—and part nurture, cultivated under the influence of his youth coaches and his competitive experiences.

Comfort zone. One of my favorite sayings is, "Nothing ever grows in your comfort zone." I challenge our players on the court using various drills to make them uncomfortable. For example, we use a lot of disadvantage-advantage drills, such as four-on-five. We establish goals such as making a certain number of shots in a specific time period or keeping track of turnovers in a drill. There are consequences for failing to accomplish the goal. This approach keeps them out of their comfort zone because they have to strive for something.

NBA scouts from all 30 teams will call me asking for my analysis of the players I have coached. When I talk to the scouts, they know each player's basketball skills and have a good idea what their basketball DNA is. What they really want to know are the traits and habits that are more difficult to observe—actions that separate talent, such as the 4 C's.

To gain an edge in your personal and professional life, consider the following **Gold Strategies**:

Get outside your comfort zone by challenging yourself to try new things. This might be dining at a new place for lunch, using a new form of transportation to get to work, or trying something for the first time, such as zip-lining. Look for new opportunities at work or outside of work that challenge your established skills and allow you to meet new people.

Open up to communicate better with others. Seek opportunities to better understand the people you work with to gain confidence and find your leadership voice within the group.

Learn what the standard of excellence is for the important tasks in your professional field. Then make choices with your personal lifestyle, the people you interact with, and in how you communicate with others to meet the standard.

Develop your competitive mindset by seeking opportunities to compete. In professional settings, develop a system or approach to evaluate your progress in key areas where you are competing with others, such as sales numbers, employee retention, or in meeting safety standards (number of days without an accident).

Gold Lesson 7: Do a Good Job Where You Are

*"Nobody is going to ask you to pursue a more difficult job
than the one you currently have." —Coach Show*

James McAdoo's bucket late in the second quarter helped ignite a
12–0 run, stretching our lead to 58–41 over Poland at the halftime
break. We finished with a 111–80 gold medal victory and an 8–0
record in the 2010 FIBA U17 World Championship in Germany.
I thought my two-year role coaching the Junior National Team had
ended.

I had proved I could lead elite talent to victory. Before our gold
medal run in Germany, my first U16 team went 5–0 and earned a
gold medal in the FIBA Americas U16 Championship in Argentina.
Would winning be enough to keep me in the role? I could not
change my past experiences or how they stacked up in the eyes of
others; all I could control was the job I had before me. I appreciated
the opportunity given to me by USA Basketball: to work with the
best of the best. I knew I needed to give my greatest effort and focus
on the task before me. My approach seemed to resonate with the
young, elite talent, including future NBA All-Star Bradley Beal.

"Coach Showalter was really vocal, and he really pushed us in
all of our practices and our games," said Bradley Beal in an interview
with USA Basketball following the gold medal game. "He wanted
the best for us on and off the court, and he really challenged us every
day we hit the floor. Having his leadership and dedication to being
the best really made us want to push ourselves."

Beal's sentiments on my effectiveness as his coach aligned with
how I worked with my high school teams; it was not about what we

287

did but how we did it. Our coaching staff challenged players to get better, and we showed them we cared about them. In the process, we earned their trust. "[Coach Show] created structure, and he let us play. That really showed that he trusted in us and believed in us," said future NBA player and U16 co-captain James McAdoo in an interview with USA Basketball. "He was a great example for us on and off the court, because most of the time we spent with him was off the court."

I think that USA Basketball felt that keeping me on as the Junior National Team coach would be good for consistency. I think I earned the opportunity to return as coach, by doing a good job where I was. My entire coaching career was based on doing a good job where I was, a behavior modeled and communicated to me by my father, working on the family farm. My father gave me a job to do, and I had to do it a certain way before I could go play. This habit stayed with me and became the approach I took at each of my coaching stops.

There is a reward benefit to doing a good job. At a minimum you feel a sense of accomplishment, and it builds your confidence. But doing a good job can also advance your career and help you acquire new opportunities. Use the following **Gold Strategies** to help you focus on doing a good job where you are for professional success:

Give your full attention to the task you are working on. Stay focused in the moment. The moment might be five minutes to send an important email or a full day to complete a project.

Operate with the mindset that your current job is your first priority in your professional life. Plan each day around the most important tasks vital to your current job first. Avoid the temptation to engage in tasks outside your role until the most important tasks are complete.

Learn what is "good work," or the standard of excellence on a particular task or in your role as a professional. Then work on the skills you need to do that good work.

Do your best work, and do it on time. Strive to give your best effort on even the smallest tasks in your job. Then make a commitment to completing tasks on time to develop trust with those with whom you work. People will notice the quality of your work and your ability to meet deadlines.

Gold Lesson 8: Success Is the Sum of Repeated Effort Each Day

"Be practice-ready—set the pace of action when teaching others." —Coach Show

During one of our prepractice sessions before we take the floor—a time reserved to prepare our athletes mentally for the upcoming practice and reinforce the culture of USA Basketball—I open with our daily Mind Candy: "For us to win the gold medal we need to be three things: unselfish, smart, and aggressive." I have each of them write what each word means to them and why they think it is important for our team.

Mind Candy is a short phrase I implement each day in practice. The phrase can provide inspiration or reinforce team standards. In this prepractice classroom session, I ask questions to reinforce the concepts we are covering. This leads to a conversation among the players and the coaching staff about how they each can do better to make the team better. By opening each practice with Mind Candy, we establish a consistent daily routine, a repeated effort each day to get better.

We reinforce Mind Candy on the practice floor. In this example, the coaching staff will praise unselfish, smart, and aggressive play while correcting self-seeking, sloppy, or nonassertive play. It is not uncommon for a coach to stop practice and recognize when a player is unselfish, and then relate it back to our prepractice Mind Candy conversation.

Mind Candy is one example of a repeated measure I include each day during a practice session. I structure practices to encourage repetition by running the same drills each day, such as footwork drills, a combination of jump stops and pivots, and the Texas Drill, a full-court drill incorporating speed dribble layups, jump shots, the perfect layup, and a five-ball combination layup/jump shot drill. While it is important to adapt as a coach and include variety in practice sessions, I find the benefits of repeated efforts each day during a two-week training camp include individual athlete improvement and the ability of the team to come together in a short period of time.

The repeated measures you use are determined when preparing your practice. I am meticulous in practice preparation, spending up to 90 minutes preparing the next session. The focus of my planning centers around one question: What do I want to accomplish in this practice? My practice preparation routine makes me practice-ready—organized and focused before we start practice—and helps me develop the pace of practice: the flow and transition between drills and instruction.

To establish routines and to build repetition for long-term success in your personal life and in leading others, consider the following **Gold Strategies**:

Grow others (those you lead) by establishing daily routines in the workplace to develop their skills. Provide feedback during the repetition of the routines and remind them to be patient, as they may not see immediate progress from a previous day; success will happen with the accumulation of small efforts. As they improve, so will your team or organization.

Organize and maximize your time by implementing little things you can do and repeat day in and day out—small daily activities that challenge you to be better. Over time, the daily repetition of the activities will lead to new habits.

Lead by modeling consistent behavior. Stay the course with the new daily habits you are forming. Those you lead will notice your preparation, organization, and focus.

Develop Mind Candy. Establish a consistent method or activity to begin group meetings. The new approach should align with and reinforce the organization's core values, purpose, and mission.

Gold Lesson 9: You Never Graduate from a Skill

"No matter how good you are at something, you can always refresh the skill." —Coach Show

All the players are elite physically—men in boys' bodies; are skilled in the fundamentals, such as shooting, dribbling, and passing; and are savvy in how they play the game, understanding player spacing, court angles, and clock management. Yet the minicamps and training camps give the coaching staff a chance to evaluate the athletes on behaviors that require zero talent, such as being on time, work ethic, effort, body language, energy, attitude, passion, and being coachable (see Gold Lesson 2).

In a basic footwork drill, the actions that require zero talent are on full display. The footwork drill, by design, is elementary but is an important foundational element all basketball players need to master. In all likelihood, the first time the drill is introduced at the camp, a few players probably question it. I know this might happen, and in the team meeting before practice, I prep them for it by explaining to them that the repetition of fundamental basketball is important in being the best player you can be. No matter how good you are at something, you can always refresh that skill—you never graduate from a skill.

To reinforce this concept, I share an example of an NBA player, one of the greatest shooters in basketball history, a player all the athletes recognize: Steph Curry. I tell them, "Steph's ability to shoot the basketball is years in the making, hours of repetition and focused practice. Curry is so good at shooting, you could say he has mastered the skill. Yet he finishes every practice by making 500 shots. He continues to practice and refresh his shooting skills. As good as he is, Steph has not graduated from the skill of shooting."

You need to continue practicing the skills you are good at. The refreshing of acquired skills relates to any professional field. For example: public speaking. Even if you are comfortable in front of a group, have good voice inflection, and can communicate a good message through storytelling, you can still work on your craft; you can practice your delivery and refresh the skill, even if you have told the story a dozen times.

Use the following **Gold Strategies** to help you refresh your skills and the skills of those you lead:

Generate a list of skills needed in your chosen field. Next, reflect on your ability to perform the skills listed. Then refresh the skills by determining a method to practice them. Finally, set aside time to practice the skills.

Orient the learning environment you manage to focus on refreshing established skills. Provide time for those you lead to practice skills that will enhance their professional as well as personal growth.

Launch a long-term commitment to lifelong learning that includes time to refresh skills you already know how to do.

Display the skills everyone needs to execute for the organization or team to be successful. Post the skills in a place for all to see. Then develop training programs that focus on repetition and opportunities to refresh the skills listed.

Gold Lesson 10: The Five Pillars of a Good Coach

"If you put others first, this is the sign of being a great leader." —Coach Show

Basketball coaches of all ages and competitive levels have converged for a USA Basketball Coach Academy. This is the fifth of our eight Coaching Academies sprinkled across eight major US cities over a five-month period. A USA Basketball Coach Academy is a coaching clinic featuring a lineup of speakers; coaches from high school through the professional ranks speak on a variety of topics related to teaching the game, connecting with athletes, and dealing with off-court issues.

In my role for USA Basketball, I invite the speakers and I attend every academy and speak at one of the sessions. In this particular session, titled "A Coach's DNA," I am sharing my five pillars of a good coach. I finish my session by providing a quick summary of the five pillars.

"First, you must be a **teacher** and know the laws of learning: a five-step process that involves providing a description, demonstration, repetition, correction (feedback), and repetition. Second, it is important to be **authentic**, as players trust coaches who are genuine. Be yourself as a coach, as your athletes will pick up on behaviors that do not align with your personality or characteristics. Third, be **organized** in your thoughts and how you conduct your practices; develop a consistency to how you do things to provide for efficiency and better communication. Next, stay **humble**. Remember how former NBA coach Jeff Van Gundy classified the two types of coaches: those who are humble and those who will be humbled. Last, be **adaptable**. Good coaches adapt to circumstances they face."

I open it up for questions.

A hand from a young coach in the front row jets up, and I acknowledge her enthusiasm. "How did you improve as a teacher throughout your career?" she asks.

"First, I had great mentors. They taught me *how* to teach beyond just *what* to teach. To be able to bounce things off someone who has experience is invaluable. Second, I attended clinics every year I was coaching. This was necessary to improve my craft and learn. Then I worked many basketball camps and learned how to teach skills to players."

A young coach, bedecked in his school's colors, gets my attention for the next question. "How did you develop trust with the elite level players in a short amount of time?" he asks.

"Developing trust starts with building a relationship with the players. Be honest with players. Never make promises to players you can't keep, such as playing time or starting games. Trust also comes from the hard work by the coach to make each player better and the team better. Players want to see the coach work hard to make them better. This develops great trust."

I call on a middle-aged woman, her hand slightly raised. "If you are not an organized person, or tend to be disorganized, what strategies do you have for that, Coach?" she asks, pointing at herself with a wide grin.

"Get in the habit of being a list-maker. This keeps you organized with what you want to do, plus being able to check things off your list is a confidence builder for you. Do a new list every day. Start with the first item on your list, the one thing you have put off or you dread getting done—making a difficult phone call—and do this first. Don't get concerned if you don't get all the list items completed; just add them to the list for tomorrow."

An older coach from a previous coaching academy sitting in the back row raises his hand. "It sounds good to strive to be humble, but what challenges have you faced or might a coach face in trying to stay humble?" he asks.

"First, being a nice person and recognizing others is a sign of humility. Second, being humble is a decision you make; you have the ability to put others first and recognize that success does not happen only by your own efforts. The challenge in staying humble is when you start having success or getting recognized. This is where a good mentor can be a great asset for you. A mentor can keep you humble, as they notice when you become too prideful in your accomplishments. Putting others first is the sign of being a great leader."

With time for one more question, I call on a coach who is in his first year coaching after a collegiate playing career. "Is there a circumstance you faced early in your coaching career where you wished you would have been more adaptable?" he asks. "And as a second question: How did you continue to adapt throughout your coaching career?"

"Early on I was not very adaptable in many game situations—for example, adjusting to various defenses—so my teams, at times, did not adjust well. Early in my career, it was what I did not know that hurt me from being adaptable. Acquiring more basketball knowledge by attending clinics and working camps helped me become adaptable to game situations. Off the court, I let the players decide anything that really makes no difference to me: what to wear on game day, shoes to wear, where to eat, etc."

While my presentation "A Coach's DNA" was created for basketball coaches, the five pillars can be applied in other leadership roles. Use the following **Gold Strategies** to apply the five pillars in your professional or personal life.

Give yourself to others by putting them first. There is no greater way to lead than to acknowledge others who have contributed to your success, and there is no greater way to build professional and personal relationships than by recognizing others for their accomplishments.

Optimize the laws of learning for your own professional growth, especially as it relates to repetition and feedback. Practice the skills you need to be successful in your profession and seek feedback from others more knowledgeable than you to help you improve. Then repeat your practice sessions.

Learn to adapt. As a leader you must expect change. You will work with different people and work for different people. How you do things in your industry will change due to technology, consumer interests, the economic climate, etc. Your knowledge of the upcoming changes in your industry will help you stay relevant and up-to-date with current issues and trends, an important attribute for connecting with those you lead.

Demonstrate authenticity. Be yourself and be your best self. Take what you observe and learn from the leaders and mentors you admire. Avoid mimicking their style. Instead, notice which behaviors they demonstrate that positively impact others the most.

Acknowledgments

Acknowledgments (Don Showalter)

When Pete Van Mullem mentioned that he would like to write a book about my story, I could not envision how this would be interesting to anyone outside my own immediate family. The story line came together with much hard work and interviews by Pete with former players, administrators, assistant coaches, other coaches, family, and friends. These interviews rekindled great memories for me; my former players sharing events with Pete that had completely slipped my mind but were important to each of them was a joy to read. Thank you, Pete, for your patience and dedication in putting these interviews together for the book.

A special thank-you to my wife, Vicky, and my daughter, Melissa, and my son, Brent, for their help in putting my story together. A big thank-you to Chris Kern, Dave Schlabaugh, Bud Bender, Wayne Mager, Kelby Bender, Steve Brower, and Tyler Griffith for your loyalty as assistant coaches who were a huge part of my 42 years of Iowa high school coaching.

This would not be a story without mentioning the outstanding individuals I work with at USA Basketball. Thank you to CEO Jim Tooley and senior men's director Sean Ford for showing faith in the abilities of a small-town coach to coach the elite youth players for 10 years. I hope 10 gold medals and a 62–0 record was a good trade-off for allowing me to coach. Working with the junior men's directors

BJ Johnson, Samson Kayode, and Doc Parris provided some great stories on our trips to Germany, Argentina, Dubai, Uruguay, Mexico, Lithuania, and Spain.

My sincere thanks to all the players at Lone Tree, Elkader Central, Mid-Prairie, and Iowa City High for giving me joy every day at practice and games. Each of you played a huge role in my coaching career. Not many people can say there is a book published about their life story. I am humbled that Pete (my coauthor), Rita Rosenkranz (our literary agent), and the staff and editors at Triumph Books believed in the project. I hope those who read it will be able to learn from my story and the lessons shared in the book.

Acknowledgments (Pete Van Mullem)

I met Don Showalter in the spring of 2005 at a coaching clinic I was hosting. He agreed to speak for no remuneration, making the 327-mile drive from Wellman, Iowa, to Ottawa, Kansas—an act that hinted at his passion for basketball and willingness to share it with others. At that moment, I never imagined that 15 years later I would begin writing his life story, a tale centered on that same passion for basketball and a commitment to share the game with others. In writing this book, I reflected on the coaches I played for, each teaching me life lessons I take with me still today. I reflected on the coaches I worked with, great mentors who changed my life. I would not go back and trade any of those experiences, but if I were still coaching today, I would strive to coach and lead like Don Showalter. I am honored and grateful to have had the privilege to be the writer for his story.

A sincere appreciation to more than 150 coaches, athletes, teammates, extended family members, community members, and colleagues who agreed to sit for an interview, providing important context to Coach Show's personal reflections. Their contributions made the story come together. A special thank-you to Vicky Showalter for her time reading drafts to fact-check and provide accuracy to the family history; Iva Showalter, Don's mom, for candid reflections of raising Don and his four siblings and for penning her memoir, a valuable resource to assist in constructing Don's childhood; Bob Garms, the former longtime athletic director at Central Elkader, for connecting me with former players and providing resources on the history of Elkader, Iowa, and the Central Elkader athletics programs; Chris Kern, Coach Showalter's assistant coach for 26 seasons, for tracking down interview subjects, making time for multiple conversations, and sharing materials to support the history of the Mid-Prairie basketball program; Gerry Beeler, the former principal at Mid-Prairie High, for providing access to historical information about the Wellman-Kalona community; and Sean Ford, Don's colleague at USA Basketball, for firsthand insights on the development of the Junior National Team.

Thank you to our literary agent, Rita Rosenkranz, for securing the right publisher for this book. At Triumph Books, editor Jeff Fedotin set us along the right path in meeting the publication timeline, and our project manager, Katy Sprinkel Morreau, took the reins the rest of the way. Finally, this book would not have happened without the support of my family. My spouse, Heather, lent her ear thoughtfully throughout the project, a consistent voice reassuring the book was on the right path. My three children—Lily, Ali, and Henry—showed patience and provided the right diversions at precise moments when I needed to stay away from the keyboard.

Sources

Books

Camp with Coach Wooden, Greg Hayes
Chuck Taylor, All Star, Abraham Aamidor
Collection of Memories, Iva Showalter
Maplecrest Turkey Farms, Inc.: A. C. Gingerich and the Turkey Industry in Wellman, Iowa, Gordon W. Miller
Mid-Prairie Golden Hawk Basketball 2012–13
The Only Dance in Iowa, Max McElwain
Opening a Window to the World, Franklin L. Yoder
The Rise and Reign of Mike Krzyzewski, Ian O'Connor

Newspapers, Periodicals, and Radio

Associated Press
Burlington Hawk Eye
Cedar Falls Courier
Cedar Rapids Gazette
Clayton County Register
Daily Iowan
Dayton Daily News
Des Moines Register
Iowa City Press-Citizen
Iowa History Journal
Kalona News

KRLS Radio
Los Angeles Times
Muscatine Journal
Olewein Daily Register
The Oregonian
Quad City Times
Seattle Times
SLAM magazine
Springfield News-Leader
Tulsa World
Washington Evening Journal
Washington Post
Waterloo Courier
Wellman Advance

Websites

ACLU.org
Census.gov
ChichenItza.com
CoachesDatabase.com
DangerousRoads.org
Elkader-Iowa.com
FIBA.Basketball.com
FIFA.com
FiveStarBasketball.com
Go-Knights.net
GuinnessWorldRecords.com
HawkeyeSports.com
Heddels.com
HillcrestRavens.org
History.com
HoopHall.com

IHSSA.org

IowaAgriculture.gov

JimBurson.com

KalonaIowa.org

McDonaldsAllAmerican.com

MilitaryBases.com

NBA.com

NBACoaches.com

NCAA.com

OrangeCoastCollege.edu

OregonSportsHall.org

PottsvilleSchools.com

PrairieRootsResearch.com

PurdueSports.com

RMHC.org

Sports-Reference.com

SSS.gov

TABCHoops.com

TeamUSA.org

UniPanthers.com

USAB.com

Wartburg.edu

WashingtonIowa.gov

Zeroto60Times.com

A complete, detailed bibliography is available from the publisher upon request.